Nascar

Also by Daniel J. Brush, David Horne, and Marc CB Maxwell

University of Oklahoma Football:
An Interactive Guide to the World of Sports
(Savas Beatie, 2007)

Also by Marc CB Maxwell

Surviving Military Separation: 365 Days
An Activity Guide for Family Members of Deployed Personnel
Illustrated by Val Laolagi
(Savas Beatie, 2007)

Nascar

An *Interactive* Guide to the World of Sports

To Jason—
Welcome to SBTN!

SB

Savas Beatie

New York and California

Printed in the United States of America

Cataloging-in-Publication Data is available from the Library of Congress.

ISBN 13: 978-1-932714-42-5

10 09 08 07 06 05 04 03 02 01 / First edition, first printing

Cover photo courtesy of David Horne. Original illustration by Val Laolagi

SB

Published by
Savas Beatie LLC
521 Fifth Avenue, Suite 3400
New York, NY 10175
Phone: 610-853-9131

Editorial Offices:

Savas Beatie LLC
P.O. Box 4527
El Dorado Hills, CA 95762
Phone: 916-941-6896
(E-mail) editorial@savasbeatie.com

Savas Beatie titles are available at special discounts for bulk purchases in the United States by corporations, institutions, and other organizations. For more details, please contact Special Sales, P.O. Box 4527, El Dorado Hills, CA 95762. You may also e-mail us at sales@savasbeatie.com, or click over for a visit to our website at www.savasbeatie.com or www.sportsbythenumbers.com for more information.

This title is not sponsored by or affiliated with NASCAR[TM]

For

Devin & Kristian

Contents

Contents (continued)

Contents (continued)

Photos, illustrations, charts, and tables have been placed
throughout the book for the benefit of our readers.

Foreword

ASCAR by the numbers, huh?

With the possible exception of baseball, stock-car racing probably puts as much emphasis on numbers as any sport. Many fans can recite the numbers on the tops and sides of the cars. Several familiar jokes refer to fans counting by the numbers of the drivers: "Truex, Kurt, Daaaaaallllle! . . ."

The number of the late Dale Earnhardt, 3, is as sacred to stock-car fans as the number, once worn by Babe Ruth, is to fans of the New York Yankees. There are no retired numbers in NASCAR, but since Earnhardt's tragic death on February 18, 2001, no one has dared use it, not even Dale Earnhardt Jr.

Fans pay attention to the length of pit stops and the laps in the race. (For instance, 500 miles at Darlington is 367 laps.) They know the margin of victory, the laps under caution, the average speed, the pole speed, the pit-road speed limit, finishing positions, starting positions, positions improved, et al. They know how points are awarded, keep up with bonus points, and rely on television announcers to keep them abreast of what the point standings are *in the middle of races*!

It's all very high-tech. NASCAR officials have recently begun distributing packets of what is known as "loop data," which are garnered from electronic instruments placed around each track. This data can get pretty arcane: "quality" passes, average speed in the turns, average running position, fastest drivers early in run, fastest drivers late in run, etc.

The term for maniacal baseball statistician is "sabermetrician," derived from SABR, or Society for American Baseball Research. Perhaps a title should be similarly signed to devotees of stock-car statistics. Nascarmetrician?

On the surface, NASCAR would seem to have almost nothing in common with baseball. The sports have similarly fanatical fans, however.

The popularity of football is easy to understand. One doesn't have to know much about it to be entertained. This can't be said of baseball and NASCAR. A high percentage of fans revel in the numbers. To those who don't know enough to pay attention, baseball seems slow and boring. NASCAR detractors say it's nothing more than "a bunch of cars going around and around for three hours."

Both baseball and NASCAR reward those who pay attention. To the guy in the bleachers scribbling on a scorecard, baseball is pulsating because, well, little things mean a lot. The same can be said of racing, where thousands of fans sit in the grandstands wearing soundproof head phones and using scanners to monitor the radio conversations between drivers and crews. The high-speed intricacies make NASCAR just as intellectually stimulating.

NASCAR fans are often stereotyped as beer-swilling, flag-waving, T-shirt-wearing rednecks, but all in all, the atmosphere in the great speedways of the land isn't markedly different from the crowd at football stadiums, baseball parks, basketball coliseums, and hockey arenas.

More hangs in the superspeedway air than helium balloons and tire smoke. The average attendance is more than 120,000. There's passion in those numbers.

Monte Dutton

Preface

The history of NASCAR lies in the numbers. Numbers tell the stories that make NASCAR great. They show us how fast the sport is, they show us how close a finish was, and they tell us where our heroes sit in the point standings. Numbers are immortalized on the hood of the car, the suit of the driver, and sometimes shaved in the head of that obsessed fan who just can't get enough of his favorite driver.

It was on this premise that we created the Sports by the Numbers™ franchise in July of 2006. It began in Rudy's "Country Store" and Bar-B-Q, one of our favorite hangout spots in Norman, Oklahoma. On the big screen TV the Atlanta Braves and the St. Louis Cardinals were in the midst of a lopsided affair for the second consecutive day. It was the Braves offense posting the big numbers, 29 runs in two games. Atlanta, of course, was hoping to make a post-season push after winning 14 consecutive division titles since 1991. We did the math on a napkin, and we decided the odds were long against the Braves making it 15 straight. Statistically, it was a mind-numbing streak, and as our conversation drifted among sports, numbers, and memories, we began talking about streaks, and about records that will never be broken.

Some of the people around us were listening to our conversation, though we did not realize it until we stood to leave at the same time as an older gentleman who was seated at a table behind us. He gave us a nod and said, "Forty-seven." Then he smiled, "The longest winning streak in NCAA history, set by OU."

His interest in our conversation validated what we knew to be true already—that sports fans are passionate about numbers and the stories they tell. It took us only a few days to draft a proposal for the Sports by the Numbers™ series, and only a few days more to draft some samples for the University of Oklahoma and Major League Baseball titles. It took only a few weeks to find the right publisher, who then got the perfect website designer for us, and began helping us to craft the format of the books to tell our stories in the best way possible.

In every SBTN title, you will find a numerical list from one to one thousand—and for each number the SBTN team will give you a story by way of statistical facts, anomalies, records, personalities, accomplishments, and fascinating trivia. If you love sports, our books are for you. If you have a hero from your favorite team, our books are for you. If you want to learn about a sport or a specific team, our books are for you.

Our books, however, are not just for diehards like us. If you want to teach a new fan about a team or sport, then SBTN is perfect for that too. But just in case you are as passionate and obsessive of a fan as we are, look for future SBTN titles on your favorite sports and your favorite teams, and reminisce with us about days gone by and championships won and lost.

The SBTN experience does not end with the books. Inside each title you will find that our favorite numbers are tagged as SBTN – All Star or SBTN – Hall of Fame numbers. When you see these, go online to www.sportsbythenumbers.com and use those specific numbers to access more content on the web and take part in our SBTN Interactive World of Sports. On our website you will also find some of our SBTN memories. We invite you to check them out, and email us some of your own so we can post them on our site too.

One final note: When we were deciding just how to compile this text, we had to make a decision on how to refer to the big three. The Craftsman Truck Series was easy . . . it started as the CTS in 1995. The Busch Series was only referenced back to 1982, when it gained its namesake, even though there were three decades of racing that predated the series in the form of the Sportsman and Late Model Sportsman Division. Toward the end of the 2007 season, Anheuser-Busch and NASCAR officially terminated their sponsorship agreement and Nationwide Insurance took over title sponsorship. While tempted to refer to all previous Busch Series statistics as Nationwide for this release, we decided not to due to the long-standing relationship between AB and NASCAR, a relationship that lasted 25 years.

The NEXTEL Cup, which changes over to the Sprint Cup Series in 2008, posed a different problem. It has had a few names since 1949 when it began as the Strictly Stock Car Series. From 1950 to 1971 it was the Grand National Series, from 1972 to 2003 it was the Winston Cup Series, and from 2004 to 2007 the series was called the NEXTEL Cup. Names and sponsorships have changed, most recently due to a corporate merger. For the purpose of this book, we refer to the senior circuit as the Sprint Cup. It allows for readers, especially the newer NASCAR fans, to follow the history a bit more easily.

Acknowledgments

It is time to acknowledge so many important people who have made SBTN a reality.

Special thanks first of all to Theodore P. "Ted" Savas of Savas Beatie. The publishing industry is supposed to be brutal, but you not only gave us a shot, you also bought into our vision and made this one of the greatest rides of our lives, and for that we are grateful.

The SBTN guys got plenty of good advice the past few months, but perhaps the best of all came from Ted himself, who told us, "Do exactly what Sarah suggests you do." Sarah Keeney is the Marketing Director for Savas Beatie, and Sarah, as long as you say jump, we'll ask "how high" on our way up. You have our sincere gratitude for your enduring patience with us.

Our website and logo designer is Val Laolagi, and he was introduced to us by our publisher as the best talent on the market for this sort of work. Val is an incredibly gifted artist, coach, and mentor. His vision for the website and sketches for our books are amazing, and we are grateful to be surrounded by such talent.

Jim Zach of zGrafix designs many of the books produced by Savas Beatie. He also created the best book covers on the sports market today—and he did it for SBTN.

All three of us were blessed and found someone to make us better people—Paulina Brush, Lisa Horne, and Christine Maxwell. You guys loved us, and believed in us—so if nobody that doesn't share our last names ever reads our books, it's all good.

Daniel J. Brush, David Horne,
and Marc CB Maxwell

Norman, Oklahoma
June 1, 2008

The Locker

*W*elcome to Sports by the Numbers™ and our Interactive Guide to the World of Sports. In compiling our first 1,000 numbers that we used to tell stories in our debut title, *University of Oklahoma Football*, it was apparent to us that for one reason or another some of the numbers resonated more deeply with us than did others—they were special.

The numbers were all great, but there were some numbers that we were drawn toward and felt the need to expand on more than the others. Our website provided us with the opportunity to do just that in an area we call The Locker.

The team of authors for this title on NASCAR has used special logos to designate five Hall of Fame numbers and ten All Star numbers that you will come across as you read the stories that unfold within these pages.

Numbers designated as Hall of Fame or All Star lets you know that they are among our favorites from this book—and once in the locker room, you will find out why.

Our website is: www.SportsByTheNumbers.com

Use the tab at the top of our homepage or the locker on the bottom right-hand corner of our homepage to enter our locker. Once there you will see the covers of all the SBTN titles that are currently available.

Click on the cover of your favorite SBTN title to view the Hall of Fame and All Star numbers that the SBTN authors have selected for that book.

You can then click on any number in the locker room to gain access to additional information that may come in the form of pictures, video, audio, text, or random musings from one of the SBTN authors, but regardless, it will enhance the story told by the number, and it will let you know why we feel the number is so significant.

Creating an Interactive World of Sports that combines the best of the traditional book world with the unlimited potential of the Internet is an exciting and fluid process—and we are constantly working on new and better ways to bring together the book world and the cyber world with one goal in mind, to give sports fans the ultimate experience when it comes to reminiscing about their favorite numbers, players, teams, and memories.

Enjoy the experience.

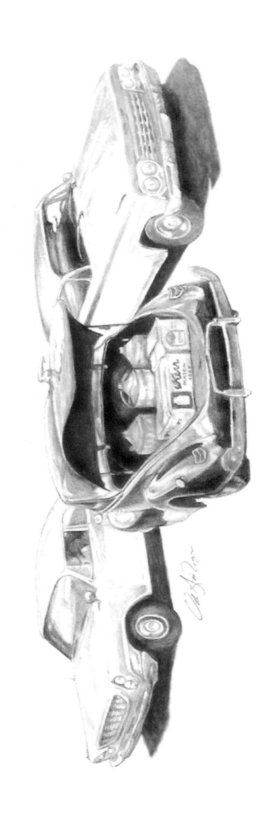

Chapter One

Bootleggin'

No story about NASCAR can begin without acknowledging the past that gave so many of the first generation drivers their start: bootlegging. While the stories have been told since before NASCAR began, it is a story that never gets old. Some of NASCAR's greatest drivers got their start running moonshine in the South. Names like Tim Flock, Curtis Turner, Wendell Scott, and Junior Johnson. Notice a few of those names appear on NASCAR's list of 50 greatest drivers of all-time. Ask best-selling author and novelist Tom Wolfe who the last American hero was and he'll tell you Junior Johnson. Bootleggers ran moonshine during Prohibition but, even after Prohibition ended, moonshine remained popular because it was cheap. In order to avoid paying taxes on the moonshine, you needed to deliver it and deliver fast. Welcome to the start of the NASCAR generation.

Drivers needed an edge, something to ensure the local sheriff didn't catch them because if he did, there went your car and you'd have to go and buy it back at auction. The local sheriff probably didn't care so much about the untaxed alcohol, but getting some revenue by impounding the car and selling it at auction. Bootleggers did everything they could to make their cars faster and handle better to ensure that they could deliver their moonshine without having to spend any quality time with the sheriff. After a while, these back-road legends started talking about whose car was faster or better and one thing led to another until, one day in 1937, out in a field in the middle of Georgia, these skilled drivers put their money where their mouths were. It would take another couple of years and Big Bill France until stock car racing became NASCAR, but it had already started with these guys, guys like Junior "the last American hero" Johnson and other drivers who went by names like "the Midnight Traveler" and "the Black Ghost."

The number of Sprint, Busch, or Craftsman Series titles (1) needed to fulfill your dreams and the dreams of all your fans who travel hundreds (if not thousands) of miles to watch you race.

The number of poles (2) and victories (2) by legendary driver Red Byron. Byron would race between 1949 and 1951 and enter into 15 races. During his first season in 1949, which consisted of eight races, he would place in the top five four times, winning two races en route to winning the first Sprint Cup Series.

The number of times (3) that Bobby Allison would take the checkered flag at Daytona. Allison won his first Daytona in 1977 and his second in 1982. It was perhaps his third Daytona run that would be the most bittersweet for Allison. In 1988, starting from the #3 position, Allison would cross the finish line in front of son Davey, who would finish the race in second place. Four years later Davey would take the checkered flag himself at Daytona.

The number of drivers (4) to win the Sprint Cup Series title while only winning one race during the season. Bill Rexford (11 top tens in 17 starts in 1950), Ned Jarrett (34 top tens in 46 starts in 1961), Benny Parsons (21 top tens in 28 starts in 1973), and Matt Kenseth (25 top tens in 2003) relied on consistency rather than victory tally to win their championships.

The number of different drivers (5) to claim the checkered flag at the Fairgrounds Raceway in Birmingham, Alabama. NASCAR ran eight races at the track between 1958 and 1968 with Ned Jarrett and Richard Petty monopolizing victory lane with five of those victories. Jarrett took checkered flags in 1961, 1964, and 1965, while Petty took the second race in 1963 and the track's last race in 1968. Other winners were Fireball Roberts (1958), Jim Paschal (1963), and Bobby Allison (1967).

The number of Sprint Cup championships (6) of Dale Earnhardt's seven overall titles that came in back-to-back seasons. Earnhardt won back-to-back titles on three separate occasions: 1986-87, 1990-91, and 1993-94. The Intimidator is the only driver to win three separate back-to-back titles in NASCAR history.

The standard number of crew members (7) allowed over the wall during pit stops, according to NASCAR rules. These rules allow for an eighth member over the wall for the sole purpose of cleaning the windshield. Also the number of season championships (7) recorded by Richard Petty and Dale Earnhardt.

The number of points (8) that Kurt Busch beat Jimmie Johnson by to win the 2004 Sprint Cup. The margin of victory, the closest in NASCAR history, beat a 12-year-old record for closest margin of victory held previously by Alan Kulwicki over Bill Elliot. In 1992, Kulwicki beat Elliot by ten points.

The number of victories (9) that Richard Petty earned during the 1964 season, his first Sprint Cup Series championship. During that season, which coincidently was his father Lee's last on the circuit, the King would take the checkered at Daytona, and finish in the top ten in 43 of 61 races helping him beat out Ned Jarrett for the title despite the fact that Jarrett had six more victories than Petty.

Number of consecutive races won (10) by Richard Petty during his incredible 1967 season. Petty, in his tenth season of racing, won 27 of 48 races (.562) including a stretch of ten straight races; the King finished seven of the remaining 21 races in second place, easily winning the 1967 title. Petty led 43% of all laps raced during the season (5,537 of 12,739) and held the lead in 41 of the 48 races he competed in.

The number of consecutive seasons (11) that Lee Petty would finish the NASCAR season in one of the top five positions. Petty entered the NASCAR scene in 1949 and dominated the early years. He would finish second in the point standing in his inaugural season and, not until his 12th season on the circuit, would he finish a season outside of the top five (he was sixth in 1960). Along the way, Petty would win three championships and hold the record for victories at 54 until son Richard broke the record in 1967.

The car (#12) that took Bobby Allison across the finish line with the checkered flag on 25 occasions. While Allison may have made the #12 famous, 12 is also the number of times that Ryan Newman has taken the #12 to victory lane, with the most recent one coming at the New Hampshire International Speedway in 2005 with a victory at the Sylvania 300.

The position (13) that Ned Jarrett held in total victories during the 1961 season. Jarrett and six other drivers could only muster a single victory apiece, placing the group of seven tied for 13th place on the victory list, eight victories apiece behind Joe Weatherly's nine wins for the season. Despite Jarrett's inability to take the checkered flag more than once, he was steady throughout the season, finishing in the top ten 34 times in 46 starts and earning the season title.

The margin of victory in laps (14) that Ned Jarrett had in the 1965 Southern 500 held at Darlington Raceway. On September 6, Jarrett, starting in the tenth position, would annihilate the field and take the checkered flag by an unheard of 17.5 miles. The margin of victory remains a NASCAR record. The rest of the season was good to Jarrett as well . . . he won the championship for the second time in his career leading the field in points, races won, and money won, while finishing second in poles won.

The maximum amount of time (15) in seconds that constitutes an "efficient" pit stop. It is commonly accepted that a pit stop in which all four tires are changed and the vehicle is refueled is efficient if it occurs between 13-15 seconds. That equates to an average of less than four seconds to change a tire while refueling.

The number of top five finishes (16) in 33 races recorded by Herb Thomas during his first championship season in 1951. Thomas would take the checkered flag seven times and earn $21,025 on the season while driving a Marshall Teague Hudson.

The number of top five finishes (17) in 20 starts by Mike Skinner during the inaugural season of the NASCAR Craftsman Truck Series in 1995. Skinner, who would take the first championship, won eight of those races en route to a 126 point victory over Joe Ruttman. Skinner would also take home almost $430,000 in winnings.

The number of victories (18) by Tim Flock during the 1955 season. Flock took the checkered flag in 18 of 38 races and set the record for most wins in a season. That record stood for 12 years until Richard Petty shattered it in 1967 with 27 victories. During his 1955 championship season, Flock won almost $38,000 in prize money. The 1955 season marked his second championship with the first coming three years earlier.

The day (19) in June of 1960 that the Lowe's Motor Speedway hosted its first NASCAR race. Joe Lee Johnson won the World 600 in just under five hours and 35 minutes. Johnson broke in the track for NASCAR with an average speed of 107.735 mph en route to taking the checkered flag.

The number of poles (20) won in a single season by Bobby Isaac, a NASCAR record. During the 1969 season, Isaac held the pole 20 times and won 17 races, yet finished sixth in the point standings and fourth on the money list as the season ended. The following season Isaac would again lead the pack in poles held, but would finish it up properly, winning the championship by 51 points over Bobby Allison. Isaac finished the season second on the wins list behind Richard Petty, with 11 and, once again, fourth on the money list, but won the coveted title.

The number of top ten finishes (21) that Darrell Waltrip had in his 1985 championship season. While only winning three races on the year, Waltrip's consistency allowed him to become the first driver to earn over $1 million dollars in winnings in a single season (he would finish with $1,318,374).

The number of tracks (22) in 19 states that currently host Sprint Cup races. The oldest track can be found in Martinsville, Virginia (Martinsville Speedway: 1949) while the newest track can be found in Kansas City, Kansas (Kansas Speedway: 2001).

The age in years (23) of the youngest driver to win the Sprint Cup Series championship. During NASCAR's 1950 season, Bill Rexford took the title with one victory and 11 top tens in 17 starts. His purse for the season was $6,175. Rexford would race only from 1949 to 1953, retiring at the age of 26.

Dale Earnhardt's margin of victory, in points (24), over Mark Martin during the 1990 season. In a controversial championship season, Earnhardt claimed the title by the margin after Martin was assessed a 46 point penalty earlier in the season for "rules infractions." Nevertheless, "Ironhead" finished the season with nine victories, 18 top ten finishes, and over $3.3 million in earnings over 29 starts.

The number of victories (25) by Lee Petty during his three Series Cup Titles. Petty would take the checkered flag seven times in both 1954 and 1958. In 1959, Petty won 11 races in what would be his third and final championship season. Also the number of victories (25) by Darrell Waltrip during his three Series Cup Titles. Waltrip would take the checkered flag 12 times in 1981 and 1982 and win three races in his last championship season in 1985.

The total number of top five finishes (26) by Randy LaJoie en route to back-to-back Busch Series championships in 1996 and 1997. Of 56 races started in over the two year span, LaJoie would finish in the top five 26 times (11 times in 1996 and 15 times in 1997) and secured ten victories (five in each season). LaJoie's 1997 championship was the first season in the history of the Busch Series to see a driver cross the $1 million mark in earnings.

The number of years (27) that the record for the fastest average-speed of the Daytona 500 winner has stood (as of 2007). In 1980, Buddy Baker took the checkered at Daytona with an average speed of 177.602 mph. Only three other times has Daytona been run with the winner averaging over 170 mph. In 1987, Bill Elliot came closest to match the record when he averaged 176.283 mph. Elliot also topped the 170 mph mark two years earlier, winning Daytona with an average speed of 172.265. In 1998, Dale Earnhardt won Daytona with an average speed of 172.712 mph.

The car (#28) that took nine drivers down victory lane 76 times . . . . eight of the drivers grace the list of NASCAR's all-time greatest drivers. Fred Lorenzen (25 victories), Davey Allison (19 victories), Cale Yarborough (9 victories), Ernie Irvan (8 victories), Bobby Allison (5 victories), Buddy Baker (5 victories), Ricky Rudd (3 victories), Dan Gurney (1 victory), and Dale Jarrett (1 victory) won races in #28, making it the fifth most successful car number in the Sprint Cup.

The number of career victories (29) in the Craftsman Truck Series by two-time champ Ron Hornaday Jr. Heading into the 2007 season, he has started 175 races winning 16.6% of all races entered. Hornaday may best be remembered as catapulting from fourth into second place during the final lap of the final race of the 1998 season to edge race-winner Jack Sprague for the title by three points in one of the most exciting season finishes in NASCAR history.

The air pressure (30) in psi (cold) of the left tires of cars riding on Goodyear Eagle race tires in NASCAR events. The psi found on the right tires averages 45 psi, while the standard Goodyear Eagle street tire that you use in your car averages 35 psi all the way around.

The position (31) that Jeff Gordon finished in at his first Sprint Cup race. Gordon, who had spent two successful seasons on the Busch Series, wrecked on lap 164 at the 1992 Hooters 500. That race would coincidently be Richard Petty's final race.

The age (32) of Davey Allison when he died in a helicopter crash. On July 12, 1993, Allison, who had just finished in third place at the inaugural race at the New Hampshire International Speedway, picked up legendary driver Red Farmer in his new helicopter and flew to Talladega, where he crashed in the infield. Red survived the crash, Davey did not.

The number of NASCAR races entered (33) by Janet Guthrie in four years. Guthrie, an avid pilot who held a degree in physics and initially qualified for NASA's astronaut program, never won a race, but was the first woman to qualify for the Daytona 500 (finishing 12th in 1977) and earned approximately $75,000 in winnings between 1976 and 1980. She would finish in the top 15 in over half of her races and finished in the top ten five times.

The number of race weeks (34) that Kevin Harvick held the #1 ranking on the Busch Series en route to perhaps the most dominating season on the circuit. In 2006, Harvick ran all 35 races, placing in the top five 23 times, in the top ten 32 times, and finishing each race en route to $2,850,864 in winnings and his second Busch Series title.

The number of years (35) that Dave Marcis raced the NASCAR circuit. In 883 races within that time frame, Marcis only won five races but earned the respect of anyone who knew anything about stock car racing. His starts are second only to Richard Petty and his hard work and dedication (along with his wingtip racing shoes) made him an engaging figure on the NASCAR circuit.

The banking in turns (36) in degrees, found at the Bristol Motor Speedway in Bristol, Tennessee. The track banks significantly more than the Indianapolis Motor Speedway, which has the least banking in turns at nine degrees.

The number of top ten finishes (37) recorded at Bristol Motor Speedway in Bristol, Tennessee by Richard Petty. Three of the King's top ten finishes led to victory lane (1967 Volunteer 500, the 1975 Volunteer 500, and the Southeastern 500 that same year). Also, the number of top ten finishes (37) by Petty at Daytona International Speedway, although Petty would win ten of those races.

The age (38) of Alan Kulwicki when he died as the Hooters corporate jet he was in crashed on April 1, 1993 while en route to Bristol Motor Speedway. Kulwicki, who started 207 races between 1985 and 1993, died the year after winning his first Sprint Cup Series. Super 'K' was not your average NASCAR driver . . . he held a degree in mechanical engineering from the University of Wisconsin, celebrated victories with the "Polish Victory Lap" in which he turned his car around so the driver side would be facing the fans, and wore a customized "Mighty Mouse" patch on his driver's suit.

The number of times (39) that Fonty Flock either won a race or finished in the runner-up position. Flock would win 19 races over his nine year career and finish second an additional 20 times. Flock would place first or second in over 25% of the races he started (39 times in 153 races).

The number of lead changes (40) during the 1991 Valleydale 500 at Bristol Motor Speedway. This number of lead changes is a track record. The race was eventually won by Rusty Wallace, who happened to start from the pole position. 40 is also the track record at Bristol for number of cars running at the finish (1999 Food City 500).

The number of top ten finishes (41) recorded by driver Kasey Kahne during his first five years on the Busch Series. Kahne has placed in the top ten in exactly one-third of all races started between 2002 and 2006 (41 of 123).

The number of top five finishes (42) out of 54 starts earned by Ned Jarrett during his 1965 championship season. Jarrett would place in the top five in 77.7% of the races he started and be victorious in 24% of them (13 victories) en route to over $93,000 in earnings on the year.

The number (43) of the car made famous by Richard Petty. Petty took #43 to victory lane 192 times during his 35 year career. Petty also earned two victories in 1965 in the car made famous by his father Lee, the #42 car. Lee Petty also won one race in the #43 car, made famous by his son.

The number of top ten finishes (44) recorded by Dale Earnhardt Jr. during his back-to-back Busch Series championships of 1998 and 1999. Each season saw Junior place in the top ten 22 times. Similarities in the seasons didn't stop there . . . they were also evident in poles won (three in both 1998 and 1999), wins (seven in 1998 and six in 1999), top 5s (16 in 1998 and 18 in 1999), and DNFs (three in 1998 and four in 1999).

The number of races started (45) by Joe Weatherly during his 1962 NASCAR championship season. That number (45) also coincides with the number of top ten finishes Weatherly had that season. The "Clown Prince of Stock Car Racing" would finish every race entered in the top ten, including nine of which ended with a trip down victory lane.

David Green's margin of victory, in points (46), over Ricky Craven in the 1994 Busch Series championship. Green, who became the second driver to win Busch with just one victory, relied on consistency (ten top five finishes, 14 top ten finishes, and only one DNF) to win the series championship. His strong qualifying didn't hurt either; he won nine poles on the season.

The number of all-time manufacturer championships (47) by the "Big 3" automakers. Heading into the 2007 season, Chevy leads all manufacturers with 30 championships, followed by Ford with 15, and Dodge is fourth on the list with two.

The number of top ten finishes (48) recorded by the top three drivers in the final point standings of the 2004 Craftsman Truck Series. Champion Bobby Hamilton, runner-up Dennis Setzer, and third-place finisher Ted Musgrave each recorded 16 top ten finishes on the season and finished the season with a mere 70 points separating the three in the championship standings.

The margin of victory, in points (49), between the inaugural Busch Series champion and its runner-up in 1982. Jack Ingram would edge out Sam Ard for the first Busch title. Ard would return the favor the following two years, beating Ingram for the championship. The point total during the inaugural season wasn't the only thing close during the year . . . Ingram collected $1 more in winnings than Ard that year ($122,100 to $122,099).

The number of drivers (50) labeled the greatest of NASCAR: Bobby Allison, Davey Allison, Buck Baker, Buddy Baker, Geoff Bodine, Neil Bonnett, Red Byron, Jerry Cook, Dale Earnhardt, Ralph Earnhardt, Bill Elliot, Richie Evans, Red Farmer, Tim Flock, A.J. Foyt, Harry Gant, Jeff Gordon, Ray Hendrick, Jack Ingram, Ernie Irvan, Bobby Isaac, Dale Jarrett, Ned Jarrett, Junior Johnson, Alan Kulwicki, Terry Labonte, Fred Lorenzen, Tiny Lund, Mark Martin, Hershel McGriff, Cotton Owens, Marvin Panch, Benny Parsons, David Pearson, Lee Petty, Richard Petty, Tim Richmond, Fireball Roberts, Ricky Rudd, Marshall Teague, Herb Thomas, Curtis Turner, Rusty Wallace, Darrell Waltrip, Joe Weatherly, Bob Welborn, Rex White, Glen Wood, Cale Yarborough, and LeeRoy Yarbrough.

The car (#51) driven to two victories by Gober Sosebee during his nine years racing on the NASCAR circuit. Sosebee, who began racing in 1949, won one race in 1952 and 1954 making him the only driver to find victory lane driving the #51 car.

The age (52) of the oldest driver to win a Sprint Cup Series race. On August 16, 1992, Harry Gant took the checkered flag at the Champion Sparkplug 500 at Michigan International Speedway to set the record for the oldest driver to win a race at 52 years and 219 days.

The number of races started (53) by legendary driver Joe Weatherly during his 1963 championship campaign. Despite winning the cup the previous year for Bud Moore, Weatherly did not have a permanent ride the following year, making his repeat as champion even more impressive. Weatherly took the Cup by driving for a record nine different teams that year. "Little Joe" would unfortunately die in a racing accident early the year after his repeat in Riverside, California.

The margin of victory (54) in points by Ron Hornaday Jr. over Mike Skinner en route to the 2007 Craftsman Truck Series championship, his third series championship. Hornaday, who claimed the series championship in 1996 and 1998, won four races and recorded 13 top tens to win the championship despite Skinner collecting more wins (five) and top five finishes (17).

Entering the 2007 season, the number of career top ten finishes (55) recorded by Jamie McMurray. McMurray, who has been on the Sprint Cup Series since 2002, has finished just over a third of all races entered in the top ten (55 of 150).

The number of Sprint Cup and Craftsman Truck Series races (56) "run in the desert" through the end of the 2006 season. The Las Vegas Motor Speedway and the Phoenix International Raceway have hosted 30 Sprint Cup races and 25 Craftsman Truck Series races over the past 18 years.

The number of times (57) that NASCAR fans would find David Pearson either in victory lane or in the runner-up position during his consecutive championship seasons in 1968 and 1969. Pearson would take the checkered flag 27 times (16 in 1968 and 11 times in 1969) and finished second 30 times en route to back-to-back championships. Pearson would finish in the top five an additional 21 times and finish these two seasons with over $360,000 in winnings.

The number of Speedway Poles (58) won by David Pearson during his legendary career. This number is a Sprint Cup Series record and a full ten more than Bill Elliot, who holds the #2 position on the list.

The age in years (59) of Red Farmer when he returned from a 16 year hiatus to race in two races on the Busch Series. Farmer, who had last raced on the Sprint Cup in 1975, came back in 1992 to race two events on the Busch Series. His first race back saw Red crash at the end of the Fram Filter 500K. The following race, Red placed 18th in his final NASCAR race at the age of 59.

60 The record for number of cars starting a race (60) at the Charlotte Motor Speedway. On June 19, 1960, sixty drivers started the World 600. By the time the race was won by Joe Lee Johnson, only 18 cars were left running.

61 The NASCAR record for number of starts (61) at the Talladega Superspeedway in Talladega, Alabama. Dave Marcis ran his first race at Talladega on April 12, 1970 where he finished in 17th place at the Alabama 500. His final race at Talladega came just over 31 years later on April 22, 2001; he finished the Talladega 500 in 38th place. He also claimed one of his five NASCAR wins at the track, the 1976 Talladega 500.

62 The average finish position (6.2) of Jack Sprague during his first of three championship seasons on the Craftsman Truck Series. Sprague racked up three victories, 16 top five finishes, and 23 top ten finishes during the 1997 season. 6.2 is also the average finish position of Travis Kvapil during his 2003 Craftsman championship season.

63 Number of top five finishes (63) recorded by Morgan-McClure Motorsports drivers between 1983 and 2006. Joe Ruttman recorded the first top five finish for Larry McClure in 1985 and Bobby Hamilton recorded McClure's last top five finish in 1999. Ernie Irvan, who drove for Morgan-McClure between 1990 and 1993, recorded the most top five finishes with 33 of the total 63 under his belt.

64 Entering the 2007 season, the number (64) of top ten finishes recorded by Travis Kvapil over four seasons on the Craftsman Truck Series. Kvapil, who returned in 2007 from two years off the truck series, recorded 64 top tens in 96 starts between 2001 and 2004. He recorded his career best in top ten finishes in 2003 with 22 top ten finishes in 24 races, which helped him to earn the Craftsman Truck Series Championship.

65 The combined number of races (65) that all Busch Series champions failed to finish between 1982 and 2006. Over 25 years, 18 different drivers started 769 races, only failing to complete 65 of those races meaning that, on average, the champion completed 91.5% of all races entered. Two drivers finished every race started and no driver failed to finish more than five races in a season.

Entering the 2007 season, the number of top five finishes (66) recorded by Matt Kenseth over his first nine seasons on the Sprint Cup Series. Of his 66 top five finishes, 26 came in his championship season of 2003 and his runner-up campaign in 2006.

The year ('67) that will live in NASCAR infamy . . . for any driver other than Richard Petty. The King dominated all of NASCAR that season and gave the circuit a taste of what the future would hold. Petty would annihilate the field en route to his second Sprint Cup title. He had 27 victories (21 more than Bobby Allison), including a stretch of ten straight, won approximately $130,000 (approximately $55,000 more than Dick Hutcherson), and qualified at pole 19 times (ten times more than Hutcherson). He would win the title with 42,472 points; over 6,000 points ahead of James Hylton in the #2 position.

The average starting position (6.8) and finishing position (6.8) of Buck Baker during his first championship season. In 1956, Baker started and finished, on average, in the same position over the 48 races he entered. His season was assisted by a career-high 14 victories and 12 pole positions. As impressive as Baker's season was, it was neither his best season for average start (his average start position was 2.2 in 1954) nor his best final position average (his average finish position was 4.7 in 1957).

The year ('69) that LeeRoy Yarbrough became the first NASCAR driver to take the Triple Crown. Yarbrough would win the Daytona 500, the World 600, and the Southern 500 en route to a seven victory season in which he led all racers in winnings ($188,105) despite not finishing in the top ten in points.

The number of top five finishes (70) that Cale Yarborough recorded during the 1976, 1977, and 1978 seasons. Yarborough also managed 28 victories during that span en route to becoming NASCAR's only three-peat champion. 70 is also the number of times Yarborough would sit pole in a race during his 32 year career.

71 The car number (71) often driven by independent owner-driver Dave Marcis over 35 years racing on the Sprint Cup. While Bobby Isaac may have recorded the most victories (35) driving the #71 car, it was Dave Marcis and his hard work and dedication that may best be remembered and associated with the number.

72 The average finish position (7.2) of Ron Hornaday Jr. during his 1998 Craftsman Series championship season. Hornaday, in winning his second championship in a three-year span, recorded 16 top five finishes and 22 top ten finishes in 27 starts en route to a three point victory over Jack Sprague.

73 The number of starts (73) by Carl Edwards during the 2007 season. Edwards started each race in the Sprint and Busch Series and added a couple on the Craftsman Series. Edwards not only showed up to race, he finished ninth in the Sprint Cup Series while winning the Busch Series championship.

74 The age (74) of Hershel McGriff when he finally retired from racing. McGriff, named one of NASCAR's 50 greatest drivers, earned all four of his career victories during the last nine races of the 1954 season. He would finish sixth in the point standings that year for his best season ever. McGriff would continue racing until he finally called it quits after a 12th place finish at a NASCAR West Series race in California. His career as a driver would span 52 years (1950-2001).

75 Entering the 2007 season, the number of career victories (75) recorded by Jeff Gordon on the Sprint Cup. Gordon entered the 2007 season in seventh place on the all-time career victory list behind Dale Earnhardt.

76 The number of victories (76) claimed by the "Intimidator" Dale Earnhardt during his NASCAR career. Earnhardt, whose career spanned over four decades, won seven Sprint Cup Series titles and was one of NASCAR's most prolific drivers earning in excess of $40 million during his career. Earnhardt died on the last lap of the 2001 Daytona 500. His son, Dale Earnhardt Jr. would return to capture the Pepsi 400 on the same track that claimed his father later that season.

77 The number of top ten finishes (77) recorded by Buck Baker during his back-to-back championship seasons of 1956-57. Baker dominated NASCAR those two years, not only in top ten finishes, but in victories (24), money won ($54,805), and poles (17). Baker's 77 top ten finishes came over 88 races, meaning that he finished in the top ten an incredible 87.5% of all races started.

78 The combined margin of victory in points (78) in Jack Ingram's two Busch Series championship series. In 1982, Ingram would capture the first Busch Series title by 49 points over Sam Ard. Three years later, he would squeeze by Brett Bodine by a mere 29 points. By way of comparison, 14 other champions on the Busch series exceed that margin of victory in one season.

79 The season ending ranking (79) of Jeff Gordon in his first season racing on the Sprint Cup Series. Gordon only started one race during the 1992 season on series, although he did run every race on the Busch Series. Gordon would finish the Busch season in fourth place and, the following season on the Sprint Cup, his first full season, Gordon would finish ranked 14th.

80 The number of top ten finishes (80) recorded by Joe Weatherly during his two consecutive championship seasons. Weatherly, who won the NASCAR championship in 1962 and 1963, did so by consistently finishing in the top ten. In fact, Weatherly only finished outside the top ten in three races over the two year span in which he was running at finish. Weatherly was running at finish in 83 of 110 races started meaning that, in races completed over the two year span, he finished in the top ten 96.4% of the time.

81 The average start position per race (8.1) by legend Rex White. White raced in 233 races during his career and finished slightly behind his starting position, averaging each finish in ninth place. His strong average start position was helped by 36 poles earned throughout his career. His single season best average start position was in 1958 at 5.1, while his worst was his second season, at 18.1.

The number of top five finishes (82) recorded by Ned Jarrett during the 1964 and 1965 seasons. During the 1964 season, Jarrett recorded 40 top five finishes in 59 races started and finished the season in second place behind Richard Petty. The following year, Jarrett recorded the most top five finishes in a season in the history of NASCAR when he finished the season with 42 top five finishes and the championship.

The number of victories (83) recorded by Cale Yarborough over his 31 year career. Yarborough would win almost 15% of all races started, and place in the top five in over 45% of races started.

The number of victories (84) recorded by two of NASCAR's all-time greatest drivers. Darrell Waltrip (1972-2000, 809 races) and Bobby Allison (1961-88, 717 races) each took the checkered flag 84 times, tying for third on the all-time list for victories.

Entering the 2007 season, the number of career starts (85) recorded by Carl Edwards. In just three seasons on the Sprint Cup Series, Edwards has recorded four victories and has finished in the top ten in over half of the races he's started (43 of 85). He also has solid career earnings of $13.7 million.

The number of second place finishes (86) recorded by Bobby Allison between 1961 and 1988. Allison would record two more runner-up finishes than victories over that span, and coupled with his 71 third place finishes, would complete one-third of all races entered in the top three. 86 is also the number of career starts on the Busch Series recorded by Bobby's son, Davey.

The car number (87) of 1992 Busch Series champion Joe Nemechek. Nemechek would hold off defending champion Bobby Labonte by a mere three points for the championship. In the closest and most exciting finish in Busch history, Nemechek finished in sixth place on the final race of the season at Hickory . . . he needed it as Labonte took the checkered flag at the race.

The number of top five finishes (88) that Bobby Allison recorded between 1961 and 1988 when driving a car he owned. Of those

88 top five finishes, 14 were victories and 20 were in the runner-up position.

The car number (89) that gave one driver his sole victory and another half of his. Buddy Shuman, who started in 29 NASCAR races between 1951 and 1955, recorded his sole NASCAR victory driving the #89 when, on July 1, 1952, he captured Grand National Race #18 at Stamford Park in Niagara Falls, Ontario. Eight years later, Joe Lee Johnson collected his second and final NASCAR victory driving #89 to victory lane in the World 600 at Charlotte Motor Speedway.

Entering the 2007 season, the number of Sprint Cup and Busch Series races (90) held at Talladega Superspeedway since it first started hosting races in 1969. The Sprint Cup Series ran one race there in 1969 and has since run two races per-year at the Superspeedway. Busch began using the Superspeedway in 1992 and runs one race per-year at the track.

The average finish position (9.1) by Greg Biffle during his five years racing on the Craftsman Truck Series. Biffle's worst average finish was during his first season racing trucks. He averaged a 15.1 finish position over 27 races. The following year, his average finish position jumped to 6.7, as did his position in the final standings (from eighth to second). His third and final full season on Craftsman saw Biffle cut his average finish position to 5.8. That was good enough over 24 races to earn him the Craftsman Truck Series championship.

The car number (92) that took Herb Thomas to 43 of his 48 overall NASCAR victories. Only one other driver has taken number 92 to victory lane. Marvin Panch is the only other driver to accomplish the feat, he recorded a single victory driving a #92 car.

The number of career starts (93) recorded by Dave Blaney over nine seasons on the Busch Series. Between 1998 and 2006, Blaney won one race and recorded 24 top ten finishes, having more success on the Busch Series than on the Sprint Cup. Entering 2007, Blaney has also started 234 Sprint Cup races, but has recorded three fewer top ten finishes and has yet to take the checkered flag.

94 The average finish position (9.4) per race by Bobby Hamilton during his 2004 Craftsman championship season. Hamilton recorded three victories, 12 top five finishes, and 16 top ten finishes en route to his first and only championship on the Craftsman Truck Series.

95 The number of victories (95) that separate number one and number two on NASCAR's all-time victory list. Richard Petty (200 victories in 1,184 races) leads all drivers with David "Silver Fox" Pearson (105 victories in 574 races) in the second spot.

96 The number of victories (96) recorded by Richard Petty during his five most successful campaigns. Petty, who holds five spots in NASCAR's "top ten" all-time single-season victory category, recorded 27 victories (#1) in 1967, 21 victories (#2) in 1971, 18 victories (#4) in 1970, 16 victories (#6) in 1968, and 14 victories (#10) in 1963. These five seasons, dominated so clearly by Petty, saw him record almost half of his NASCAR record 200 victories.

97 The number of short track poles earned (97) by Richard Petty. The 97 poles is a Sprint Cup Series record and is over twice as many as David Pearson, who sits in second place on the list with 47.

98 The car number (98) that Marvin Panch took to victory lane on December 2, 1956 in Concord, North Carolina. Hosting the Grand National Race #2, Concord Speedway's half-mile dirt track saw Panch take the checkered flag in Pete DePaolo's 1956 Ford and earn $650 for his efforts.

99 The number of top three finishes (99) recorded by Dale Earnhardt during his seven championship seasons. Earnhardt tallied 44 victories, 31 second place finishes, and 24 third place finishes in 1980, 1986, 1987, 1990, 1991, 1993, and 1994, the seasons he claimed the most prestigious title in NASCAR.

100 The average finish position (10.0) by Greg Biffle during his Busch Series championship season of 2002. Biffle, who won the Craftsman Truck Series championship two years before, was consistent all year long, finishing 20 of 34 starts in the top five and an additional five races in the 6-10 position.

LEE PETTY

STARTS	WINS	TOP 5	TOP 10	CHAMPIONSHIPS
427	54	231	332	3

LEE vs. RICHARD
(76 TOTAL RACES)

	LEE	RICHARD
	LEE	RICHARD
HEAD-TO-HEAD	52 WINS	24 WINS
ACTUAL RACE STATS		
WINS	16	5
TOP 5's	45	25
TOP 10's	61	43
AVERAGE FINISH	7.6	11.6

RICHARD PETTY

STARTS	WINS	TOP 5	TOP 10	CHAMPIONSHIPS
1124	200	555	712	7

Chapter Two

Father Knows Best

There is little doubt to who the King of NASCAR is, but when it comes down to who is the King of the Pettys, it isn't Richard who holds the crown. Richard may hold more NASCAR records, to include the big ones (championships and wins), but it was Lee who dominated the head-to-head competition between father and son. The father-son rivalry began on July 18, 1958 at the Canadian Exposition Stadium in Toronto, Canada. It would be Lee's race and year . . . he won both the race and the season championship. Richard finished 17th. It wasn't until Richard's 12th race against his father that he found the edge. On March 29, 1959, Richard placed third at the Wilson Speedway in Wilson, North Carolina. Lee finished the race in fourth place.

In head-to-head competition, Lee finished ahead of Richard in 68.4% of all the races they both started (52 of 76 races). In fact Lee dominated pretty much the entire race line. Lee won 16 races to Richard's five. Lee placed in the top five in 45 of 76 races compared to Richard's 25 top five finishes. Lee placed in the top ten in 61 of the races, Richard in just 43 (coincidently the same number as the car that he made famous). Lee's average finish was four positions higher than Richard's, 11.6 to 7.6.

The final father-son race occurred on July 19, 1964 at Watkins Glen International in New York. The 1964 at the Glen saw Richard strike the final blow in the father-son rivalry. Richard started the race in fourth place, but faded and finished in 21st place. Lee, on the other hand, started in the 20th position, but he too would drop. Lee fell just two spots but by the time the race was over Lee was in 22nd place, one spot behind his son. The King may have struck the final blow, but in the end it was Lee who dominated the father-son series. It just goes to show that Pettys (and NASCAR) are very much like an American icon . . . Father Knows Best.

The number of career starts (101) recorded by Robert Ingram on the Busch Series. Between 1983 and 1988 Ingram recorded 35 top ten finishes, but was unable to find a victory. His career year was in 1987 when he started in all 27 races, earned his sole pole, and recorded seven top ten finishes.

The number of top ten finishes (102) recorded by Bob Welborn. Welborn, named one of NASCAR's 50 greatest drivers of all-time, started 183 races between 1952 and 1964 and recorded nine victories, 58 top five finishes, and 102 top tens. Welborn would place in the top ten in over 55% of races entered during his 13 year career.

The number of career starts (103) recorded by Larry Frank over 11 seasons racing NASCAR. Frank recorded 32 top ten finishes and one victory, which came at the 1962 Southern 500 at Darlington Raceway in South Carolina.

The average start position (10.4) of Red Byron in his 15 career NASCAR starts. Byron only raced three seasons, but had an immediate impact. He won the 1949 championship, starting the six of eight races entered from the 2.2 position. The following year, he entered four of 19 races with an average starting position of 3.3. It certainly helped that in two of his first ten races he started from the pole position. In his final season and last five races, Byron held an average starting position of 23.8. On a positive note, due to his lower starting position, Byron's third season saw him better his average finish position by 8.6 over his starting position, while his previous two seasons it had dropped.

The average start position (10.5) of LeeRoy Yarbrough in 198 races started. Over his 12-year career, Yarbrough would earn 11 poles with his season average start position ranging from 5.5 to 19.4. Yarbrough also had a stretch of five consecutive years (1966-70) where his average start would be in the top ten.

The number of races started (106) by Scott Riggs, as of the beginning of the 2007 Sprint Cup Series. Riggs, who managed 16 top ten finishes over his first three years on the circuit, enjoyed more success on the Busch Series before making the switch. He won the Raybestos Rookie of the Year Award in 2002 with 13 top ten finishes in 34 races and a tenth-place finish in the final point standings. The following year, he finished sixth in the final standings.

The average start position (10.7) of Emanuel Zervakis during his best season racing NASCAR. In his 38 starts on the 1961 season, Zervakis managed 28 top ten finishes and, on average, finished three positions better (7.8) than when he started. He finished the season with two victories and was ranked third in the final standings.

The average start position (10.8) by Jimmie Johnson during his first Sprint Cup championship in 2006. 10.8 is also the average finish position by Jimmie Johnson the year after, which marked his second consecutive championship season.

The number of points (109) earned by Terry Labonte on three separate occasions during the 2003 season. Labonte, who finished tenth in the final season rankings in the Sprint Cup, recorded 109 points at the Sirius at the Glen, the Silvania 300, and the UAW-GM Quality 500 by placing 18th in each race.

The number of laps run (110) by Joe Eubanks at the Orange Speedway (Occoneechee Speedway) in Hillsboro, North Carolina on September 28, 1958. The 47th race of 51 on the season took place on a .900 dirt track with Eubanks managing to lead 12 laps en route to his only NASCAR victory (and a payday of $800).

The record for the most races started before earning a victory (111) in the Craftsman Truck Series. Bryan Reffner, who entered the series in 1996, was unable to win a race until October 13, 2000, when he pulled off a victory at the 2000 O'Reilly 400 at Texas Motor Speedway. Reffner was unable to duplicate the result in his final 15 career starts over the next three years.

The average finish position (11.2) of Dan Gurney over ten seasons racing NASCAR. Gurney only had 16 career starts to his name and never started in more than four races in a season (he also took a ten year hiatus between his 15th and 16th season). What makes Gurney even more impressive than an 11.2 average finish is that he won five of his 16 career starts and placed in the top ten in half of all races started.

The number of poles won (113) by David Pearson over 27 years racing on the Sprint Cup. Pearson sits at number two on NASCAR's list of all-time pole winners just 13 poles behind Richard Petty. But taking into account that Pearson accomplished the feat in eight fewer seasons and 610 fewer starts than Petty, Pearson is simply the King of the pole position.

The number of top five finishes (114) recorded by Dale Earnhardt Jr. through the end of the 2006 season on the Busch and Sprint Series. Earnhardt Jr. placed in the top five 45 times on Busch (34 of those coming in his only two full seasons . . . both of which he won the championship) and 69 times on the Sprint Cup Series.

The number of top ten finishes (115) recorded by Donnie Allison in 21 years on the NASCAR circuit. The 1970 Rookie of the Year had ten victories in his career and earned just over $1 million. His career was cut short after a crash in the 1981 World 600 (he would only enter into 13 more races after that). He is perhaps best remembered for his part in the infield rumble during the nationally televised 1979 Daytona 500 when he and brother Bobby got into a fight with Cale Yarborough after a crash.

The number of Sprint Cup victories (116) recorded by an Oldsmobile. The Olds ranks fifth on the list of most successful cars by manufacturer and had dominating seasons in 1950, 1951, and 1978. In those three years, an Oldsmobile car won 42 of 80 races.

The number of laps completed (117) by Greg Sacks at the 1996 Humminbird Fishfinder 500K at Talladega. Sacks recorded his sole Busch Series victory on the July 26th race to go along with his one victory on the Sprint Cup, also recorded in July (1985).

The winning percentage (.118) of Parnelli Jones during his 12-year NASCAR career. Between 1956 and 1970, Jones started in 34 races, averaging less than three starts per season. He managed four victories in four different seasons with winning percentages of .100 (1957), .333 (1958), .500 (1959), and .1000 (1967).

The number of times (119) that Junior Johnson finished a race in the top five. Of those 119 finishes, 50 were victories and 18 were in the runner-up position. Johnson, whose career would span 14 years, finished in the top five in approximately 38% of all races he entered.

The record for the most races between wins (120) on the Craftsman Truck Series, held by Rick Crawford. Crawford, who won the 1998 Florida Dodge Dealers 400, could not find victory again until claiming the checkered flag at the same race in 2003.

The average finish position (12.1) by Billy Wade over his three-season NASCAR career. Wade started 70 races between 1962 and 1964, with his most successful season being his last. In 1964, Wade started in 35 races and recorded 25 top ten finishes, 12 of which were top five finishes, as well as all four of his career victories. He also had an average finish position of 9.5 per race entered, his career best.

Entering the 2007 season, the number of top ten finishes (122) recorded by Michael Waltrip in 22 years on the Sprint Cup Series. Of his 122 top ten finishes, 38 have been top fives and four have been victories.

The number of top ten finishes (123) recorded by Davey Allison over 277 career starts in the Sprint Cup and Busch Series over ten years of racing. On the Busch Series, Allison recorded 31 top ten finishes in 86 career starts while on the Sprint Cup Series, he finished in the top ten 92 times out of 191 starts.

The number of career starts (124) recorded by Charlie Glotzbach. Glotzbach began his NASCAR career at the age of 22 in 1950 and stopped racing in 1993 at the age of 54. During the 33-year span, he started in at least one race in 15 seasons, but he was most active between 1968 and 1971. During that four-year span, Glotzbach started in 73 races and recorded all four of his NASCAR victories.

The winning percentage (.125) of "Big Bill" France at the Daytona Beach course over 16 starts between 1936 and 1941. In the predecessor to what is now NASCAR, France recorded two victories and six top ten finishes as a driver before turning his attention to promoting racing. As they say, the rest is history.

The margin of victory in points (126) by Mike Skinner over Joe Ruttman in the inaugural Craftsman Series Cup in 1995. Skinner would take the checkered flag eight times in 20 starts for his first and only Craftsman Series title.

The number of career starts (127) by Paul Goldsmith. Goldsmith, who raced between 1956 and 1969, recorded 59 top ten finishes, nine of which were victories. Over his career, Goldsmith would earn almost $200,000 and earn more victories than legends like Herschel McGriff and Tiny Lund.

The number of NASCAR races (128) that A.J. Foyt would compete in during his 20-year NASCAR career. Foyt, arguably the best race car driver ever and certainly the best to race Indy Car, never started in more that seven races in any season. He would compile seven victories on the NASCAR circuit and win three-quarters of a million dollars.

129 The average start position (12.9) by Dale Earnhardt over 676 career starts on the Sprint Cup Series. His best average start position was during his fourth championship season in 1990, where the Intimidator averaged a start position of 5.9. The worst average start position during a real season (during his first four seasons, Earnhardt started five or fewer races per season) was in 1998, where his average start position was 26.5.

130 The number of career starts (130) recorded by Tom Pistone in 11 years racing NASCAR. Pistone raced between 1955 and 1968, recording 53 top ten finishes, two of which were victories. The bulk of Pistone's starts came over four seasons (1959-60, 1965-66), where he recorded 103 of his career starts. His best season came in 1959, where he recorded 18 top ten finishes in 22 races started, earned both of his career victories, and finished sixth in the final points standing.

131 Entering the 2007 season, the number of top ten finishes (131) recorded by Mike Bliss. Bliss has not had too much success on the Sprint Cup, recording only five top ten finishes in 77 races, but he gets much better from there. In his first eight years on the Busch Series, Bliss recorded 29 top ten finishes in 84 races entered. On the Craftsman Truck Series, he has been blissful, recording 97 top ten finishes in his first 174 races.

132 Heading into the 2007 season, the number of races won (132) by Junior Johnson as a car owner. Johnson, who himself won 50 races of 313 entered between 1953 and 1966, has become a greater legend as an owner than a driver. His 132 victories as an owner place him in second on the all-time list behind Petty Enterprises. Two of his drivers, Cale Yarborough (1976-78) and Darrell Waltrip (1981-82, 1985), earned Junior six Sprint Cups.

133 The average finish position (13.3) of Cotton Owens over 15 seasons and 160 NASCAR starts. Owens, who entering the 2007 season ranked 54th on the Sprint Cup list for all time wins, averaged a little over ten starts per season with his best average finish season being his last at

1.5 (Owens started two races and recorded one victory and one third place finish).

134 The average finish position (13.4) of Bob Flock in 36 career starts. Flock, the eldest of the three Flock brothers, was one of NASCAR's original drivers, beginning his career in 1949. In his seven years of racing, Flock recorded 18 top ten finishes and took the checkered flag on four occasions. His lowest finish in any single event occurred in his first race, when he finished in 32nd place at the Charlotte Speedway on June 19, 1949.

135 The number of points (135) that separated rookies Travis Kvapil and Ricky Hendrick in the 2001 final point standings in the Craftsman Truck Series. The season marked the first and only time in the 11 years that the Rabestos Rookie of the Year Award has been given that two rookies finished the season in the top ten in points. Kvapil would win the Raybestos Rookie of the Year finishing the season with 3,547 points (versus Hendrick's 3,412) and follow it up two years later with a series championship.

136 The number of points (136) separating the top three drivers at the end of the 2006 Craftsman Truck Series season. Todd Bodine would claim the title with 3,666 points followed by Johnny Benson with 3,539 and David Reutimann with 3,530 points.

137 The average finish position (13.7) of Jimmy Florian during his most successful season racing NASCAR. Florian's rookie season (1950) was his most active and best season racing. He started in ten of the 19 races scheduled that season from, on average, the 33rd position, yet finished almost 20 spots better. He finished six of ten races in the top ten, including his only NASCAR victory.

138 The average finish position (13.8) of Gober Sosebee over his 71 race NASCAR career. Sosebee started each race slightly better than he finished, on average between tenth and 11th position (10.8). His best season was in 1952, when he finished an average of tenth place; his worst was two years prior, when he could only manage a 23.9 average finish position in two races.

139 The percentage of laps raced (.139) by Bobby Allison on the Sprint Cup Series in which he watched the rest of the field in his rearview mirror. Allison, who completed a total of 197,438 laps in his 25 years on the circuit, led a total of 27,539 laps en route to 85 career victories. It is also the number of laps led per-race (13.9) by Buddy Baker over 33 years on the NASCAR circuit.

140 The length in miles (1.40) of the Marchbanks Speedway located in Hanford, California. The track hosted three NASCAR races in 1951, 1960, and 1961. The track was a .500 mile oval when the 1951 race was held, but the 1960 and 1961 races were both held on the 1.40 mile track. It is the location where Fireball Roberts became the only NASCAR driver ever to lead from start to finish on a long-distance Superspeedway. He did it in 1961 leading all 178 laps of the eighth race of the season and his margin of victory was over two laps.

141 The number of career starts (141) recorded by Bobby Johns over 14 years. Between 1956 and 1969, Johns started between one and 19 races per season, averaging just over ten starts per season. He managed 36 top ten finishes and recorded two victories in his racing career and posted his best overall season in 1960, recording one of his two victories and ten top ten finishes en route to a third place ranking in the final season points.

142 The margin of victory in seconds (1.42) by Bill Elliot over Michael Waltrip at the 2001 Pennzoil Freedom 500 on November 11, 2001. Elliot held the lead in 59 laps over the course of the race and, averaging 117.449 mph, edged out Waltrip for his sole victory on the season and his 40th career win.

143 The percentage of races entered (.143) in which Sara Christian would place in the top five. Christian was NASCAR's first female driver and she was there from the start. She raced in six races during the 1949 season and one race the following year. She remains the only female driver to record a top five finish in NASCAR.

144 The number of career starts (144) recorded by Casey Mears after four years on the Sprint Cup circuit. Mears, who has yet to find victory lane, has finished in the top ten 26 times and has earned over $16 million since coming over from the Busch Series after his rookie season.

The average finish position (14.5) of Benny Parsons over 526 career starts. Parsons, whose NASCAR career spanned three decades, spent nine consecutive years in the top five season ending rankings on the Sprint Cup, averaging anywhere between a 7.8 and 14.6 finish position per season.

The margin of victory in seconds (.146) by Terry Labonte over Bobby Labonte in the 1997 Die Hard 500 at Talladega Super Speedway. Terry beat his kid brother by a fraction of a second to secure his sole victory of the season. Terry needed it come season's end as he edged out his little brother by 76 points in the final standings, finishing one spot above Bobby in sixth place.

The number of top ten finishes (147) by racing pioneer Wendell Scott. Scott, the first African American driver to compete in the Sprint Cup Series, raced for 13 seasons before retiring due to injuries suffered in a 1973 crash at Talladega.

The number of laps (148) that Dan Gurney led during the 1966 Motor Trend 500 at the Riverside International Raceway in California. In the only race entered by Gurney that season, he led 148 of 185 laps (.800) en route to a victory over David Pearson.

Entering the 2007 season, the percentage of laps raced (.149) by Jack Sprague on the Craftsman Truck Series in which he would be leading. In his 11 seasons racing trucks, Sprague completed 40,871 laps and he was in the lead for 6,104 of them. Sprague had two seasons in which he led in over 1,000 laps. In 1997, he led a total of 1,004 laps and in 2001, it was 1,386. Coincidently, he won the championship both of those seasons.

Entering the 2007 season, the number of races started (150) by Greg Biffle on the Sprint Cup Series. Biffle, driving for Jack Roush and sponsored by Ameriquest, has driven for five seasons and won 11 races. His best season was 2005, where he compiled six victories and was the championship series runner-up.

The average finish position (15.1) over 13 seasons in races started by Wendell Scott. On average, Scott started each of his 495 races between the 20th and 21st position (20.4 to be exact) and, over the course of each race, improved five spots by the time the race was over.

The average start position (15.2) of Indy Car legend Mario Andretti in his NASCAR starts. Between 1966 and 1969, Andretti entered 14 races, recording one win and three top ten finishes. His average finish position in these races was 19.9. His 1967 season with NASCAR was his best. He entered six races, recording all of his top ten victories and sole victory, averaging a finish position in 14.8, en route to earning approximately $52,000.

The number of top ten finishes (153) recorded by NASCAR legend Joe Weatherly. Weatherly, a World War II veteran and American Motorcycle Association Hall-of-Famer, started his NASCAR career in 1952. Over the next 12 years, Weatherly would start in 230 races, collecting 153 top ten finishes, 25 of which were victories.

Entering the 2007 season, the record for the number of races without a win (154) on the Craftsman Truck series. Between the 1996 Florida Dodge Dealers 400 and the 2002 Ford 200, Lance Norick could not muster up a win, although he did place in the top ten 15 times over the seven-year span.

The number of laps (155) Red Byron finished during the final race of the 1949 season. At the Wilkes 200, held at the half-mile dirt track in North Wilkesboro, North Carolina on October 16, 1949, Byron pulled off a 16th place finish and, although he didn't earn any money for his efforts, he was able to win the season's championship over Lee Petty (who finished second that day).

The number of top ten finishes (156) recorded by Neil Bonnet in 362 races started. Bonnet, who raced in 18 seasons on the Sprint Cup Series between 1974 and 1993, would finish in the top ten in just over

43% of all races entered. Bonnet was statistically more successful on the Busch Series, placing in the top ten in 54% of races started (seven of 13).

The margin of victory in seconds (1.57) by Mark Martin over Jimmy Spencer at the 1997 Coca-Cola 300. Martin would collect one of his four season victories at the Texas Motor Speedway and help himself to 180 points en route to a third place finish on the season.

The number of races run (158) by Fred Lorenzen between 1956 and 1972. Lorenzen, known as "Golden Boy," "Fabulous Freddy," or the "Elmhurst [IL] Express," was a popular figure with the fans and not too shabby on the track either. Lorenzen won a total of 26 races and became the first driver to win over $100,000 in a season when, in 1963, he won six races and finished third in points, earning more money than the champion (Joe Weatherly) and runner-up (Richard Petty) . . . combined.

The number of Dodge cars that found victory lane (159) on the Sprint Cup between 1949 and 1998. As NASCAR hit the half-century mark, Dodge cars ranked fourth on the most successful manufacturer list behind Ford, Chevy, and Plymouth despite not recording a victory between 1978 and 1998.

The number of career starts (160) recorded by Cotton Owens. Between 1950 and 1964, Owens started an average of almost 11 races per season, but most of his starts came over a six-year span. Between 1957 and 1962, Owens started 130 of his 160 total races.

The number of laps raced (161) at the 2004 Brickyard 400 due to green/white/checker. The 160 lap race was extended an additional lap due to a crash by Brian Vickers on lap 156 and it became the first race to finish under the green/white/checker system. Jeff Gordon eventually won the race with Dale Jarrett finishing second.

The average start (16.2) and finish position (16.2) for Ron Hornaday Jr. over 173 Busch Series starts. Hornaday may be best known for his success on the Craftsman Truck Series where he has won two series championships and his average start and finish position are in the top ten, but he has also been pretty successful racing Busch (four victories and 64 top ten finishes). His best average start and finish positions came in 2003 when, racing a full 34 race schedule, he started on average in the ten spot and finished one spot back (11.1).

163   Entering the 2007 season, the number of top five finishes (163) recorded by Sprint Cup driver Dale Jarrett. Of the 163 top five finishes recorded during Jarrett's 23-year career, 120 of them came in seasons in which he finished in the top five in the final season point standings.

164   The percentage of laps raced (.164) by Dick Hutcherson during his final NASCAR season in which he would hold the lead. Hutcherson led 1,455 of 8,893 laps raced in 1967 and managed 22 top five finishes, of which two were victories. Hutcherson would finish the season ranked third behind Richard Petty and James Hylton. Not incredibly impressive at first glance, but dig a little deeper and it was an amazing season. Hutcherson only raced in 33 of the 49 races ran that season while Petty and Hylton ran 48 and 46 races, respectively. Hutcherson earned an average of 1,020 points per race and, if he maintained that average and raced in just 43 races, would have captured the championship.

165   The number of laps led (165) by Mario Andretti while racing NASCAR. Between 1966 and 1969, Andretti started in 14 races on the Spint Cup. He was most successful during the 1967 season when he started in six races, finishing three in the top ten, and earned his sole victory racing NASCAR at the 1967 Daytona 500. He led 112 laps during that race and 137 laps throughout the season.

166   The margin of victory in seconds (1.66) at the 1984 Talladega 500 and the 1993 First Union 400. At Talladega, Dale Earnhardt earned one of his two season victories by squeaking by Buddy Baker. Nine years later Rusty Wallace would beat Dale Earnhardt by that same margin at the Bristol International Speedway. That season Wallace found victory lane ten times (one-third of all races run), but it was Earnhardt who edged out Wallace for the championship by 80 points.

Entering the 2007 season, the number of top ten finishes (167) in the Sprint Cup and Busch Series by Dale Earnhardt Jr. Junior has recorded 109 top ten finishes in 255 starts on the Sprint Cup and 58 top ten finishes in 92 races entered on the Busch Series. Over his career, Earnhardt Jr. has placed in the top ten in .481 of all races entered.

The margin of victory in seconds (1.68) at the 1993 Busch Series' Carolina Pride/Budweiser 250 at Myrtle Beach Speedway. Jeff Burton edged big brother Ward Burton to record his sole season victory and his fourth career victory on the Busch Series, along with a $25,000 paycheck.

The percentage of laps raced (.169) by Richard Petty throughout his career in which he would find himself in the lead. Petty would complete 307,848 laps over 1,184 races and lead a total of 52,135 of those while racing on the Sprint Cup.

The margin of victory in seconds (.170) by Mark Martin over Ernie Irvan in the 1993 Sprint Cup "Slick 50" 500 at Phoenix International Raceway. The margin of victory is a track record over the 22 races held at that venue.

The pole speed (171) in miles per hour at the 1971 Texas 500 at the Texas Motor Speedway at College Station, Texas. On December 12, 1971, Pete Hamilton would start the race from the pole but it was Richard Petty starting from the third position who would take the race (averaging 144 mph) and the season championship. Petty became only the fourth driver to win both the final race of the season and the championship in the same year.

The average start position (17.2) that Terry Labonte has become accustomed to over 30 years of racing NASCAR. Labonte has a virtually identical average starting position of 17.2 over 848 career starts on Sprint Cup and 124 starts on Busch. On both circuits Labonte finished his races on average better than he started them, 16.0 and 14.1 on the Sprint Cup and Busch Series, respectively.

173 The number of career starts (173) recorded by Johnny Allen over his 13-year NASCAR career. Allen, who began racing NASCAR in 1955, started in 173 races and retired from the sport with 61 top ten finishes and a single victory to his name.

174 The average number of laps led (17.4) per-race by NASCAR legend LeeRoy Yarbrough. Yarbrough led a total of 3,439 laps over 198 starts during his 12-year career. His best season came in 1968, when LeeRoy led 1,300 laps of 6,423 total laps completed and finished the season ranked 16th overall.

175 The amount of money earned, in dollars (175), by legend Glen Wood during his first four seasons racing NASCAR. Wood would enter into six races between 1953 and 1956, but would fail to earn any more than $100 in any race. He finished the first season with $125 in winnings and earned $50 during the 1956 season, with no money earned in two starts between 1954 and 1955.

176 Entering the 2007 season, the number of top ten finishes (176) recorded by Jeff Burton. Burton, having completed 14 seasons on the Sprint Cup Series, has recorded 101 top fives and 18 victories within the 176 top ten finishes.

177 The number of career starts (177) by Jerry Nadeau on the Sprint Cup over seven years. Nadeau recorded 19 top ten finishes with his sole NASCAR victory coming during the last race of the 2000 season when he beat out Dale Earnhardt at the Atlanta Motor Speedway in the NAPA 500.

178 Entering the 2007 season, the number of Busch Series starts (178) recorded by Bobby Labonte. Labonte, who began racing on the Busch Series in 1982, has concentrated predominately on the Sprint Cup since becoming a regular in 1993. On the Busch Series, Labonte has recorded 95 top ten finishes, including nine victories, and has earned almost $1.7 million.

179 The margin of victory (1.79), in seconds, by Terry Labonte over teammate Jeff Gordon at the 1994 Miller Genuine Draft 400 at the

Richmond International Raceway in Richmond, Virginia. Labonte would record two additional wins on the season and edge out Gordon one more time . . . in the final season standings. Labonte finished the season in seventh place, one place and 100 points better than Gordon.

180 The number of top five finishes (180) recorded by Ned Jarrett between 1953 and 1966. Jarrett earned 50 victories, 37 runner-ups, 38 third place finishes, 28 fourth place finishes, and 24 fifth place finishes in 352 races. He finished in the top five in over half of all the races he entered.

181 The number of NASCAR starts (181) recorded by Carl Edwards in just three seasons. Edwards has raced on the Sprint Cup, Busch, and Craftsman Series' and, between 2004 and 2006, averaged over 60 starts per season. Edwards hasn't just shown up at the racetrack a lot, he has had a great deal of success as well. On the Sprint Cup, he started in 85 races, recording 43 top ten finishes of which four were victories. He also finished third in the final season standings during the 2005 season. On the Busch Series, Edwards started in 70 races, recording nine victories and 46 top ten finishes. He finished the season ranked third in 2005 and second in 2006 as well. On Craftsman, where he began his NASCAR career, Edwards started in 26 races, recording three victories and 18 top ten finishes and, in 2004, finished the season ranked fourth.

182 The approximate amount of winnings (182) in thousands of dollars by Benny Parsons during his 1973 championship season. Parsons would finish 75% of the races he started in the top ten (21 of 28). The only seven times he did not finish in the top ten were when he did not finish the race. Parsons' consistency paid off with solid earnings and his sole NASCAR championship.

183 Entering the 2007 season, the number of career starts (183) recorded by Jimmie Johnson. A rising superstar who has the highest average winnings per start at $241,173, Johnson has recorded 23 victories (for a winning percentage of .126) in just six seasons and has earned over $44 million.

184 The number of top ten finishes (184) recorded by Ken Schrader between 1984 and 2006. Schrader had a streak of ten consecutive years in which he reached double digits in top ten finishes. Of the 184 top tens, approximately one-third were top-fives, but only four resulted in victories.

185 The number of laps led (185) by Ted Musgrave during his 2005 Craftsman Truck Series championship season. Musgrave only led in 185 of 4,158 laps raced and won the title despite the fact that, in the category of laps led, that season was his worst performance to date. In his previous four seasons in which he placed either in the second or third ranking come seasons end, he led an average of 780 laps per season.

186 Entering the 2007 season, the number of top ten finishes (186) recorded by Joe Nemechek since he began racing the Busch Series in 1989. Nemechek has recorded 121 of his top ten finishes on the Busch Series in 271 races started. In 1993 Nemechek also began racing on the Sprint Cup, where he has recorded 61 additional top ten finishes in 430 career starts. Three years later, Nemechek tried his hand racing trucks and recorded an additional four top ten finishes in seven races started.

187 The number of career starts (187) recorded by Tim Flock over 13 years of racing on the Sprint Cup. Flock averaged between 14 and 15 races started per season, with the bulk of his career starts (167) coming between 1950 and 1956.

188 Entering the 2007 season, the number of career starts (188) recorded by Ryan Newman. Between 2000 and 2006, Newman was one of the most consistent qualifiers, posting 37 poles (despite an off-season in 2006). Newman has recorded 12 victories and won over $31 million in seven seasons.

189 The average finish position (18.9) by Matt Kenseth during his first full season racing on the Sprint Cup. Kenseth started all 34 races on the season, averaging a start position of 25.2. He raced better than he qualified and ended the season with 11 top ten finishes and an average finish position of 18.9. It didn't take very long for Kenseth to find his

groove . . . three seasons later he would be crowned the Sprint Cup champ averaging a 10.2 finish per race.

The number of top ten finishes (190) recorded by Geoff Bodine in 25 years racing on the Sprint Cup Series circuit. Bodine finished one-third of all races entered in the top ten (190 of 570) and enjoyed his best season in 1990, when he finished in the top ten in 19 of 29 races started.

The number of career starts (191) on the Sprint Cup Series by Davey Allison. Allison, whose career and life were cut way too short, died in a helicopter accident in the middle of the 1993 season. During his career, Allison racked up 92 top ten finishes, 66 of which were top five finishes, and 19 victories.

Entering the 2007 season, the number of top ten finishes (192) recorded by Bobby Labonte in 15 seasons racing in the Sprint Cup Series. Of Labonte's 192 top ten finishes, 113 were top five finishes and 21 were victories.

The number of points (193) Jeff Gordon came up short in his quest for the 2002 Sprint Cup. Gordon finished in fourth place behind Kurt Busch, Mark Martin, and champ Tony Stewart. In the following season Gordon would also place fourth, this time finishing 237 points behind champ Matt Kenesth.

Entering the 2007 season, the number of top five finishes (194) recorded by Ricky Rudd in 31 years on the Sprint Cup Series. Rudd placed in the top five in approximately 22.2% of all races entered (194 of 875). In the years that Rudd had double digit top five finishes (ten or more), he finished in the top ten in the final season standings (three sixth place finishes, two fifth place finishes, and one fourth and one ninth place finish).

As of 2007, the number of times (195) that the number 92 car has recorded a top ten finish. Most of those top tens were recorded by legend Herb Thomas, although other drivers such as Marvin Panch, Gerald Duke (who recorded six of his career seven top tens in the #92),

Skip Manning, and Terry Labonte have also recorded top ten finishes while driving 92.

The average finish position (19.6) of Greg Sacks during his most successful season on the Sprint Cup. During the 1985 season, Sacks started in 20 races, finishing in the top ten in five of those races and recording his sole Sprint Cup victory at the Pepsi Firecracker 400 at Daytona on the fourth of July.

The percentage of Sprint Cup career starts (.197) in which Ryan Newman started the race from the pole. Newman, likely NASCAR's best qualifier, has qualified pole 37 times in 188 races over seven seasons. He is one of a handful of drivers who can claim to have more pole qualifications than unfinished races.

The number of times (198) car number 43 took the checkered flag in the Sprint Cup Series. While it is true that Richard Petty is the most famous driver to lead #43 to victory, he is not the only one to have done so. While the King was responsible for 192 of the 198 victories, Bobby Hamilton (2), Jim Paschal (2), John Andretti (1), and Lee Petty (1) also earned victories while driving #43.

The number of laps raced (199) by Bill Amick at the Capital Speedway in Sacramento, California during the 25th race of the 1957 NASCAR season. In the only race hosted on the half-mile dirt track, Amick won the race by over a lap even though the race technically hadn't ended. Due to a scoring error, the race was shortened to 199 laps, cutting the 100 mile race short one-half a mile and giving Amick the distinction of winning the one and only NASCAR event held at the track in a 99.5 mile race.

The number of Winston Cup Series wins (200) by Richard Petty. Between 1958 and 1992, the King won 200 races, a Sprint Cup Series record. Petty also holds the record for races started (1,184), top five finishes (555), top ten finishes (714), pole-positions (184), laps completed (307,836), laps led (52,194), races led (599), and consecutive races won (ten) making Petty the undisputed king of stock car racing.

The Intimidator

YEAR	STARTS	WINS	TOP 5	TOP 10	RANK
1975	1	0	0	0	
1976	2	0	0	0	103
1977	1	0	0	0	118
1978	5	0	1	2	43
1979	27	1	11	17	7
1980	31	5	19	24	1
1981	31	0	9	17	7
1982	30	1	7	12	12
1983	30	2	9	14	8
1984	30	2	12	22	4
1985	28	4	10	16	8
1986	29	5	16	23	1
1987	29	11	21	24	1
1988	29	3	13	19	3
1989	29	5	14	19	2
1990	29	9	18	23	1
1991	29	4	14	21	1
1992	29	1	6	15	12
1993	30	6	17	21	1
1994	31	4	20	25	1
1995	31	5	19	23	2
1996	31	2	13	17	4
1997	32	0	7	16	5
1998	33	1	5	13	8
1999	34	3	7	21	7
2000	34	2	13	24	2
2001	1	0	0	0	57
TOTAL	676	76	281	428	

Chapter Three

"Finishing races is important, but racing is more important."

ale Earnhardt may not have been "the King," but with all due respect to Richard Petty, he was something equally, if not more, special. Earnhardt raced, and he raced to win . . . not to place in the top five or ten (even though he was incredibly successful at doing both), but to win. While some people didn't like his aggressive driving, he was anything but careless. In 676 races on the Sprint Cup, Earnhardt was only involved in 22 race-ending crashes . . . just over 3% of all races entered. Twenty-two crashes in 27 seasons . . . less than one a year. Earnhardt was by far more likely to have car problems, particularly engine problems. The Intimidator had 49 races come to an end because of engine problems; maybe it was because he pushed his car to the max, shooting for that checkered flag and another trip down victory lane.

If you were another driver on the circuit, you may have disliked looking in the rearview mirror to see the #3 on your tail and, when he passed you, maybe you cursed his name; but deep down you respected the man and his determination and drive to compete. If you were a fan, you probably shared the same sentiment as the #3 passed your team. When Earnhardt hit the wall in the final turn at the 2001 Daytona, many people thought it to be a relatively minor accident. After all, the car was generally intact . . . the hood had flipped up, not much more. In fact, Dale had hit the wall head-on at 150 mph and died on impact. The invincible had somehow fallen. No matter whether you loved the Intimidator or hated him, there was a sudden hollowness in the heart of NASCAR. The sport lost a living legend, one who still had many successful years ahead of him.

Earnhardt left an impact on NASCAR, consisting of both numbers and memories. He may have "only" recorded 76 wins over his 27 year Sprint Cup career, but he captured seven championships and left the sport far better than how he found it. He left the sport on top of his game and with a lasting memory of what a true NASCAR competitor should be.

The length in miles (201) of the fifth and final NASCAR race held in the state of Arkansas. On July 14, 1957, 28 drivers took to the 1.5 mile Memphis-Arkansas Speedway in LeHi, Arkansas and ran 134 laps. Marvin Panch recorded one of his six victories on the season by beating out Bill Amick and Fireball Roberts.

The number of top five finishes (202) by Rusty Wallace over his 16-year career. In 707 career starts, Wallace would take 55 checkered flags, finish in the runner-up position 42 times, and finish 3-5 another 105 times. 202 is also the number of top five finishes recorded by Buddy Baker over 699 starts between 1959 and 1992.

The total number of top five finishes (203) recorded by the Sprint Rookies-of-the-Year between 1958 and 2006. Seven different drivers recorded double digit top five finishes, led by James Hylton who, in 1966, placed in the top five 20 times, en route not only to Rookie of the Year honors, but a series runner-up finish.

The actual number of laps (204) run at the 2005 Kroger 200. The Busch series race, typically a 137.2 mile race over 200 laps on the 0.686 mile track, was extended to 204 laps due to a green/white/checker. Martin Truex Jr. needed the win . . . he won the Busch Series by a mere 68 points to secure his second consecutive championship.

The average finish position (20.5) of Bobby Johns in 141 NASCAR starts. Johns' career line is not all that impressive on the surface: 141 starts, two wins, 21 top five finishes, 36 top ten finishes, and $145,000 in career earnings over 14 years. Look a little closer at 1960, and you can see how Johns could have become a NASCAR champion. That season, Johns started in 19 of 44 races and still finished in third place in the final season point standings with 14,964 points, an average of 787.58 points per start. By comparison, champion Rex White started in 40 races and earned 21,164 points, or 529.1 points per start. Runner-up Richard Petty also started in 40 races, earned 17,228 points, and averaged 430.7 points per start. If Johns would have kept up his pace, he would have only needed 27 starts to claim the title compared to White and Petty's 40 starts.

The number of races (206) run by Edward Glenn "Fireball" Roberts. Roberts won 33 of those races in 15 years on the circuit and was certain to notch numerous others. His driving legacy, and sadly his life, was lost a little over a month after a crash at the 1964 World 600 at Charlotte. Roberts started the May 24th race in the 11th position, right in the middle of the pack. On lap seven, Ned Jarrett and Junior Johnson were involved in a crash, which Roberts tried to avoid. Roberts spun out and hit the retaining wall backwards, causing his car to flip and burst into flames. Roberts died a little over a month later, leaving a hole in the heart of NASCAR.

The number of career starts (207) by Alan Kulwicki on the Sprint Cup Series. Kulwicki raced between 1985 and 1993 and recorded five victories, 38 top five finishes, and 75 top ten finishes and captured the championship in 1992. The defending champ was taken from the racing community too soon when, in 1993, he died in a Hooters corporate plane crash.

The average start position (20.8) of Sterling Marlin in 74 Busch Series starts through 2005. Marlin would finish a bit better than he started with a 20.6 average finish position each race. Marlin recorded three seasons in which his average start position was within the top ten (7.0 in 1995, 8.5 in 1996, and 9.4 in 1999). His worst average start position came during his first Busch season in which he started one race, the Winn Dixie 300, in 29th place.

The number of times (209) that car #64 placed in the top ten of a race started. The first to score a top ten finish was Al Keller, who finished in the runner-up position on December 11, 1956. The last was Tommy Gale, who placed tenth in the Warner W. Hodgdon America 500 on October 30, 1983. Elmo Langley is the only driver to guide #64 to victory lane, doing so twice during the 1966 season.

The number of laps led (210) by Bobby Isaac at the 1972 Carolina 500 at North Carolina Motor Speedway in Rockingham, North Carolina. In what would be Isaac's 37th and last victory racing on the Sprint Cup, he would start the race from the pole and finish in the same position, leading 210 of the 492 laps.

The NASCAR record for career winning percentage (.211). Between 1949 and 1962, Herb Thomas won 48 races of 228 races entered, technically second behind Tim Flock by .0011, but considered by many to co-hold the record for the best winning percentage in NASCAR history.

The NASCAR record for career winning percentage (.212) for a driver. Between 1949 and 1961, Tim Flock won 40 of the 189 races he started, winning two championships (1952 and 1955) and occasionally riding with his monkey and "co-pilot" Jocko Flocko.

The average start position (21.3) by Matt Kenseth during the 2003 Sprint Cup season. What stands out about Kenseth that season is not where he started each race, but where he finished each race. His average finish position was 11.1 positions better than the start and, although Kenseth was only able to record a single victory on the season, he placed in the top ten in 25 of 36 races and won the championship with an average finish position of 10.2.

Entering the 2007 season, the number of career starts (214) recorded by Kevin Harvick. Harvick, who has been on the Sprint circuit for six seasons, has placed in the top ten in 86 of those races (to include ten victories) en route to over $33 million in earnings.

The average start (21.5) and finish (21.5) position by Dave Marcis during the 1969 season in races in which he was both owner and driver. In the Gwyn Staley 400, Marcis started in the fifth position and finished in 24th place. Eight races later, at the Motor State 500, Marcis started in 38th place and finished in 19th place. Those two races constituted the only ones that season in which Marcis was both the owner and driver.

The number of top ten finishes (216) recorded by Sterling Marlin in 14 years on the Sprint Cup. Through the end of the 2006 season Marlin, who began his racing career in 1976 and became a regular on the Sprint Cup in 1983, started in 711 races, recording 216 top ten finishes of which ten were victories.

The number of career starts (217) recorded by Jimmy Pardue between 1955 and 1964. Pardue raced sparingly between 1955 and 1959, only starting in nine races and recording one top ten finish. Between 1959 and 1964 though, Pardue started in no fewer than 29 races in a season and averaged 41.4 starts-per-year. He ended his career with 88 top ten finishes, 30 of those were top five showings and two victories.

Heading into the 2007 season, the number of Sprint Cup and Busch Series starts (218) recorded by Ryan Newman. Since beginning his NASCAR career in 2000, Newman has compiled quite the resume. He has started in 188 races on the Sprint Cup, recording 83 top ten finishes including 12 victories. On the Busch Series he has been even stronger, recording 19 top ten finishes (including seven victories) in just 30 starts.

The percentage of laps raced (.219) that Cale Yarborough found himself at the front of the pack. Yarborough completed 144,948 laps over his career and, of those laps, he led 31,677 of them.

Entering the 2007 season, the number of career starts (220) on the Sprint Cup Series by Kurt Busch. Over seven seasons, Busch has earned just over $36 million while finishing in the top ten 91 times. He placed third in the series in 2002 and captured the series championship two years later.

The margin of victory (2.21) in seconds by Bill Elliot over Rusty Wallace at the 1989 AC Spark Plug 500. Elliot, the most popular driver five years running, may have won the race over Wallace, but lost the title of most popular, at least for two years. Darrell Waltrip would take over the spot in 1989 and 1990, but Elliot would recapture the "most popular driver" title again in 1991 and hold it for ten more (consecutive) years.

The percentage of laps raced (.222) during Rusty Wallace's championship season of 1989 in which he was in the lead. Wallace ran 9,104 laps over 29 races, leading 2,021 of them. Over the 20 race season, Wallace averaged almost 70 laps in the lead per-race.

The average start position (22.3) of Ricky Craven while driving for Rick Hendrick in 1997. Over 30 starts, Craven recorded seven top tens and had an average finish position of 20.9. It is also the start position (22.3) of Jerry Nadeau while driving for Hendrick. In 2001, Nadeau started in 36 races and recorded ten top ten finishes and had an average finish position of 21.2.

The amount of money won (224) in thousands of dollars by NASCAR legend Rex White over nine years on the circuit. White began his career in 1956 and would start 233 races with 28 career victories. His most successful seasons were his back-to-back campaigns of 1960-61 where he won the Sprint Cup and then finished second. During those two seasons, White started in 87 races, recorded 13 victories, and earned just under $114,000.

225 The amount of earnings, in dollars (225), collected by LeeRoy Yarbrough during his first season racing NASCAR. Yarbrough entered one race during the 1960 NASCAR season and collected $225 with a 33rd place finish. Yarbrough crashed the #82 car after completing 60 of the 334 laps scheduled at the Atlanta Motor Speedway, ending his season and ranking him 137th come season's end.

226 The winning percentage (.226) recorded by Jim Reed during his best two seasons racing on the Sprint Cup. During the 1958 and 1959 seasons, Reed entered 31 races and recorded all seven of his NASCAR victories. In 1958, Reed started 17 races and recorded four victories. The following year he had 14 starts and recorded three victories. During these two seasons, not only did Reed record all of his victories, he recorded almost half of his 13-year career total for top five finishes (17 out of 38) and top ten finishes (21 out of 47).

227 The number of top five finishes (227) recorded by Lee Petty between 1949 and 1964. Petty, who ran 429 races over that span, recorded 54 victories, 48 second place finishes, 50 third place finishes, 46 fourth place finishes, and 29 fifth place finishes resulting in a top five finish rate of .529.

228 The number of career starts (228) by Todd Bodine on the Sprint Cup Series between 1992 and 2006. Bodine, who has split time between the Sprint Cup, Busch, and Craftsman Series, has started anywhere between one and 35 races on the Sprint Cup Series, averaging approximately 15 starts-per-year over the past 15 years.

229 The number of top ten finishes (229) recorded by Michael Waltrip over the past 22 years. Waltrip, who has started in 952 races entering the 2007 season over the three Series, has recorded 122 top ten finishes on the Sprint Cup, 104 top ten finishes on the Busch Series, and an additional three top ten finishes on the Craftsman Truck Series.

230 The number of races run (230) by Herb Thomas between 1949 and 1962. Thomas, one of NASCAR's original racers, took the checkered flag in 48 of those races for a winning percentage of .209. He would be NASCAR's first two-time champ, winning the cup in 1951 and 1953, and he would finish in second place in the standings in 1952 and 1954.

231 The number of laps raced (231) by Buddy Baker on the IROC circuit. Baker competed in the International Race of Champions in 1977 and 1980 and completed 149 out of 150 laps in 1977 and 80 of 80 laps during the first two races of the 1980 season. Baker's third race ended two laps into the 66 laps scheduled at the Oval Final. Baker, along with seven of the 11 other drivers, were involved in a crash on lap two, ending his IROC racing career.

232 The margin of victory in points (232) by Jack Sprague over Rich Bickle to capture the 1997 Craftsman Truck Series championship. Sprague and Bickle both won three races on the season, but Sprague recorded six more top ten finishes to edge out Bickle for the championship.

233 Number of races started (233) by NASCAR legend Rex White. White, one of NASCAR's 50 greatest drivers, raced over a nine-year span from 1956 until 1964. He would collect 28 victories and win the NASCAR championship in 1960.

234 The number of career starts (234) recorded by Lennie Pond. Between 1969 and 1989, Pond would start in at least one race in 17 different seasons. He had a career best fifth place showing in the final season point standings in 1976 on the strength of 19 top ten finishes in 30 races started. Two years later, Pond would finish seventh in the final point standings, but that season was perhaps more memorable. At the 1978 Talladega 500, Pond recorded his only NASCAR victory by beating out some of the "who's who" of NASCAR. Second through eighth position read as follows: Donnie Allison, Benny Parsons, Cale Yarborough, David Pearson, Bobby Allison, Richard Petty, and Neil Bonnett . . . doesn't get much better than that.

235 Heading into the 2007 season, the number of starts (235) on the Sprint Cup circuit by Dave Blaney. Driving for Bill Davis and sponsored primarily by Catepillar, Blaney has yet to win a race in his nine years on the Series. He has finished in the top ten 21 times though and has collected over $17 million in career earnings.

236 The percentage of starts (.236) by Tim Richmond in which he would finish in the top five. Richmond started in 185 races on the Sprint Cup and an additional ten races on the Busch Series, and recorded 42 and four top five finishes, respectively. Richmond's career was cut short when he contracted AIDS and, despite his desire to continue racing, was not allowed to compete. He died in 1989 at the age of 34.

237 How many more laps (237) Sam Ard led during his 1984 Busch Series championship season than he did the year before. During his second consecutive championship season, Ard would lead a total of 2,099 laps, bettering his previous year's total by 237 laps despite the fact that he entered seven fewer races.

238 The number of top ten finishes (238) recorded by Geoff Bodine in his NASCAR career. Bodine, who spent most of his time on the Sprint Cup Series, recorded 190 top ten finishes there, but added an additional 39 top tens on the Busch Series and nine from the Craftsman Truck Series to total 238 top ten finishes during his career.

239 The margin of victory in points (239) by Tommy Ellis over Rob Moroso in the final season point standing of the 1988 Busch Series. Ellis finished in the top ten in 20 of 30 races started to beat out some stiff competition and win $200,000 on the season.

240 The closest margin of victory in seconds (.240) in a NASCAR race held at the Riverside International Speedway in Riverside, California. Between 1958 and 1988, Riverside hosted 48 NASCAR races with the closest margin of victory occurring on November 22, 1981 at the Winston Western 500. On that day, Bobby Allison edged out Joe Ruttman to take one of his record six victories on the track.

241   The approximate amount of thousands of dollars (241) that Jimmie Johnson averages per race entered. As of the end of 2006, Johnson earned a total of $44,134,716 in 183 races, averaging $241,173 per race. The amount is the highest average earnings-per-race in NASCAR's history.

242   The number of career starts (242) recorded by Donnie Allison on the Sprint Cup. Between 1966 and 1988, Allison raced in 20 different seasons, averaging 12.1 starts per year while recording a total of 115 top ten finishes, of which ten were victories.

243   The amount of money earned (2.43) in thousands by Dale Earnhardt at the 1975 World 600 at Charlotte Motor Speedway in Concord, North Carolina. In his first NASCAR race, Earnhardt would finish in 22nd place and complete 355 laps of the 400 lap race. It would be a few more years before Earnhardt would start earning really good money, but after it began, the green just kept flowing. Earnhardt would earn over $42 million on the Sprint Cup as well as approximately $890,000 on the Busch Series. In addition to his NASCAR driving, Earnhardt would also earn a fair amount driving IROC. In 59 starts on the International Race of Champions, the Intimidator would earn an additional $1.29 million.

244   The average number of starts per season (2.44) recorded by Eddie Gray over nine years racing NASCAR. Between 1957 and 1966, Gray started in 22 races, recording four victories and nine top ten finishes. The most number of starts he recorded in any season was five, which occurred during his rookie season on 1957. The last four years, he entered in only one race each season.

245   The length in miles (2.45) of the NASCAR course at Watkins Glen International in New York. The track was completed in 1948 and, through the end of the 2006 season, has hosted 42 races since Buck Baker took the first checkered flag in 1957.

246   The number of top five finishes (246) recorded by NASCAR original and racing legend Buck Baker. Baker, who began racing NASCAR in 1949, would finish in the top five in almost 40% of

the 636 races he started over his 26 year career. His two best seasons were back-to-back efforts in 1956-57. In those seasons, Baker would record 31 and 30 top five finishes, respectively.

The average number of laps led (24.7) per start recorded by Jack Sprague in 247 starts. Between 1995 and 2006 Sprague led a total of 6,104 laps, averaging just under 25 laps-per-race in the lead. During that time frame, Sprague would win a total of 27 races en route to three Series championships.

The length (2.48) in thousands of feet of the grandstands at Chicagoland Speedway in Joliet, Illinois. The grandstands stand 15 stories tall and seat 75,000 fans. The track hosted its first NASCAR races on the weekend of July 14-15, 2001. Kevin Harvick recorded the first Sprint Cup victory with a win at the Tropicana 400 on July 14 while Jimmie Johnson took the checkered the following day on the Sam's Club presents Hill Bros. Coffee 300.

The number of laps raced (249) by Alan Kulwicki during his last season on the Busch Series. Kulwicki started his NASCAR career in 1984 on the Busch Series, starting in four events and recording three top ten finishes. The following season, he raced in just two Busch races, completing 249 of 320 laps, and earning $3,675. He then moved on to the Sprint Cup where seven years later he would claim the championship.

Weight in pounds (250) of driver Dewayne Louis Lund. "Tiny," who raced between 1955 and 1975, was a mammoth for a driver, not only in weight, but in height, standing 6'5". Lund would die in an accident at Talladega in 1975, but he left a lasting legacy in NASCAR. He may have only won five races in his career, but he was also awarded the Carnegie Medal for Heroism (along with Ernest Gahan, Stephen Petrasek, and Jerry Raborn) for rescuing driver Marvin Panch from a burning car during a practice run for the 1963 Daytona 500. Panch would ask Lund to drive in his place at Daytona, where Tiny would take his car to victory lane.

The number of top five finishes (251) by Cale Yarborough during his 32-year career. Yarborough would compete in 559 races during his career, taking the checkered flag 83 times, and finishing in the second through fifth spot 59, 46, 35, and 28 times respectively.

The length in miles (2.52) of the Sears Point International Raceway track through its first nine years of use. Located in Sonoma, California and now called the Infineon Raceway, the track was a 2.52 mile speedway between 1989 and 1997. The current track length is 1.99 miles.

The point difference (253) between Ricky Craven and Steve Grissom at the end of the 1993 Busch Series. It would be Grissom who would take home the championship despite tying for fifth in victories on the season. Grissom was in fact the only driver to hit double digits on top five finishes (11) which helped him secure the championship.

The total number of laps led (254) by Elliot Sadler during the 2004 Sprint Cup season. Sadler led 2.4% of all laps (10,517) and recorded his first two career victories en route to his most successful Sprint Cup season to date; Sadler finished the year in ninth place in the final season point standings.

Entering the 2007 season, the number of career starts (255) recorded by Kyle Petty. In just eight seasons on the Sprint Cup circuit, Petty has recorded 17 victories and 109 top ten finishes en route to almost $43 million in career earnings.

Entering the 2007 season, the number of career starts (256) recorded by Matt Kenseth on the Sprint Cup. In his last five seasons, Kenseth has finished in the top eight or better each year, to include winning the championship in 2003 and finishing in the runner-up position in 2006. In his first nine years on the Sprint Cup, Kenseth has recorded 66 top five finishes of which 14 were victories.

The average start position (25.7) of Jeff Burton during his rookie season on the Sprint Cup circuit. After spending six seasons on the Busch Series and recording one start on the Sprint Cup in 1993, Burton started in 30 of 31 events in 1994. Burton finished a bit better than he started though, averaging a 24.5 finish position.

The length (258) in miles of the only NASCAR event held at Road America in Elkhart Lakes, Wisconsin won by Tim Flock. The race consisted of 63 laps on the 4.1 mile road course with Flock beating Billy Myers by 17 seconds. It was a pretty good day for owner Bill Stroppe, who owned both Flock's and Myers' cars.

The percentage of races started (.259) by Harry Gant on the Sprint Cup in which he would place in the top five. Over a 22-year career which spanned from 1973 through 1994, Gant would place in the top five in 123 races of 474 races started.

The number of top ten finishes (260) recorded by Dale Jarrett entering the 2007 season. Jarrett, who has been racing on the Sprint Cup Series since 1984, has finished 40.7% (260 out of 639) of all races entered in the top ten during his illustrious career.

The average number of laps led per-race started (26.1) by Davey Allison on the Sprint Cup Series. Allison recorded 191 career starts and led a total of 4,978 laps of just over 56,000 laps completed. Allison fared better on the Sprint Cup than the Busch Series, where he was only able to muster an average of 3.77 laps led per-race over 86 starts.

The amount of beer sold, in thousands of gallons (26.2), at the NASCAR Sprint Cup Series weekend at Kansas Speedway in Kansas City, Kansas . . . enough to fill a Sprint Cup regulation car's gas tank 1,191 times over. That beer goes well with the 250 yards of bratwurst sold during the weekend of the Banquet 400 held each year at the track.

The average number of laps led per race (26.3) by Glen Wood. Wood, one of NASCAR's all-time greatest drivers, led a total of 1,635 laps over 62 races. In his first five years racing NASCAR, Wood didn't lead a single lap over 12 races, but over the next six years, he would lead 1,635 laps of 10,717 laps completed over 50 races.

The number of points (264) that Busch Series Champ Greg Biffle beat runner-up Jason Keller by during the 2002 season. In 34 races, Biffle relied on the consistency of 25 top ten finishes (20 of which were top five finishes and four of which were victories) en route to his first Busch Series title. He also became the first driver to win both the Busch and Craftsman Truck Series, which he had won two years earlier.

The number of top ten finishes (265) separating the King from the runner-up on the Sprint Cup's all-time list. Richard Petty recorded 712 top ten finishes in 1,184 races while Bobby Allison finished in the top ten in 447 of 718 races started. While the difference is large by number, it is not so by percentage. Allison actually has a higher career percentage of top ten finishes than Petty, .623 to .601, respectively. 265 is also the margin of victory by Bobby Labonte over Dale Earnhardt in the final season point standings in 2000. Subsequently, it is the number of points in what would be Earnhardt's last full season that prevented him from capturing #8.

The distance in miles (2.66) of the longest track used in NASCAR: the Talladega Superspeedway in Talladega, Alabama. The track also has the longest front stretch at 4,300 feet and it saw the fastest oval qualifying time when, on April 30, 1987, Bill Elliot clocked in at an amazing 212.809 mph.

The percentage of Buck Baker's pole starts (.267) that would lead him down victory lane. Entering the 2007 season, Baker ranked tenth on the all-time pole winner list with 45 poles won. In races started from the pole, Baker would record 12 of his 46 career victories. Half of Baker's 12 races won from the pole came during 1956, when Baker won six races of 12 poles won.

The number of career victories (268) recorded by Petty Enterprises between 1949 and 2006. Richard Petty is the winningest driver followed by his father, Lee. As a team, Petty Enterprise drivers win almost 10% of races entered, 268 of 2,743 races over 58 seasons.

The margin of victory (2.69) in seconds by Mark Martin over Jeff Gordon at the 1992 AC-Delco 200. Martin picked up his only victory in 14 starts on the Busch Series at the North Carolina Motor Speedway in Rockingham, North Carolina. Martin concentrated his efforts on the Sprint Cup and finished sixth in the final season standings. Gordon, on the other hand, raced all events on the Busch Series, recorded three wins, and finished fourth in the final season standings.

The amount of money won (270) in dollars by Speedy Thompson in back-to-back races during the 1957 season. On May 30, Thompson placed fifth at the Lincoln Speedway in New Oxford, Pennsylvania, earning $270 and finishing behind Marvin Panch. Just two days later, on June 1, Speedy finished the race at the Lancaster Speedway in Lancaster, South Carolina, once again in fifth place, and once again, on the tail of Marvin Panch.

The amount of money earned (27.1) in thousands of dollars by Tim Fedewa in his first NASCAR victory. On May 21, 1995, Fedewa beat Doug Heveron by 7.90 seconds to record his first victory and over $27,000. In his fourth Busch Series season, Fedewa topped $250,000 in earnings.

The margin of victory (2.72) in seconds by Mark Martin over Tracy Leslie at the 1993 Autolite 250. The September 10 race marked Martin's fifth of seven victories on a truly amazing season for him. Martin only started 14 races, but won every race that he was running at finish. Half of his races ended prematurely due to crashes or mechanical failures, the other half in victories. Leslie on the other hand was denied his second victory on the season and would never take a checkered flag again. He finished his career (211 starts) with a single victory, recorded earlier that season.

The percentage of races started from the pole (.273) that Fonty Flock would win. During Flock's nine year NASCAR career, he started from the pole position in 33 of 153 races. Of those 33 pole starts, Flock would win nine races (seven of eight victories in 1951, one of two victories in 1952, and one of three victories in 1955 came from the pole).

The length (274) in miles of the last three races held at the Middle Georgia Raceway in Macon, Georgia. The track hosted nine

NASCAR races between 1966 and 1971. The first six races varied in length between 100 and 267 miles. The final three events consisted of 500 laps run on a .548 mile track. Richard Petty and Bobby Allison dominated races at the site, winning seven of nine events, including all three races (Allison 2, Petty 1) run at 274 miles.

275 Entering the 2007 season, the number of NASCAR career starts (275) recorded by Robby Gordon. Gordon has spent most of his career on the Sprint Cup, recording 235 starts over 13 years. He has also started in 36 races over four seasons on the Busch Series and added four additional starts in three seasons racing on the Craftsman Truck Series. Gordon has recorded a total of 50 top ten finishes between the three, of which four were victories (three on the Sprint Cup and one on the Busch Series).

276 The number of top five finishes (276) recorded by Darrell Waltrip between 1972 and 2000. In 809 races, Waltrip would win 84 races and place second 58 times, third 62 times, fourth 41 times, and fifth 31 times.

277 The number of races started (277) by Davey Allison in ten years racing NASCAR. Between 1985 and 1993, Allison started in 191 races on the Sprint Cup. Allison also raced sporadically over ten years on the Busch Series where he started in 86 races.

278 The percentage of races started (.278) by Jimmie Johnson during the 2007 Sprint Cup season in which he would take the checkered flag. Johnson, en route to his second consecutive Sprint Cup championship, started all 36 races on the season and won a personal best ten races on the season.

279 The number of top ten finishes (279) recorded by Harry Gant on the Sprint Cup and Busch Series. Gant, who raced between 1972 and 1994, would record 208 top ten finishes on 474 career starts on the Sprint Cup as well as 71 top ten finishes on 128 Busch Series starts.

280 The margin of victory in points (280) by Dale Earnhardt Jr. over Jeff Green in the race for the 1999 Busch Series championship.

Junior led all competitors with six wins, 18 top five finishes, and 22 top ten finishes en route to his second consecutive Busch Series championship.

The number of times (281) that Dale Earnhardt finished a race in the top five. Of 676 races run, Earnhardt won 76 races, placed second 70 times, third 59 times, fourth 43 times, and fifth 33 times. That equated to Earnhardt placing in the top five in 41.6% of all races entered over a 27 year career.

The percentage of Sprint Cup races started (.282) by Carl Edwards in which he would finish in the top five. Edwards, a three-series driver, has found his best success on the Busch Series, but has been successful on the Sprint Cup as well. Entering the 2007 season, Edwards has recorded 24 top five finishes in 85 races started. Edwards' 2005 season was his best showing on the Sprint Cup; he recorded four victories and 13 top ten finishes in 36 starts, en route to a third place finish in the final season rankings.

The number of top ten finishes (283) recorded by Benny Parsons during his 21 year NASCAR career. Parsons, who began racing on the circuit in 1964, started a total of 526 races, placing in the top ten in almost 54% of all starts.

The number of career starts (284) recorded by Tony Stewart in his first eight seasons on the Sprint Cup. Of the 284 races entered, Stewart has finished in the top ten 168 times and has 29 victories to his name.

Entering the 2007 season, the number of career starts (285) recorded by Elliot Sadler. Between 1998 and 2006, Sadler averaged almost 32 races per season on the Sprint Cup and earned just over $31 million.

The winning percentage (.286) during Sam Ard's 1983 championship season on the Busch Series. Ard, who became Busch's first back-to-back champion the following year, would win ten of 35 races entered in a dominating season which also saw Ard finish in the top ten 30 out of 35 starts.

287 The number of laps led (287) by 2006 Craftsman Truck Series champion Todd Bodine. Bodine, who claimed his first title that season, relied on 15 top ten finishes and a 100% run at finish rate to win the championship. Although he won three races, his number of laps led was seventh overall and significantly behind Mark Martin's 661 laps led throughout the season.

288 The weight of Culver Blocks (2.88) in tons used to repave the Indianapolis Motor Speedway in 1909 after the original crushed rock and tar surface became unsuitable for racing shortly after it opened. The bricks, manufactured by the Wabash Valley Clay Company of Veedersburg, Indiana, made up 90% of all the bricks used to repave the track, with the rest of the 3.2 million tons coming from other local companies. Over the years, the bricks have been replaced by asphalt, currently leaving only a three-foot wide section at the start/finish line.

289 Legend Bobby Isaac's winning percentage (.289) during his two most dominant seasons racing NASCAR. On back-to-back seasons, Isaac started in 97 races and recorded 28 victories. In 1969, Isaac dominated the win column, recording 17 victories in 50 starts, but he failed to finish 19 races and he ended the season in a disappointing sixth place. The following year, Isaac recorded 11 victories and finished 38 of 47 starts and finished each race he completed in the top ten, leading Isaac to his sole NASCAR championship.

290 The total number of laps raced (290) on the Busch Series by Ricky Rudd. One of NASCAR's all-time greatest drivers started in three races on the Busch Series during the 1983 season on top of his full Sprint Cup schedule, winning the only race he completed. His first Busch race was a 200 lap victory at Dover Downs in which Rudd beat Bobby Allison by less than one second. The following two races saw Rudd bow out with engine problems after completing 20 laps at Darlington and 70 laps at Charlotte.

291 The average finish position (29.1) by Todd Bodine during his 1999 Sprint Cup season. Bodine started in seven races on the season, starting anywhere between fifth and 34th. On average, he finished 6.7 spots behind where he began (22.4). The following year, big brother Geoff averaged the same start position (29.1). In 14 races, Geoff's starts ranged between fourth and 43rd position. His average finish was a bit lower at 29.7.

292 Total miles driven (29.2) by Joe Littlejohn in his second and final NASCAR race. Littlejohn started the second race of the 1949 season at Daytona Beach, starting and finishing in fourth place and earning $300 for his efforts. The following season, Littlejohn once again made his season debut at the Beach and Road Course at Daytona Beach, this time in the pole position. He was only able to complete four laps on the 4.170 mile track, finishing in 35th place and collecting $25 in earnings.

293 The margin of victory (.293) in seconds by Jimmie Johnson over Mark Martin in the 2004 Bass Pro Shops MNBA 500. On October 31, 2004, Johnson, who started from the eighth position, took Rick Hendrick's #48 car to victory lane in front of 104,000 fans at the Atlanta Motor Speedway in Hampton, Georgia. It was Johnson's third consecutive victory and seventh of eight on a season in which he would finish second to Kurt Busch.

294 The percentage of Sprint races started (.294) by Tony Stewart at Bristol Motor Speedway in which he would place in the top ten. In 17 starts between 1999 and the fifth race of the 2007 season, Stewart placed in the top ten in five races. It is also the percentage of Sprint races started (.294) by Tony Stewart at the Richmond International Speedway in which he would place in the top five. Between 1999 and the tenth race of the 2007 season, Stewart recorded five top five finishes. His top ten placement is even better . . . 64.7% of all starts at the track.

295 The number of top five finishes (295) recorded by NASCAR's second winningest driver, David Pearson. Pearson, whose career spanned between 1960 and 1986, won 105 races, took second 89

times, third 44 times, fourth 38 times, and finished fifth 19 times. He would thus finish 51.4% of all races entered in the top five.

The number of points (296) that Richard Petty came up short in the chase for the Cup in 1973. The point difference actually put Petty in fifth place in the final season point standings, but it was also the number of points that Petty needed to have become the first driver in NASCAR history to win five consecutive championships, having won the championship in 1971-72 and again in 1974-75.

The percentage of races started (.297) by Wendell Scott in which he placed in the top ten. Scott, the only African American to win a NASCAR race, started in 495 races, finishing in the top ten on 147 occasions. Scott's most successful season racing was the 1964 season. Scott had a career high in starts (56), wins (one), top five finishes (eight), laps led (27), and top ten finishes (25).

The percentage of all laps raced (.298) by Tim Flock in which he was in the lead. Over his 13 year career, Flock led 6,937 laps of 23,280 total laps raced. His best season in the category was during his second championship season in 1955. That season, Flock set a number of career bests; he started a career-high 39 races, recorded 18 victories and 32 top five finishes, won 18 poles, and led an incredible 3,495 laps of 6,208 laps completed. Flock's winning percentage for the season was 46.15%, outdone only by the percentage of laps raced of which he led (56.3%).

The average start position (29.9) of Cecil Gordon as an owner-driver during the 1981 season. The season marked Gordon's last as the primary driver of his team. He would start in 18 of the 28 starts recorded and have a starting position worse than the four other drivers who recorded at least one start for him. Despite finishing stronger than he started (an average finish position of 22.2), Gordon was still weaker in that category as well. Gordon's role as an owner only lasted two more seasons.

The car number (300) that Tim Flock drove to victory lane in the 30th race of the 1955 season at Bay Meadows Race Track. In the second of only three NASCAR races run at this San Mateo track, Flock set a speed record of 68.571 mph en route to one of his 17 victories driving the #300 car.

David Pearson

YEAR	STARTS	WINS	TOP 5	TOP 10	RANK
1960	22	0	3	7	23
1961	19	3	7	8	13
1962	12	0	1	7	10
1963	41	0	13	19	8
1964	61	8	29	42	3
1965	14	2	8	11	40
1966	42	15	26	33	1
1967	22	2	11	13	7
1968	48	16	36	38	1
1969	51	11	42	44	1
1970	19	1	9	11	23
1971	17	2	8	9	51
1972	17	6	12	13	20
1973	18	11	14	14	13
1974	19	7	15	15	3
1975	21	3	13	14	14
1976	22	10	16	18	9
1977	22	2	16	16	13
1978	22	4	11	11	16
1979	9	1	4	5	32
1980	9	1	4	5	37
1981	6	0	0	2	70
1982	6	0	2	2	37
1983	10	0	1	4	33
1984	11	0	0	3	41
1985	12	0	0	1	36
1986	2	0	0	1	82
TOTAL	574	105	301	366	

Chapter Four

The Crown Prince

*I*f Richard Petty was the King of NASCAR, the crown prince was undoubtedly David Pearson. When asked who the greatest driver he raced against was, Petty said it was David Pearson, "David and I ran more firsts and seconds than anybody else, and we raced together on dirt tracks, superspeedways, road courses, big tracks and little tracks. It didn't make any difference; you had to beat him every week."

If any one driver had Richard Petty's number, it was David Pearson. Pearson actually outperformed Petty in many categories, at least statistically, over his 574 starts. Pearson recorded 105 wins for an 18.29% winning percentage, Petty stood at 16.89%. Pearson recorded 301 top five finishes for a percentage of 52.44, Petty's top fives equaled 46.88 of his starts. Pearson recorded 366 top ten finishes, or 63.76% of all races, Petty was at 60.14%. No one can argue that Pearson was the King of poles. Petty recorded 126 poles in 1,184 starts while Pearson recorded just 13 fewer in 610 fewer starts. Pearson sat pole in one of every five races, Petty sat pole one of every ten races. When the two drivers finished 1-2 in a race, it was Pearson who edged out Petty, 33 wins to 30. The two men started 550 races together and were pretty even going head to head: Petty finished ahead of Pearson 289 times, Pearson in front of Petty 261 times; Petty won 107 of the 550 races, Pearson won 97; Petty finished in the top five 291 times, Pearson 289 times; Petty finished in the top ten 366 times, Pearson 349 times; and, Petty's average finish was 9.8, Pearson's was 11.2.

Pearson retired from driving in 1986, but before doing so, built a garage and got a team together for his son. Pearson's last gift to NASCAR was getting his son Larry in a position to win back-to-back Busch Series championships in 1986 and 1987. The next time people speak of the greatest drivers in NASCAR history, don't let the conversation neglect David Pearson. The Crown Prince was an equal to the King in many ways and, like the King, Pearson epitomizes everything that a legendary NASCAR driver is and should strive to be.

301 The number of top five finishes recorded (301) by NASCAR's second winningest driver, David Pearson. Pearson, who started in 574 races on the Sprint Cup over 27 years, recorded 301 top five finishes, with 105 of those being victories. The 1960 Rookie of the Year certainly lived up to the expectations and 30 years later, the Silver Fox was inducted into the International Motorsports Hall of Fame with three championships under his belt.

302 Entering the 2007 season, the number of races started by Tony Stewart (302) in which he was running at finish. Between 1996 and 2006, Stewart started in 355 races between the Sprint, Busch, and Craftsman Truck Series and was running at finish in an impressive 85.1% of those starts.

303 The number of career starts (303) by Tiny Lund over 20 years racing NASCAR. Lund's career began in 1955 and, with the exception of 1974, he started in at least one race per season through 1975. Over this span, he recorded five victories and 54 top five finishes. Lund's career and life were cut short at Talladega on August 17, 1975 when Lund and J.D. McDuffie were involved in a spin out, with rookie Terry Link broadsiding Lund's driver side. Lund died at the scene, clouding the celebration of Buddy Baker, who would fall to his knees in sorrow.

The percentage of races entered (.304) that Marshall Teague won. Teague only started 23 races with NASCAR, but won seven of those races. In the 1949 and 1950 seasons, Teague only started in four races and failed to record a top ten finish. In 1951, Teague started 15 races and won five. The following season, which was his last, Teague tacked on two more victories in the four races he entered.

The percentage (.305) of all of Richard Petty's victories than came from the pole. Throughout his storied career, Petty won 200 races and of those 200 victories, 61 came from races in which he started from the pole position.

The number of career starts (306) by driver Steve Grissom over 21 seasons of Busch Series racing (1986-2006). Heading into 2007, Grissom registered 11 career victories and won the 1993 Busch Series championship.

The average finish position (30.7) by Tammy Jo Kirk in 15 races on the Busch Series. Kirk, who became the first woman to race on the Craftsman Truck Series in 1997, started in 32 races in two years driving trucks before moving over to the Busch Series in 2003. Her best finish was 21st at Pikes Peak International Raceway in Fountain, Colorado on July 26. Her average finish position on the season was 4.3 spots better than her start (35.0).

The number of races (308) started by Bobby Isaac between 1964 and 1979. Isaac would hold the pole position in 50 of those races (seventh best all-time) and be victorious 37 times with 28 of those victories coming during the 1969 season and his 1970 championship season.

309 The margin of victory (3.09) in seconds at the 1994 "Slick 50" 500 held at the Phoenix International Raceway in Phoenix, Arizona. On October 30, Terry Labonte held off Mark Martin by the margin to collect his third victory of the season and help push him over $1 million in earnings on the Sprint Cup that season.

310 The average start position (31.0) of Dick Brooks in his only career start racing for Rick Hendrick. In 1985 Brooks became the second driver to start for Hendrick after Geoff Bodine, who started in 58 races over the first two seasons driving for Hendrick. Brooks faired well in his one start, finishing tenth at the Coca-Cola World 600 at the Charlotte Motor Speedway. The start would be his final start on the Sprint Cup and Brooks would finish his career with 358 career starts, one victory, 150 top ten finishes, and $1.25 million in earnings.

311 The number of top ten finishes (311) recorded by Buddy Baker in 699 career starts. Baker had two seasons in which he recorded 20 top ten finishes. In 1973 he recorded 20 top ten finishes in 27 starts and in 1977 he did it in 30 races started. Over his 33 years as a NASCAR legend, Baker finished almost 45% of all races entered in the top ten.

312 The margin of victory (3.12) in seconds by Greg Biffle over Jeff Burton at the 2004 Diamond Hills Plywood 200. Biffle recorded his first of five victories on the Busch Series at Darlington and would finish the Busch season in third place. The race was neither the narrowest nor greatest margin of victory for Biffle on the season. His fifth victory was a .356 second win over Casey Mears at the Target House 300 while his second victory at the Stater Brothers 300 was a 5.32 second win over Tony Stewart.

313 The total margin of victory (313) in points in Jack Sprague's three Craftsman Truck Series championships. Sprague, the truck series only 3-time champion, won his first series championship in 1997 by a margin of victory of 232 points over Rich Bickle. Two-years later, Sprague won the championship by edging out Greg Biffle by a mere eight points. Sprague would claim his third championship in 2001 by beating Ted Musgrave by 73 points.

The percentage of races started (.314) that Ralph Earnhardt placed in the top ten. The Earnhardt that started the racing-family legend began his career in 1956 and, in six seasons on the Sprint Cup Series, he would record 16 top ten finishes in 51 starts. Ralph recorded his first top ten finish on November 11, 1956 at the Schuman 250. Earnhardt, driving for Pete DaPaolo, also earned his first career pole that day. He would finish the race a mere four seconds behind winner Speedy Thompson. While he never found victory lane in what is now the Sprint Cup Series, Earnhardt did win the 1956 Sportsman championship and began a family that has been a dominating force in NASCAR ever since.

The average number of races entered per season (3.15) by Hershel McGriff. McGriff would start in 85 races over 27 seasons in 43 years. He was absent from the driving scene from 1954 until 1971, when he reappeared on the NASCAR circuit as a driver. Over the next 22 years, he would never start in more than five races in a season. McGriff would retire from racing in 1993 at the age of 65.

The amount of soda, in thousands of gallons (31.6), consumed during the Sprint Cup race weekend at the Kansas Speedway. The track, which hosts the Banquet 400, better sell that much . . . it takes a lot of liquid to wash down the 25,000 hamburgers and 23,200 orders of fries spectators consume.

The total number of laps raced (317) by Whitey Brainerd during the 1954 season. Brainerd started in two NASCAR events and recorded a seventh place finish at Langhorne Speedway in Langhorne, Pennsylvania and a 13th place finish at Williams Grove Speedway in Mechanicsburg, Pennsylvania. Brainerd completed .960 of all laps run at the two sites and earned $175 in his NASCAR career.

The average finish position (31.8) by Darrell Waltrip in his last season racing on the Sprint Cup Series. In Waltrip's 29th year on the circuit, he started in 29 of 34 races but only recorded two top 20 finishes. It was a far cry from his career average finish position, which was 15.1 over 809 starts.

The total number of top ten finishes (319) recorded by NASCAR legend Cale Yarborough. Yarborough, whose racing career began at the age of 18 in 1957 and spanned over three decades, started 560 races. He would finish an amazing 57% of all races started in the top ten.

Entering the 2006 season, the number of top ten finishes (320) recorded by Bill Elliot over 31 seasons racing on the Sprint Cup. Elliot, who began his career in 1976, has averaged 24.5 starts per season over his career, placing in the top ten an average of 10.3 times per season. Throughout his career, Elliot has placed in the top ten in 42.2% of all starts on the Sprint Cup.

The number of miles (3.21) led in thousands by Dale Earnhardt during the 1990 season. Earnhardt led 2,438 laps of 9,162 laps raced on the season, earning nine victories and 23 top ten finishes in 29 starts. His performance was good enough to earn Earnhardt his fifth season championship.

The number of points (3.22) in thousands earned on the Craftsman Truck Series by Kenny Irwin during the 1997 season. Irwin, who won the second annual Raybestos Rookie of the Year Award, finished the season in tenth place in his only full season racing trucks. Irwin would move on to the Sprint Cup the following year, where he would earn Rookie of the Year honors as well. His life tragically ended in an accident during practice at the New Hampshire International Speedway on July 7, 2000, while practicing for the upcoming New England 300.

The amount of money earned (323) in thousands of dollars by Chuck Bown during the 1990 Busch Series season. On the strength of 18 top ten finishes, to include six victories, Bown won the championship by 200 points over Jimmy Hensley and earned a career high $323,000 on the season.

The average start position (32.4) by Robbie Gordon and the average finish position (32.4) by Andy Houston during the 2001 Sprint Cup season. Both drivers started in 17 of the 36 scheduled races that year, but the similarities pretty much ended there. Gordon improved 7.6 spots between start and finish while Houston finished, on average, 8.4 spots lower than his start position. Gordon recorded three top ten finishes, including a victory, while Houston could only place in the top ten once. Gordon earned $1.37 million on the year, Houston $865,263.

The number of laps (325) led by Bill Blair during the 1949 season. Blair led 145 of the first 150 laps in the first race of the season, but his race ended when his Lincoln overheated. The last race of the season saw Blair lead 180 of the first 191 laps on the race. Engine problems ended his race and his chance to win his first NASCAR race. Interestingly enough the only two races in which he led any laps were his two worst finishes on the season, 12th and tenth place respectively.

The amount of earnings (326) in thousands by Fireball Roberts over 206 career starts on the Sprint Cup. Roberts, who began his career in 1950, raced for 15 years, earning just over $1,580 per starts and approximately $22,500 per season. Roberts' best individual season was his second to last. In 1963, Roberts started in just 20 of the 55 scheduled races, finishing in fifth place on the season and earning just over $73,000.

The number of career starts (327) by Kenny Wallace between 1990 and 2006 on the Sprint Cup Series. Wallace has averaged about 20 races a season on the series over that span while still averaging 22 races a season on the Busch Series during that span. In his average 40 starts per season, Wallace has averaged just over ten top ten finishes per year.

The number of Craftsman Truck points earned (3.28) in thousands by Jimmy Hensley during the 1999 season. The point total put Hensley in tenth place in the final season point standings and marked the fourth consecutive year he would place in the top ten come season's end. The season would also see Hensley win his second and last Craftsman race and would mark his last top ten placement in the Craftsman Series final season point standings.

The number of races (329) that David Pearson would hold a lead in his over 574 Sprint Cup racing career. Pearson led a total of

25,444 laps of 135,020 raced (or almost 19% of all laps raced) and held a lead in 57.3% of the races he started.

330   The percentage of all races started (.330) by Bobby Isaac during the 1969-70 seasons in which he would start the race from the pole position. In an absolutely dominating display in qualifying, Isaac would earn the pole in 19 of 50 races started (.380) during the 1969 season. He would follow that effort up the following year by starting 13 of 47 (.277) races from that coveted position. Throughout his 15 year career, Isaac would hold the pole position in 49 of 308 starts (.159).

331   The amount of money earned (3.31) in millions of dollars by Dale Earnhardt in his fourth championship season. In 1990, Earnhardt dominated the field, earning nine victories, leading 2,437 laps of 9,162 laps completed, and earning well over twice as much as his nearest competitor, Mark Martin ($3.31 to $1.30 million).

332   The number of points (3.32), in thousands, recorded by Chuck Bown during the 1997 Craftsman Truck Series. In his first and only full season of racing trucks, Bown would record 13 top ten finishes in 26 starts and finish the season ranked ninth in the final point standings.

333   The length (.333), in miles, of the State Line Speedway, located in Busti, New York. The dirt track hosted only one NASCAR race, the 30th race of the 1958 season, won by Shorty Rollins. Rollins owned and drove his 1958 Ford to victory lane, winning $600 and claiming his sole NASCAR victory in 43 races started.

334   The number of top five finishes (334) recorded by drivers racing for Woods Brothers Racing. WBR started with one driver, Glen Wood, during the 1953 season and, over the next 53 seasons, Glen and company started in 1,271 races and recorded 334 top five finishes, including 96 victories.

335   The Lowe's Motor Speedway record for most laps led (335) by a race winner. On May 21, 1967 at the World 600, Jim Paschal led 335 of 400 laps en route to one of his two career victories at the track and 25 career NASCAR victories.

336 The number of top five finishes (336) recorded by Bobby Allison over 25 years racing on the Sprint Cup Series. Between 1961 and 1988 (he didn't start between 1962 and 1964), Allison placed in the top five in .468 of all races entered (336 of 718).

337 The number of laps raced (337) by Bobby Hamilton during the 1997 Craftsman Truck Series. Hamilton, who started a full schedule on the Sprint Cup Series that season, started in two Craftsman races placing in the top ten in both events, with an average finish position of 5.5. Hamilton would start between two and five races on the Craftsman Series before making it his primary ride in 2003. It was a good move for Hamilton. In just his second full season racing trucks, he won his first and only NASCAR championship.

338 The number of laps led (338) by Pete Hamilton during his most successful NASCAR season. Hamilton, who started in 64 races between 1968 and 1973, recorded 24 of those starts in 1970. During that campaign, he recorded three of his four career victories, and placed in the top ten a total of 12 times. He led 338 laps of the 4,069 laps he raced and, despite racing in only one-third of the scheduled races that season, finished 21st in the end of season standings.

339 The amount of money earned (339) in thousands of dollars by Richard Petty during his 1972 championship season, the fourth of his career. Petty's earnings were just below his career high, earned just one year prior, during his third championship season.

340 Entering the 2007 season, the number of career starts (340) on the Sprint Cup Series recorded by John Andretti. Andretti, the nephew of legend Mario and cousin of Michael, has been successful in Indy, NHRA, and NASCAR. He also was the first driver to ever drive the Indy 500 and turn around and drive the Coca-Cola 600 . . . on the same day. Andretti has recorded a couple of victories on the Sprint Cup and has also competed in 36 Busch Series events and four Craftsman Truck Series races.

341 The number of starts (341) recorded by drivers who drove for Bobby Allison between 1969 and 1996. Allison recorded more driver

starts than any of the other nine drivers who drove for him. Allison had 130 starts as an owner/driver, with Derrike Cope (72 starts) and Hut Stricklin (71 starts) recording a majority of the rest of the races. Allison was the only driver of the ten that recorded a victory though. He had six wins between 1970 and 1973.

The average finish position (34.2) of A.J. Foyt IV during his first season racing on the Busch Series. In 2005, the grandson of legend A.J. Foyt started in four races (28.2 average start position) and recorded his best finish in his first race, the Sam's Town 250 at the Memphis Motorsports Park in Memphis, Tennessee.

The amount of money earned (3.43) in millions of dollars by Jeff Gordon during the 1996 season. Gordon would finish second in the final season point standings and second in money earned, just behind Terry Labonte. The following season Gordon would almost double his winnings, earning $6.34 million and winning his second championship.

The number of laps led (344) by A.J. Foyt during his most successful NASCAR season. In 1972 Foyt started in six races, recording two victories and five top five finishes and three poles won. He would end up leading 344 of 1,417 laps raced, holding a lead of at least eight laps in every race he entered on the season.

The attendance (34.5) in thousands at the 1981 Busch 500 held at the Bristol International Speedway. Darrell Waltrip took the checkered flag, beating Ricky Rudd by over a lap, and earned his eighth victory on the season and his second of the year at Bristol. The victory would help Waltrip narrow the gap between himself and first-place Bobby Allison to just 50 points. Waltrip would finish strong (four straight victories in the final six races) and he would claim his first of two consecutive Sprint Cup Series championships, beating Allison by 53 points.

The number of miles led (3.46) in thousands by Jeff Gordon during the 1995 Sprint Cup season. In 31 starts on the season, Gordon led 2,610 laps of 9,405 laps raced en route to his first Sprint Cup championship.

347 The amount of money earned (34.7) in thousands of dollars by Jack Smith during his most financially successful NASCAR season. In 1962, Smith started a career high 51 races on the season and recorded a career high 35 top ten finishes of which 27 were top fives and five were victories. Over his 15 year NASCAR career, Smith would earn just short of $140,000.

348 The number of points (3.48) in thousands by Dennis Setzer in the final season point standings of the 2005 Craftsman Truck Series. Setzer would fall 55 points short of his first championship and end up in the runner-up position for the third consecutive season. The previous season, Setzer finished 46 points behind Bobby Hamilton and, in 2003, he fell just nine points shy of his championship quest, losing to Travis Kvapil.

349 The number of points (349) separating 2001 Sprint Cup champ Jeff Gordon from runner-up Tony Stewart. Gordon placed in the top ten in 24 of 36 races, winning six races while earning 5,112 points. Stewart recorded 22 top ten finishes, including three wins, and earning 4,763 points. Gordon's winnings on the season were over twice as much as any one driver, $10.9 million to Stewart's $4.9 million.

350 The average finish position (35.0) by Ned Jarrett during the 1953 season, his first on the NASCAR circuit. In two races started on the season, Jarrett would finish in 11th and 59th place for an average finish position of 35th. Fortunately, it would not be a sign of things to come for Jarrett, who over the next 13 years would become one of NASCAR's all-time greatest drivers and retire with an average finish position of 9.2.

351 The percentage of laps completed (.351) by John Sears in his two starts during the 1965 season. Sears only started the last two races of the season, the American 500 and the Tidewater 300, and had a few problems. While Sears completed 280 of 300 laps at the Dog Track Speedway in Maycock, and recorded a tenth place finish, his luck was not so good at the American 500. Sears only completed one lap of the 500 lap race in Rockingham before crashing, yet still earned $510 versus the $140 payday in Maycock.

352 The amount of money earned (35.2) in thousands of dollars by Johnny Benson Jr. at the 2007 Power Stroke Diesel 200 at the O'Reilly Raceway Park in Clermont, Indiana. Ron Hornaday Jr. held off Benson by .350 seconds to deny him his second win on the 2007 season. Benson Jr. didn't have to wait too much longer to collect his second victory though. After a relatively unimpressive 30th place finish in his next start at Nashville, Benson reeled off back-to-back victories at Bristol and Gateway, beating out Hornaday Jr. in the latter, winning under caution, and giving the eventual season champ a little payback.

353 The number of laps led (3.53) in thousands by Cale Yarborough during the 1974 season. Yarborough led 37.5% of all laps completed (3,530 of 9,398) and won ten races over the season. Despite the success, Yarborough came up short in the final season point standings, finishing second to Richard Petty. Throughout his illustrious career, Yarborough would record over 3,000 laps led in five different seasons. He would win the championship in three of those seasons and place runner-up in the remaining two.

354 The number of laps led (354) by Buddy Baker during the 1978 Sprint Cup season. Baker started in 19 of 30 races on the season, leading 354 of the 4,319 laps he completed, and finishing the season in 24th place. Over the course of his 33 year career, Baker would lead a total of 9,748 laps in 699 starts.

355 Entering the 2007 season, the number of career starts (355) recorded by Tony Stewart since his 1996 rookie season. Stewart began racing in 1996 with ten starts on the Busch and Craftsman Truck Series. It was not until 1999 that he started racing a full season schedule, and when he did, he did it well. Stewart won Rookie of the Year honors en route to eight consecutive seasons starting every race (284 consecutive starts) and winning at least two races per season, a streak that continues through the 2007 season. Stewart continues to race periodically on the Busch Series, but has not entered a Craftsman Truck event since 2005.

356 The amount of money earned (3.56) in thousands of dollars by Dick May at the 1978 American 500. May finished the race in 11th place and recorded his best finish at the North Carolina Motor Speedway in Rockingham. The amount of money won at the raceway was a career high over 14 starts at the track.

357 The amount of money earned (35.7) in thousands of dollars by Ron Hornaday Jr. at the 1998 Loadhandler 200 at the Bristol Motor Speedway in Bristol, Tennessee. Hornaday started in the pole position with Jack Sprague starting in the number two spot and the two men were the only drivers who held the lead over the course of 206 laps. Sprague led the race for 19 laps and Hornaday for 187 laps, but it was Hornaday who held the lead when it mattered the most. He pulled off the win by .854 seconds over Sprague to win the race and, most importantly the season championship over Sprague by three points.

358 The number of career starts (358) recorded by Dick Brooks in 17 NASCAR seasons. Brooks started his NASCAR career in 1969, starting in 28 of 54 races, and wrapped it up on May 26, 1985 at the Coca-Cola World 600. Brooks recorded his sole NASCAR victory at the Talladega 500 in 1973 but came close to victory on five other occasions when he was the runner-up. All told, he recorded 150 top ten finishes over his career and earned over $1.2 million.

359 Entering the 2007 season, the number of career starts (359) by Ward Burton on the Sprint Cup Series. Over the span of 13 seasons, Burton has compiled five victories, 24 top five finishes, and 82 top ten finishes en route to over $24 million in earnings. Burton also has a few starts on the Busch Series. Over nine seasons, Burton has 145 starts on the Busch Series, adding another four victories to his tally.

360 The record for consecutive starts (360) in the Busch Series. Between February 13, 1982 and February 26, 1994, Tommy Houston did not miss a start. The streak began at the inaugural race of the Busch Series, the Goody's 300, at Daytona. The streak ended after a 35th place finish at the Goodwrench 200 . . . 12 years and 13 days later.

361 NASCAR legend Tim Flock's winning percentage (.361) during his two championship series. In 1952 Flock won eight of 33 starts en route to his first championship and most lucrative season to that point.

Three years later, Flock won 18 of 39 starts (an amazing .462 winning percentage) en route to the best season of his career.

The amount of career winnings (362) in thousands of dollars by Buck Baker in 26 seasons of racing NASCAR. Baker came on the NASCAR scene in 1949 and, through 1976, started in 636 races. His most financially lucrative season was in 1964 when he would earn almost $44,000. His average earnings per race over his career were $570, although he would earn more per race as his career progressed. In his final eight starts in 1976, Baker would earn $1,586 per-race despite only one top ten finish.

The number of thousands of miles driven (3.63) by Bob Welborn during the 1955 season. Welborn started in 32 of 45 races on the season, running at finish in 27 of those races, and finished the season fourth in miles completed. He also finished the season ranked fourth in the final season point standings, a career best.

The number of points (364) separating Jeff Gordon from Mark Martin in the final 1998 Sprint Cup point standings. Gordon, at the age of 26, won his third Sprint Cup championship and second consecutive championship by earning 5,328 points on the strength of 13 victories. Martin tied a personal best with a second place finish with 4,964 points.

The average winnings per start ($365) by Wendell Scott, the first African American to compete in a NASCAR event. Scott, who had 495 career starts over 13 seasons, had $180,629 in career winnings by the time he retired in 1973.

The number of top ten finishes (366) recorded by David Pearson over 574 career Sprint Cup starts. In 27 seasons, Pearson recorded over 40 top ten finishes on two occasions (42 in 1964 and 44 in 1969) and over 30 in both 1966 and 1968. Pearson also recorded an additional four top ten finishes in six starts on the Busch Series and 15 top ten finishes in 17 starts on the IROC.

The amount of money earned (3.67) in thousands of dollars by Eddie Pagan in five starts at the Portland Speedway in Portland, Oregon. Pagan won his last two starts at the track and earned $1,930 of his total earnings at the venue. He averaged $733 per start at Portland.

The average finish position (36.8) by Shawna Robinson over two Sprint Cup seasons. During the 2001 and 2002 seasons, Robinson started in eight races and earned a total of $464,000 for her efforts. Her career best finish on the Sprint Cup Series was at the 2002 Daytona 500, where she finished the race in 24th place.

The career earnings (3.69) in thousands of dollars by owner W.J. Ridgeway in races run at Speedways between one and two miles in length. Ridgeway's drivers recorded nine starts, almost half of which occurred in Atlanta. In Atlanta, Marvin Panch, Darel Dieringer, J.C. Hendriz, and Curtis Turner recorded four starts and earned $2,175.

The margin of victory (.370) in seconds by Dale Earnhardt over Rusty Wallace at the 1995 Brickyard 400. Earnhardt would record one of his five victories on the season, but would come up short in the final season standings. Earnhardt would finish second behind Jeff Gordon in the final season point standings by just 34 points to end his quest for a three-peat.

The number of laps led (371) by Ward Burton in 2002. Burton started all 36 races on the season and collected two of his career five victories and six top five finishes while leading 371 of 8,931 laps raced. While the number of laps led is not a career best, nor was his season ending ranking, Burton earned a career high $4.9 million on the season.

The number of top ten finishes (372) recorded by Buck Baker over 26 years of racing on the NASCAR circuit. Baker had five seasons in which he recorded 30-plus top ten finishes. Baker's highest number of top ten finishes was in 1956 with 39 in 48 starts. The following season, Baker recorded 38 top ten finishes in just 40 races for an incredible 95% top-ten finish rate.

As of the end of the 2006 season, the number of top ten finishes (373) recorded by Ricky Rudd in his 31 year career on the Sprint Cup. Rudd has placed in the top ten in approximately 42.6% of all races started (373 of 875 races started). The 373 top ten finishes include 23 victories (25th on the all-time list) and 194 top five finishes. He also has earned over $40 million in winnings over his career.

The number of laps led (374) by Benny Parsons during his sole Sprint Cup championship. Parsons, one of only four Sprint drivers to ever win the championship with only one victory on the season, finished three-quarters of his 28 starts during the 1973 season in the top ten. Most of Parsons' laps led tally (320 of 374) came during his victory at the Volunteer Cup 500 at Bristol, Tennessee.

The number of career starts (375) recorded by Neil Bonnet during his 18 years racing NASCAR. Bonnet would start 362 races over 18 years as a regular on the Sprint Cup Series and added an additional 13 starts spread out over six seasons on Busch. In these 375 starts, Bonnet recorded 163 top ten finishes, of which 80 were top fives and 19 were victories.

The number of races started (376) by David Pearson in which he would be running at finish. Of Pearson's 574 starts on the Sprint Cup, he was RAF on 371 of those. Of his six Busch Series starts, Pearson was RAF in five of those races. His NASCAR career RAF rate 376 races of 579 starts, or .648.

The percentage of races won (.377) by a Chrysler race car between 1954 and 1956. In the three most successful seasons by the manufacturer, Chrysler cars recorded 56 victories out of 138 total races.

The total number of laps led (378) by Al Keller during his six year NASCAR career. Keller only started in 29 races between 1949 and 1956 (he didn't start a race in 1951 or 1955), but managed 12 top ten finishes and a couple of victories. It was during his two career wins that he recorded a bulk of his laps-in-lead. Of his 378 laps led, 212 of them came during his two career victories, both recorded in 1954, at the Oglethorpe Speedway in Savannah, Georgia and at the Linden Airport in

Linden, New Jersey. The rest of his laps led were also recorded in 1954, over three other races.

Entering the 2007 season, the number of career starts (379) recorded by Jack Sprague. Sprague saw limited action in the Sprint Cup Series, starting in only 24 races in four years with no top ten finishes. Sprague found more success in the Busch Series, starting in 108 races over a nine year span and recording 24 top ten finishes. But it was on the truck series that Sprague found his groove. Through 2006, Sprague has raced in every race of each season, with the exception of the 2002 and 2003 seasons. He has started in 247 races with 173 top ten finishes and has three championships to his name.

The NASCAR record for best single season average finish position (3.80) held by Lloyd Dane. Dane raced between 1951 and 1964 and over that time span, never started more than ten races in any given year; 1957 was one of those years with ten starts though. In his best season racing NASCAR, Dane entered ten races, recording ten top ten finishes including seven top fives and a single victory. His average start position per race was 4.8 and his average finish was a spot lower at 3.8.

The number of miles driven (381) by Frank Mundy during the 1949 season. Mundy started in four of the scheduled eight races on the season and finished the first season of NASCAR in tenth place. Two years later, Mundy had what was to be his best season, earning all three of his career victories and finishing the season in fifth place.

The percentage of total starts (.382) by Fonty Flock during the 1951 season in which he sat pole. Flock began 13 of 34 races from the pole position and won eight races on the season. He finished a total of 22 races in the top ten and led over 2,000 laps throughout the season but was edged out by Herb Thomas for the championship by 146.2 points.

The average number of laps (38.3) that Kevin Harvick led per-race during his 2001 championship season. The 2000 Rookie of the Year led a total of 1,265 laps over 33 races en route to 24 top ten finishes in 33 starts, including five wins, on the season.

384 Entering the 2007 season, the narrowest margin of victory in seconds (.384) recorded at Watkins Glen International. Steve Park recorded his first career victory at the 2000 Global Crossing over Mark Martin by .384 seconds. Park would record his second and last Sprint Cup victory the following year at the 2001 Dura Lube 400, edging Bobby Labonte by an even closer margin, a mere .138 seconds.

385 The percentage of races entered (.385) by Danny Letner in which he would place in the top ten. Letner only started in 26 races over eight seasons between 1951 and 1963, never starting in more than six races in any given season. He recorded ten top ten finishes in his limited action, and has two victories to his name.

386 The number of laps led (386) by Emanuel Zervakis during the 1961 NASCAR season. Zervakis started in 38 of the scheduled 52 races that season and collected all 386 laps led during his two victories on the season. He led 25 laps in the Greenville 200 and 361 of the 500 laps at the Yankee 500.

387 The percentage of races run (.387) during the 1996 Sprint Cup season that were won by Hendrick Motorsports drivers. Teammates Jeff Gordon (ten wins) and Terry Labonte (two wins) accounted for 12 victories in the 31 race season. A Hendrick driver would claim the championship that season, although it was Labonte, not Gordon, who would take home the title despite the differences in the victory column.

388 Entering the 2007 season, the career earnings (38.8) in millions of dollars by Bill Elliot on the Sprint Cup. Over 31 seasons racing on that circuit, Elliot has averaged a little over $1.25 million in winnings per season. His most lucrative season came in 2003 when he earned $5.01 million over 36 starts.

389 The average price in US Dollars (389) of a Goodyear Eagle race tire, compared to the $150-$200 Eagle street version. The race tire, outside of costing on average twice the amount of a street tire, has an average life of 150 miles versus the street tire's 50,000 miles. That equates to drivers using between 9 and 14 sets of tires to complete a race.

Other differences found in the race and street versions of the Goodyear Eagle tires are inflation (race: dry air or nitrogen; street: air), weight (race: 24 lbs. per tire; street: 30 lbs. per tire), and tread thickness and width (race: 1/8 inch and 11.5 inches; street: 3/8 inch and nine inches, respectively).

390   The percentage of laps raced (.390) that Marvin Burke led in his one race NASCAR career. In an anomaly in and of itself, Burke started one race, led 156 of 400 laps, won the race along with $1,875, and never started another NASCAR race. Burke is the only driver in NASCAR history to win his only start. The race took place at Oakland Stadium on October 14, 1951, one of only three races held at that venue. Burke holds the track record for average speed at 78.748 mph, a good 25 mph faster than the next fastest driver.

391   The margin of victory (3.91) in seconds by Jeff Gordon over Rusty Wallace at the 1994 Coca-Cola 600. The victory marked Gordon's first career win on the Sprint Cup Series and was one of two victories for him on the season. The 22-year-old Gordon would finish the season ranked eighth, a season that represented his breakthrough on the Sprint Cup.

392   Entering the 2007 season, the number of career starts (392) recorded by three-series driver Ron Hornaday Jr. Between 1992 and 2007 he started in 45 Sprint Cup races, 172 Busch races, and 175 Craftsman Truck Series events. Hornaday has been successful on the Busch Series (placing in the top five in the final season standing three times), but truck racing is his forte. In the seven complete seasons on Craftsman, Hornaday has won two championships and finished no lower than seventh in the final season point standings.

393   The slowest average race speed (39.3) in miles per hour in the 29 year race history of Bowman Gray Stadium in Winston-Salem, North Carolina. On August 22, 1958, Lee Petty beat out Short Rollins to win the race and record one of his seven victories on the season. By way of comparison, the race record, coincidently held by son Richard, is 51.5 miles per hour and was set on August 28, 1970.

The percentage of races entered (.394) by Jeff Gordon during the 1998 season in which he would be victorious. In what would be his second consecutive championship season, and third in four years on the Sprint Cup Series, Gordon won 13 of 33 races entered.

The total number of laps raced (395) by Neil Bonnett on the International Race of Champions. Bonnett, who raced in 18 seasons on the Sprint Cup and started in 13 races over six season on the Busch Series, made ten International Race of Champions starts between 1979 and 1984. He recorded nine top ten finishes (four victories) and won his final IROC race at the Michigan International Speedway.

The amount of money earned (396) in thousands of dollars by both Ricky Rudd and Richard Petty during the 1981 NASCAR season. Petty actually earned a touch over $396,000, $72 more to be exact. Rudd, on the other hand, finished the season two spots ahead of Petty but earned almost $400 less on the year.

The percentage of races (.397) that Curtis Turner entered in which he would finish in the top ten. In his 20 years as a pioneering driver on the NASCAR circuit, Turner would race in 184 events, finishing in the top ten 73 times. By number, 1958 was his most successful season in this category. Turner recorded ten top ten finishes in 17 starts on the season. Percentage wise, Turner's most successful season was in 1954. That season Tuner started in ten races, finishing eight of those races in the top ten.

The amount of money earned (3.98) in thousands of dollars by Herb Thomas over seven starts at the Central City Speedway in Macon, Georgia. Thomas holds the record for earnings as well as victories, having recorded two wins in the first two races held at the track.

The amount of career winnings (3.99) in millions by Buddy Baker over his 33 year NASCAR career. Baker began his NASCAR career back in 1959, long before the sport became the lucrative job it is today, and it was due to his success and longevity that he was able to earn what he did. Baker never earned more than around $340,000 in any given season (his best season's line would likely equate to a $7-8 million payout today) and, as a rookie in 1959, made 12 starts (with five top ten finishes) earning just $1,705.

400 The percentage of races entered (.400) that Mike Skinner won during the inaugural year of the Craftsman Truck Series in 1995. Skinner, who raced sparingly on the Busch and Sprint Cup circuits before Craftsman began (he never competed in more than six races in a season between Sprint and Busch), started in all 20 races in 1995, winning eight of them.

Chapter Five

The Alabama Gang

*I*f you are ever passing through Jefferson County Alabama and happen upon a little town called Hueytown, take a second to look around. It probably is not too different from any other town with 15,000 residents, with one exception: it is the home of some of NASCAR's greatest legends. The patriarch of the Alabama Gang (as they became known) was Bobby Allison, who left Florida in search of a place he could have a chance to race. The area around Hueytown had a lot of dirt tracks, so Allison went back to Florida, picked up brother Donnie and friend Red Farmer, returned to Hueytown, and the Alabama Gang was born. Mechanic Neil Bonnet joined the crew and eventually Davey Allison was born, grew up, and became a second generation member, not by birth per se, by right. Jimmy Means, David Bonnett, and Hut Stricklin (who married Donnie's daughter) rounded out the gang.

Now look at the list of the 50 greatest NASCAR drivers of all-time and you see the gang holds a few spots. Bobby, Davey, Neil, and Red are all there. The Allison clan started in 1,151 Sprint Cup races and 149 Busch Series events, on top of countless other racing events. Bonnet started in 362 Sprint Cup races as well as 13 Busch Series events. Red Farmer started 38 races between the Sprint and Busch Series and was the Late Sportsman Division (the predecessor of the Busch Series) champ between 1969 and 1971. Jimmy Means, David Bonnett, and Hut Stricklin recorded another 859 starts between them and surely dozens of others outside the Series. Together the Alabama Gang raced in 2,159 Sprint and Busch Series races and hundreds if not thousands of other races throughout the gang's 50 years racing.

Davey and Neil have left the gang; Davey in a helicopter crash while landing in the infield at the Talladega Superspeedway in 1993 and Neil in a practice run before the 1994 Daytona 500. So, the gang may be a bit smaller than it was in its heyday, but the legacy of these drivers and of Hueytown, Alabama will live forever in racing folklore.

401 The number of laps led (4.01) in thousands by drivers starting for owner Rex White. Between 1958 and 1963, Rex White the owner had 171 starts. White was the driver of 170 of those races, with Tommy Irwin starting one race during the 1962 season. White recorded all the laps led and all 26 victories as an owner. Irwin's only start for White was a 28th place finish in Atlanta.

402 The number of career starts (402) recorded by Lake Speed on the Sprint Cup. Speed managed 75 top ten finishes, but could only pull off a single victory. He collected his win at the 1988 TransSouth 500 by beating out Alan Kulwicki by just under 19 seconds.

403 The number of career starts (403) entering the 2007 season recorded by Jeremy Mayfield. In those 403 starts, Mayfield has recorded 96 top ten finishes, including five victories and 48 top five finishes.

The number of points (404) that Jeff Green would have needed to become the only Busch Series Three-peat champion. While the feat was accomplished four times in the Sportsman Division, which pre-dated the Busch Series, it has not occurred since the Busch Series came into existence in 1982. As luck would have it, Green was only able to pull off one championship season in 2000. He would finish in the runner-up position in 1999 to Dale Earnhardt Jr. (by 280 points) and in 2001 to Kevin Harvick (by 124 points).

Entering the 2007 season, the number of career starts (405) recorded by Greg Biffle. The number is rather high, considering that Biffle has only been racing NASCAR since 1996. Biffle has been a "two-sport athlete," racing a majority of both Busch and Sprint Cup Series races since 2002, averaging just under 60 races started per season over the past five years. He has driven in as many as 70 races in a season. In 2004, he raced all 36 races on the Sprint Cup and all 34 races on the Busch Series en route to over $5.6 million in earnings.

The percentage of races started (.406) by Harry Gant on the Busch Series in which he would finish in the top five. Gant recorded 128 career starts on the Busch Series over 11 seasons, recording 52 top five finishes (including 21 victories). Gant was a bit more successful racing the Busch Series than the Sprint Cup, recording more Busch victories (21 versus 18 on the Sprint Cup) despite starting in 346 fewer races.

The amount of career earnings (40.7) in millions by Terry Labonte over 30 years on the Sprint Cup. Labonte has averaged $47,970 per each of his 847 career starts on the Sprint Cup entering the 2007 season and earned more racing 17 races during the 2006 season ($1.54 million) than he did over 124 career starts on the Busch Series ($1.25 million).

The amount of Busch Series points earned (4.08) in thousands by Steve Park during his 1997 Raybestos Rookie of the Year Award winning season. Park put up rookie record numbers in wins (three), top five finishes (12), top ten finishes (20), winnings ($678k), and series points. Those rookie season records have since fallen and Park has since moved on to the Sprint Cup series, but that season remains one of the most impressive ever by a Busch Series rookie.

409 The number of points (409) earned by Indy Race legend A.J. Foyt on the 1987 Sprint Cup season. Foyt recorded six starts on the season with a season best finish of 20th in the only race he was running at finish. His point total was good for 50th in the final season point standings.

410 The amount of earnings (41.0) in thousands of dollars during Ned Jarrett's first championship season of 1961. In a rare feat, Jarrett managed to capture the championship in a 52 race season while only recording one victory. Jarrett started in 46 races and was able to win the championship based on his consistent finishes. He placed in the top ten in 34 races and averaged a 7.6 finish position over the course of the season.

411 The margin of victory (.411) in seconds by Jamie McMurray over Martin Truex Jr. at the 2004 Goody's Headache Powder 200. McMurray earned one of his three season victories by handing Truex one of his three second place finishes on the year, but 32 races later, it was Truex who won the season championship, his first of two consecutive Busch Series crowns, on the strength of six victories.

412 The race record (41.2) in miles per hour at the Gamecock Speedway in Sumter, South Carolina. The only race held at the track was the 38th race of the 1960 NASCAR season. Ned Jarrett beat out David Pearson to record his fifth and last win on the season. Jarrett would finish the season ranked fifth.

413 The margin of victory (.413) by Jeff Gordon over Ryan Newman at the 2001 Protection One 400. On September 30, 2001, Gordon started in the #2 position and held on for the victory at the Kansas Speedway. The victory was one of six on the season and helped Gordon secure his fourth Sprint Cup championship.

414 The number of different races (414) in which Bobby Allison would hold the lead. Allison recorded 718 career starts on the Sprint Cup and, in those races, led a total of 27,516 laps of 196,838 total laps raced.

Allison led almost 14% of all laps raced and held a lead in almost 58% of all races started.

The number of miles driven (415) by Tim Flock during the 1949 NASCAR season. Flock would start in five of eight races on the season and was running at finish in two of those races. Over a third of his miles (166) driven were at the Daytona Beach & Road Course, where Flock finished in the runner-up position on the lead lap of the 4.15 mile, 40-lap road course.

The number of laps completed (416) by Dick Linder during the inaugural NASCAR season. In 1949, Linder started in three of the eight races on the season and completed 69.3% of all laps started (416 of 600). He would earn $830 for his efforts in a season that would prep him for a career best the following year.

The length in miles (4.17) of the Beach & Road Course in Daytona, Florida. The sand and paved course hosted its first race in 1949 with season champion Red Byron taking the checkered flag. Nine years and nine races later, the track saw Paul Goldsmith record the final victory on the track, which occurred on February 23, 1958.

The number of Sprint Cup Series points (4.18) in thousands recorded by Darrell Waltrip during the 1986 season. Waltrip started in all 29 races and recorded 21 top five finishes, including three wins. Despite his success on the season, Waltrip fell short of Dale Earnhardt's efforts. Earnhardt recorded five wins and five second place finishes and earned 4,468 points in the final season point standings, beating Waltrip by 288 points.

The average speed (41.9) in miles per hour by Tim Flock on his July 20, 1952 victory at Playland Park Speedway in South Bend, Indiana. Flock held off Lee Petty for his seventh of eight victories on the season and his first NASCAR championship. Petty finished the season in third place with Herb Thomas sandwiched between them.

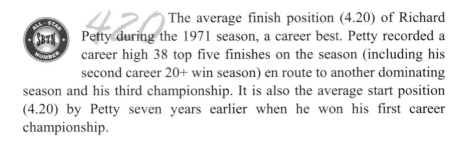

The average finish position (4.20) of Richard Petty during the 1971 season, a career best. Petty recorded a career high 38 top five finishes on the season (including his second career 20+ win season) en route to another dominating season and his third championship. It is also the average start position (4.20) by Petty seven years earlier when he won his first career championship.

The number of career starts (421) recorded by Jim Paschal over 23 years racing NASCAR. Paschal, one of the originals of NASCAR, raced between 1949 and 1972 and averaged just over 18 starts per season. His career record for starts came in 1967 when he raced in 45 of 49 events and, in his 23 seasons racing, he recorded ten seasons with ten or fewer starts and six seasons with 30 or more starts. The remaining seven seasons fell in between.

The average finish position (4.22) per race started by Richard Petty during the 1971 season. Although the King is ranked third for best average finish in an individual season, Petty has the highest average finish for a driver who raced at least one-half of a season. (Lloyd Dane only raced ten of 53 races in 1957 and Marvin Panch raced 12 of 55 races with better finish positions.)

The percentage of Busch Series races started (.423) by Carl Edwards in which he would finish in the top five. Edwards, a three-series driver, has found his best success on the Busch Series. Entering the 2007 season, Edwards has recorded 30 top five finishes in 71 races started. Of those 30 top fives, nine were victories. In the two full seasons he raced (2005-06), Edwards has finished in third and second place in the final season rankings, respectively.

The percentage of all Sprint Cup races run (.424) during the 1998 season that was won by a Hendrick Motorsports driver. Jeff Gordon found victory lane 13 times during the season and Terry Labonte won an additional race as Hendrick driver's won 14 of 33 races run on the year. For the fourth straight year, a Hendrick driver would win the Sprint Cup as Jeff Gordon captured his third title in that span.

Entering the 2007 season, the number of career starts (425) recorded by Mike Skinner. Skinner, one of the few drivers who has consistently raced in all three NASCAR series, has 244 career starts on Sprint, 52 on Busch, and 129 on the Craftsman Truck Series. In 2006, Skinner was a busy man; he started in all 25 Craftsman races, nine Busch Series races, and four Sprint Cup races. Skinner has found his best success in the trucks, winning 19 races and the inaugural championship in 1995.

The number of points (426) that separated number one from number two at the end of the 1984 Busch Series. On the strength of 24 top five finishes, including eight victories, Sam Ard (4,552 points) beat out Jack Ingram (4,126 points) for the series' third championship.

The number of Sprint Cup Series points (427) recorded by Clyde Minter during the 1950 season. Minter started in eight of the 19 races on the season and recorded a career-high three top five finishes. His point total put him in 17th place in the final season point standings (second only to his 14th place finish in 1949) and he earned a career-high $1,280 on the season.

The number of top ten finishes (428) recorded by Dale Earnhardt over his 27 years racing on the Sprint Cup. The Intimidator started in a total of 676 races, finishing 63.3% of all starts in the top ten.

The number of races (429) that Lee Petty ran in his 16 years of racing. Lee would hold the pole position in 18 of those races and earn 54 victories. 126 of these races and 25 of the victories can be found during his three most dominating seasons in NASCAR . . . the three seasons he won the Cup (1954, 1958, and 1959).

The number of career starts (430) recorded by Joe Nemechek between 1993 and 2006. Heading into the 2007 season, Nemechek has recorded 61 top ten finishes (18 of which fell into the top five), but has yet to win a race or place better than 15th in the final season standings over the past 14 seasons. Nemechek's success has been greater on the Busch Series. He won its championship in 1992 and earned 16 wins over 271 starts between 1989 and 2006.

The percentage of races (.431) that Neil Bonnet entered in which he would finish in the top ten. Bonnet, who would win 18 races, placed in the top ten in 156 of the 362 races that made up his 20-year NASCAR career. Bonnet's career was cut short when, on February 11, 1994, he died in an accident at Daytona while practicing for the Daytona 500.

The average speed (43.2) in miles per hour by Lee Petty at the only NASCAR races held at the Canadian National Exposition Speedway. Petty won the July 18, 1958 race at the three mile paved track in Toronto, Canada and Cotton Owens came in second. It was also the first race by a rookie named Richard Petty.

The number of laps completed (433) by Lee Petty in three starts during the 1961 season. The season marked the first time in his career that Petty started in less than 3/4 of all races run. Petty started just three races, but recorded one win and a third place finish. He completed 98.4% of all laps raced and led almost 30% of the laps he completed.

The number of laps led (4.34) in thousands by Bobby Allison during the 1972 season. Allison would lead at least one lap in 30 of 31 races on the season and, in fact, led over 43% of laps he completed. Despite his success on the season, which included ten wins, Richard Petty edged him out for the season championship by 128 points. In a bit of solace, Allison claimed the most in winnings on the season, earning roughly $349,000 to Petty's $339,500.

The percentage of races started (.435) by Speedy Thompson over a four-year span in which he would place in the top five. Between 1956 and 1959, Thompson would finish the season ranked third in the points standing. He started in 147 races over the four-year span and recorded 64 top five finishes. What makes Thompson's line so interesting during the four seasons is that he finished in third place each season despite the fact that he only started in 72% of the races run during those four seasons.

The number of Sprint Cup Series points earned (4.36) in thousands by Gwyn Staley during the 1955 season. Staley had career highs in starts (24), top five finishes (seven), and top ten finishes (14). Staley finished the season in tenth place in the final season point standings, which was also a career high.

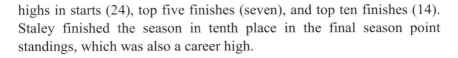The amount of money won (4.37) in thousands of dollars by Lloyd Dane during the 1956 season. Dane recorded half of his career wins (two of four) during the season and recorded nine top ten finishes in ten starts. His earnings were a career high to date and would remain his second best season by the time he retired after 11 seasons.

The percentage of races started (.438) by Curtis Turner during the 1950 season in which he would place in the top five. Turner started in 16 of the scheduled 19 events and placed in the top five in seven of those races. In his second and arguably his most successful season racing, Turner recorded a career best four victories and one-quarter of his career poles won (4 of 16) came during the season. He finished the season ranked fifth in the final season point standings, which was also a career best.

Entering the 2007 season, the number of races started (439) by Jeff Burton. Over the 439 races, Burton has earned 18 victories, 176 top ten finishes, and over $47 million in career winnings. He has yet to win a series championship, but has finished in the final season standing's top five on four occasions.

The margin of victory in seconds (.440) by Geoff Bodine over Terry Labonte at the 1996 Bud at the Glen. The victory by Bodine was the closest in the history of the Sprint Cup at the Glen until Steve Park pulled off a victory in the 2000 Global Crossing by .384 seconds.

The percentage of races entered (.441) by Junior Johnson that resulted in a top ten finish. Between 1953 and 1966, Johnson recorded 138 top ten finishes out of 313 races entered.

Entering the 2007 season, the number of career starts (442) recorded by Jeremy Mayfield on the Sprint, Busch, and Craftsman Truck circuits. Mayfield has 403 career starts on the Sprint Cup, 36 on the

Busch Series, and three starts racing trucks. In 15 years of racing, Mayfield has recorded five victories, all on the Sprint Cup Series.

The number of Sprint Cup points (4.43) in thousands by Dale Earnhardt during his 1990 championship season. Earnhardt would edge out Mark Martin for the season championship by 26 points and continue a trend of frustrating Martin for years to come (see 444).

The margin of victory, in points (444), by Dale Earnhardt over Mark Martin in the final standings of the 1994 Sprint Cup season. To put that in perspective, the combined margin of victory the three seasons (1991-93) before and the three seasons after Earnhardt's seventh championship (1995-97) was only 370 points.

The average speed (44.5) in miles per hour by Tim Flock at the only NASCAR race held at the Monroe Speedway in Monroe, Michigan. On July 6, 1952, Flock outlasted Herb Thomas to record his sixth win on the season. Flock started the race from the pole while Thomas started from the number three position. Buddy Shuman started in the second position, but finished 12th after running into engine problems after lap 146 of 200.

How much more money (4.46) in thousands of dollars Johnny Mantz made than Bill Rexford during the 1950 season. Mantz started in just three races compared to the season champ's 17 starts, but hit pay dirt when he claimed his sole victory at the Southern 500 at Darlington. The winner took a purse of $10,510 for that race alone, putting the winner of that one race (Mantz) above every other driver's season's take. Mantz would earn $10,635 over the season to Rexford's $6,175.

The number of career starts (447) recorded by Bobby Hillin Jr. on the Sprint Cup and Busch Series between 1982 and 2000. Hillin started in 334 races on the Sprint Cup and an additional 113 on the Busch Series. He placed in the top ten in 67 races, pulling off two victories on the Busch and one on the Sprint Cup Series.

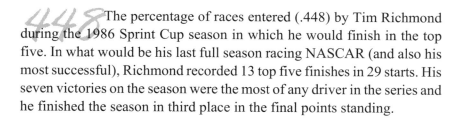

The percentage of races entered (.448) by Tim Richmond during the 1986 Sprint Cup season in which he would finish in the top five. In what would be his last full season racing NASCAR (and also his most successful), Richmond recorded 13 top five finishes in 29 starts. His seven victories on the season were the most of any driver in the series and he finished the season in third place in the final points standing.

The percentage of laps completed (.449) by Mark Martin at the 1991 Mountain Dew 400 at Hickory Motor Speedway. Martin completed 124 laps of the 276 lap race before rear end problems shut him down. He finished the race in 28th place and earned $650. It was the only Busch Series start Martin had on the season.

Entering the 2007 season, the number of laps led (450) by 2003 Craftsman Truck Series champ Travis Kvapil over four seasons. Between 2001 and 2004, Kvapil started each race but rarely found himself in the lead. In fact, during his championship season, he only led 49 laps of over 4,300 laps raced and, over his Craftsman career, he has averaged less than five laps in the lead per race. To put that in comparison, seven of the 11 other championship seasons saw the champion with more "in-lead" laps during the season than Kvapil has recorded in his Craftsman career.

The amount of money earned (4.51) in thousands of dollars by Junior Johnson at the 1964 Rebel 300. Johnson placed third in the race, winning more money than any other race that season (in fact, his three victories on the season had a purse of only $2,850 . . . combined).

The percentage of races started (.452) by Jeff Gordon during the 1994 season in which he would finish in the top ten. In the season before his first championship, Gordon recorded 14 top ten finishes in 31 starts on the season. Gordon's average finish position was 15.8, and he would complete 91.8% of all laps en route to an eighth place finish on the season.

The amount of money earned (453) in thousands of dollars by Cale Yarborough during the 1976 season. The season marked the first of three dominating years by Yarborough, who became the only driver to record a three-peat in the history of the Sprint Cup. The money Yarborough earned was a career best up to that point (19 seasons) and marked his first year earning over $400,000.

454 The number of top ten finishes (454) recorded by Sprint Cup Rookies-of-the-Year between 1958 and 2006. On two occasions, the Rookie of the Year didn't record a single top ten finish (Woodie Wilson in 1961 and Walter Ballard in 1971). The record for top tens by a rookie is 32, recorded by James Hylton in 1966.

455 The average speed (45.5) in miles per hour by the victor of the first NASCAR race held at Richmond International Raceway. On April 19, 1953, Lee Petty took the checkered flag in his '53 Dodge. It was Petty's second of five victories on the season. He would finish the season in the runner-up position for the second time in five seasons.

456 The average speed (45.6) in miles per hour by Buddy Shuman on July 1, 1952 at the Stamford Park half-mile dirt track in Niagara Falls, Ontario . . . good enough to claim the checkered flag. In the only race run at the park, Shuman beat out fellow '52 Hudson driver Herb Thomas to claim his sole NASCAR victory.

457 The number of Sprint Cup points (4.57), in thousands, recorded by Benny Parsons during the 1977 season. Parsons started in all 30 races on the season, recording 22 top ten finishes, including four victories, en route to his sixth (of nine) consecutive top five season finishes. Parsons would finish the season 430 points behind champ Cale Yarborough and 44 points behind Richard Petty.

458 The number of laps led (458) by Dave Marcis during one of his best NASCAR seasons on record. In 1975 Marcis finished the season ranked second behind Richard Petty, his best season ending ranking driving NASCAR. He ran a total of 8,324 laps throughout the season, recorded one of his five career victories, and earned over $240,000.

459 The amount of money won (4.59) in thousands of dollars by Buck Baker during the last race of the 1956 season. It would be the second consecutive year that the season champion would win the final race of the season from the pole position and, on the season, Baker would win over $34,000. Baker would repeat the same feat the following year, winning the final race of the 1957 season as well as the championship.

The amount of money earned (460) in thousands of dollars by Greg Biffle during the 1998 Craftsman Truck Series season. Biffle recorded 27 starts on the season and 12 top ten finishes en route to an eighth place finish in the final season point standings and the Raybestos Rookie of the Year Award.

The number of races started (461) by owner Harry Melling over 19 seasons. Between 1982 and 1999, Melling's drivers started in 461 races, placing in the top ten in 180 of those races and finding victory lane in 34 events. His most successful seasons as an owner came in 1985 when Bill Elliot won 11 races in 28 starts and placed second in the final season standings and in 1988 when Elliot won the championship with 22 top ten finishes in 28 events.

The number of Sprint Cup points (4.62) in thousands recorded by Junior Johnson during the 1955 season. Johnson started in 36 of 45 races on the season and recorded 14 top ten finishes, half of which were victories. His point total was good for a sixth place finish in the final season point standings, which was a career best.

The percentage of races started (.463) by Wendell Scott during the 1962 season in which he would place in the top ten. Scott, who started in 41 of the scheduled 53 races on the season, recorded 19 top ten finishes, four of which were top five finishes.

The race purse (4.64) in thousands of dollars for the 34th race of the 1964 season. Richard Petty won the 100 mile race held at the Piedmont Interstate Fairgrounds in Spartanburg, South Carolina and claimed $1,000 of that purse. Runner-up LeeRoy Yarbrough took home $600 and third-place finisher Doug Cooper walked away with $400 with the remaining 18 drivers splitting the rest of the purse.

The number of miles driven (4.65) in thousands by Al "Speedy" Thompson during the 1956 season. Thompson had a career high 42 starts on the season and recorded career bests in top ten finishes (29), top five finishes (24), and wins (eight). Thompson would end the season in third place in the final point standings for the first of four consecutive years.

466 The percentage of races started (.466) by Davey Allison during his best two seasons on the Sprint Cup Series. Allison really came into his own during the 1991 and 1992 seasons, recording five wins each season and 27 top five finishes in 58 races started. He finished his last two full seasons ranked third on the Sprint Cup and was on pace to have just as a successful season in 1993 until his untimely passing in a helicopter accident.

467 The percentage of Art Watts' career winnings earned (.467) during the season in which he recorded his sole NASCAR victory. During the 1957 season, Watts started in five races, recording three top five finishes and his only victory, which occurred at the Portland Speedway.

468 The number of races won (468) by drivers behind the wheel of a Chevy in the Sprint Cup during its first 50 years. Between 1949 and 1998, Chevy cars found victory lane more often than any other manufacturer with the exception of Ford. Chevy cars claimed approximately 1/4 of all victories in the first 50 years of NASCAR.

469 Entering the 2007 season, percent of races entered (.469) by Matt Kenseth in which he would finish in the top ten. Between 1998 and 2006, Kenseth would place in the top ten in 120 of 256 races entered.

470 The average speed (47.0) in miles per hour by Jim Reed at the only NASCAR race held at the Buffalo Civic Stadium. The stadium, which was home to the then-AFL Buffalo Bills, hosted one race on July 19, 1958. Jim Reed recorded his third career (and season) victory and, despite racing in just 17 events on the season, he wound up finishing tenth in the final season point standings.

471 The average speed (47.1) in miles per hour by Shorty Rollins in his first career NASCAR victory. On July 16, 1958, Rollins, driving in

his 14th career NASCAR start, held off Bob Duell to claim the checkered flag at the State Line Speedway in Busti, New York. Rollins only raced in 29 more events over the next two years and failed to record another win, although he did finish with 27 top ten finishes in 43 races.

The percentage of races entered (.472) by driver Rex White between 1956 and 1964 that saw him finish in the top five. White finished 110 of 233 races in the top five and finished in the top ten in approximately 70% of his races.

Entering the 2007 season, the number of Sprint Cup races started (473) by Jeff Gordon. Gordon, who moved to the Sprint Cup Series from the Busch Series in 1992, is the first driver to win Rookie of the Year Awards in both the Busch and Sprint Cup Series. He has been extremely successful since changing over to Sprint, where he has earned over $82 million in 15 seasons.

The number of NASCAR events (474) that Harry Gant raced in during his 22 year career. "Handsome Harry" would earn over $8.5 million during his career and take the checkered flag on 18 occasions. Also the number of career starts (474) heading into the 2007 season by Bobby Labonte. Labonte has 21 wins to his name and has earned almost $52 million over his 15 year career.

The number of miles driven (47.5) and the percentage of laps completed (.475) by Short Rollins in his only start at the Wilson Speedway in Wilson, North Carolina. The speedway, which was a 1/2 mile dirt track, held 12 events over a ten year period, but Rollins only started in one. A busted fuel line knocked Rollins out of the race just 95 laps into the 200 lap event.

Entering the 2007 season, the number of career starts (476) recorded by Ted Musgrave on the three NASCAR circuits. Musgrave has started in 305 Sprint Cup races, 22 Busch Series races, and 158 Craftsman Truck Series races. He has found his greatest success racing trucks, where he has recorded all 16 of his career NASCAR victories and almost 80% of his career top five finishes.

The percentage of races started (.477) by Rusty Wallace at the Michigan International Speedway in which he would place in the top ten. Between 1984 and 2005, Wallace started in 44 Sprint Cup Series events at the track, placing in the top ten in 21 of those races. He also recorded five wins between 1988 and 2000.

The percentage of Sprint Cup Series races started (.478) by Darrell Waltrip in which he would place in the top ten. Waltrip, whose career spanned 29 seasons, finished 387 of 809 races entered in the top ten. Wallace also recorded 53 top ten finishes in 95 Busch Series starts (.558) and another eight in 17 starts on the Craftsman Truck Series (.471).

Buck Baker's average speed (47.9) in miles per hour at the Gastonia Fairgrounds in Gastonia, North Carolina. On September 12, 1958, Buck Baker won the only event the track hosted, one of his three victories on the season. Baker finished the season in second place after two consecutive championship seasons.

The total acreage (480) of the Speedway Facility of Daytona International Speedway. For those unfamiliar with the conversion, that equates to 20,908,800 square feet. The infield of Daytona is 180 acres, including Lake Lloyd, which is a 29 acre lake.

The number of Sprint Cup Series points (4.81), in thousands, by Junior Johnson during the 1955 season. Johnson started in 36 races on the season, recording 18 top ten finishes, 12 of which were top five finishes (and five being victories), en route to a career best sixth place finish in the final season points standing.

The average amount of money earned (482) in dollars per race started by Fonty Flock. In nine seasons in and over 153 races, Flock earned $73,758 in winnings. His best season for average earnings-per-start was his last, where Flock won $1,800 in two starts.

The percentage of laps raced (.483) by Ryan Newman on the 2005 Busch Series in which he led. Starting in only nine races, Newman led 800 of 1,658 total laps en route to six victories and eight top ten finishes.

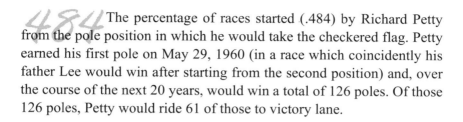

The percentage of races started (.484) by Richard Petty from the pole position in which he would take the checkered flag. Petty earned his first pole on May 29, 1960 (in a race which coincidently his father Lee would win after starting from the second position) and, over the course of the next 20 years, would win a total of 126 poles. Of those 126 poles, Petty would ride 61 of those to victory lane.

The number of races won (485) on the Sprint Cup by drivers racing a Ford at the half-century point in NASCAR history. Between 1949 and 1998, Ford was the king of race cars, winning over 26% of all races (485 of 1,864) and bettering rival Chevy by 17 victories during that time frame.

The total number of laps completed (4.86) in thousands by Richard Petty at the Daytona International Speedway while running the Daytona 500. That equates to 12,150 miles and, in the case of the King, seven Daytona 500 victories.

The number of career starts (487) recorded by Phil Parsons on the Sprint Cup and Busch Series. In 13 years racing on the Sprint Cup, Parsons started in 202 races, recording 40 top ten finishes and a single victory. On the Busch Series, Parsons started 285 races over 17 seasons, placing in the top ten on 96 occasions and recording two victories.

The average speed (48.8) in miles per hour by Herb Thomas on March 8, 1953 at the Harnett Speedway. The track only hosted one event and Thomas led from start to finish, beating out Dick Rathmann by three-plus laps.

The amount of money earned ($489) per race by one of NASCAR's originals, Lee Petty. Between 1949 and 1964, Petty would compete in 429 races, earning three championships, and finish with $209,780 in career winnings.

The percentage of all laps raced (.490) by Marshall Teague during the 1951 season that he led. In Teague's third season racing NASCAR, he would lead a total of 789 laps of 1,611 laps raced en route to recording five victories in just 15 starts.

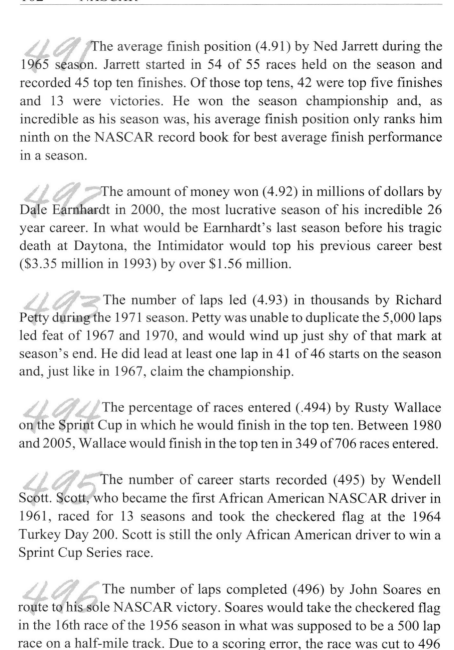

The average finish position (4.91) by Ned Jarrett during the 1965 season. Jarrett started in 54 of 55 races held on the season and recorded 45 top ten finishes. Of those top tens, 42 were top five finishes and 13 were victories. He won the season championship and, as incredible as his season was, his average finish position only ranks him ninth on the NASCAR record book for best average finish performance in a season.

The amount of money won (4.92) in millions of dollars by Dale Earnhardt in 2000, the most lucrative season of his incredible 26 year career. In what would be Earnhardt's last season before his tragic death at Daytona, the Intimidator would top his previous career best ($3.35 million in 1993) by over $1.56 million.

The number of laps led (4.93) in thousands by Richard Petty during the 1971 season. Petty was unable to duplicate the 5,000 laps led feat of 1967 and 1970, and would wind up just shy of that mark at season's end. He did lead at least one lap in 41 of 46 starts on the season and, just like in 1967, claim the championship.

The percentage of races entered (.494) by Rusty Wallace on the Sprint Cup in which he would finish in the top ten. Between 1980 and 2005, Wallace would finish in the top ten in 349 of 706 races entered.

The number of career starts recorded (495) by Wendell Scott. Scott, who became the first African American NASCAR driver in 1961, raced for 13 seasons and took the checkered flag at the 1964 Turkey Day 200. Scott is still the only African American driver to win a Sprint Cup Series race.

The number of laps completed (496) by John Soares en route to his sole NASCAR victory. Soares would take the checkered flag in the 16th race of the 1956 season in what was supposed to be a 500 lap race on a half-mile track. Due to a scoring error, the race was cut to 496 laps, but Soares won the race nevertheless, and did so by over a lap.

The career earnings (497) in thousands of dollars by Fred Lorenzen over 12 seasons and 158 career starts on the NASCAR circuit.

Lorenzen earned an average $3,143 per start and had his greatest success during the 1963 season. During that year, Lorenzen recorded 29 starts and 23 top ten finishes (including six victories), and earned over $122,000 on the season.

498 The number of laps led (4.98), in thousands, by Davey Allison in his nine year Sprint Cup Series career. Allison completed 56,066 laps over 191 starts, leading just under nine percent of all laps raced. His most successful seasons were in 1991 and 1992, where he recorded five victories each year and led 1,528 and 1,377 laps, respectively. Allison finished both seasons in third place in the final season point standings.

499 The amount of money earned (49.9) in thousands of dollars by Herb Thomas in his championship seasons of 1951 and 1953. In his first championship, Thomas earned just over $21,025, starting in 34 of 41 scheduled races and recording seven victories. Two years later, Thomas would repeat as champion, starting in all 37 races and recording 12 wins en route to earning $28,910.

500 The percentage (.500) of Rusty Wallace's earnings during his 1989 championship season that came from post-season bonuses. In what would be Wallace's first $2 million season, he would purse $1,120,090 in race earnings and $1,117,860 in post-season bonuses.

1967

RACE	SITE	FINISH		RACE	SITE	FINISH
1	Augusta	1		26	Greenville	1
2	Riverside	21		27	Montgomery	2
4	Daytona	5		28	Daytona	11
5	Daytona	8		29	Trenton	1
6	Weaverville	1		30	Oxford	2
7	Bristol	34		31	Fonda	1
8	Greenville	19		32	Islip	1
9	Winston-Salem	2		33	Bristol	1
10	Atlanta	22		34	Maryville	2
11	Columbia	1		35	Nashville	1
12	Hickory	1		36	Atlanta	17
13	North Wilkesboro	7		37	Winston-Salem	1
14	Martinsville	1		38	Columbia	1
15	Savannah	2		39	Savannah	1
16	Richmond	1		40	Darlington	1
17	Darlington	1		41	Hickory	1
18	Beltsville	2		42	Richmond	1
19	Hampton	1		43	Beltsville	1
20	Charlotte	4		44	Hillsboro	1
21	Asheville	3		45	Martinsville	1
22	Macon	1		46	North Wilkesboro	1
23	Maryville	1		47	Charlotte	18
24	Birmingham	3		48	Rockingham	28
25	Rockingham	1		49	Weaverville	2

Chapter Six

1967

*I*f anyone doubted the greatness of Richard Petty before the start of his tenth season racing on the Sprint Cup Series, 1967 certainly silenced any naysayer. Petty already solidified himself as the real deal in his first nine seasons. After all, he had started in 332 races and recorded 45 wins, won one championship, three second place finishes, and a third place finish. What 1967 did though was show the world that Petty wouldn't just be a great driver, he would be a legend and quite possibly the best driver ever to sit behind the wheel.

It defies comprehension how one man can dominate a season as much as Petty did. Petty started in 48 of 49 races on the season and won 27 races, including ten in a row. Petty didn't lose between August 12 and October 1 and won each race by an average of three laps . . . domination! As if winning 56.2% of all races and winning ten straight wasn't impressive enough, Petty finished an additional seven races in second place. Petty decimated the records that came before 1967: 27 wins vs.

Tim Flock's 18 win season of 1955, 5,537 laps led vs. Junior Johnson's 3,998 laps led in 1965, and ten consecutive races won vs. David Pearson's four consecutive wins in 1966. By the way, all these records still stand 40 years later and no one has come close to them. Petty tried four years later to outdo himself but came up short with just 21 wins during the 1971 season.

Petty was so dominating that year he became known as King Richard or simply, the King. The final season point standings relay what the rest of the numbers on the season so obviously pointed out: Richard Petty really was the King. Petty beat James Hylton for the championship by 6,028 points (42,472 to 36,444). Petty would be in the chase for the next 15 years, winning five additional championships and finishing no lower than eighth in the final season point standings. The King would bow out in 1992 with virtually every career record to his name and he will forever be associated with the single greatest NASCAR season ever.

The total amount of career earnings (50.1) in millions of dollars by Rusty Wallace. Wallace began his NASCAR career in 1980 and raced predominately on the Sprint Cup Series, although he did start a few races on the Busch and Craftsman Truck Series as well. Wallace made virtually all of his money, $49.7 million, over 706 Sprint Cup starts. He earned an additional $330,000 on 42 Busch Series starts and $5,100 more on one start on the Craftsman Truck Series in 1996.

The average finish position (5.02) by Richard Petty during his monster 1967 season. Petty set all sorts of records on the year and finished the season with 38 top five finishes of which 27 were victories. Despite his success, four finishes outside of the top 20 hurt his average finish ranking, but it wasn't important as he won the championship in the most dominating single season performance in NASCAR history.

The percentage of laps possible (.503) that Frog Fagan completed during the 1968 season. The 12 races Fagan started consisted of 3,596 total laps and Frog completed just over one-half of them, 1,808 laps to be exact. Fagan made just 20 career starts during his NASCAR career, most of which came during the 1968 season. The season also marked Fagan's only top ten finish, an eighth place finish at the 1968 Fireball 300.

The number of career starts (504) recorded by Ward Burton up through the end of the 2006 season. Burton, who began his racing career in 1990 on the Busch Series, has 145 starts on that series and another 359 starts on the Sprint Cup. In those races, Burton has recorded nine total victories, five on the Sprint Cup and four on the Busch Series.

The average speed (50.5) in miles per hour by Lee Petty at the Piedmont Interstate Fairgrounds in Spartanburg, South Carolina on July 7, 1956, good enough for the win. The 100 mile race lasted just under two hours (1:58:51) and was Petty's second and last victory of the season.

Entering the 2007 season, the percentage of races entered (.506) in which Jack Sprague would finish in the top five. Sprague has been a regular on the Craftsman since its inception in 1995 and is the series only three time champion. He did so with consistency, finishing in the top five in 125 of 247 races started.

The number of laps led (5.07) in thousands by Bobby Isaac during the 1969 season. Isaac led in 38 of his 50 starts on the season and led 41.2% of all laps completed. As successful as he was on the year and as incredible as it was and still is to imagine a driver leading in over 5,000 laps in a single season, Isaac didn't set a record nor win the championship that year. Two years prior, Richard Petty set the record for laps led in a season at over 5,500 and in 1969, Isaac could only muster up a sixth place finish on the season, a full 800+ points behind David Pearson.

The margin of victory (5.08) in seconds by Ricky Rudd over Neil Bonnett at the 1986 Delaware 500 at Dover Downs International Speedway. Also the margin of victory (5.08) in seconds by

Kyle Petty over Ken Schrader at the 1993 Champion Spark Plug 500 at the Pocono International Raceway in Long Island, Pennsylvania.

509 The average finish position (5.09) of drivers driving for Petty Enterprises during the 1971 season. Richard Petty started in 46 races on the season, finishing, on average, 4.2 per race. Buddy Baker also drove for Petty that season and, in 18 starts, had an average finish position of 7.3. Together the team recorded 56 top ten finishes and 22 victories.

510 The speed record (51.0) in miles per hour at the Princess Anne Speedway set by Herb Thomas on August 23, 1953. The half-mile dirt track located in Norfolk, Virginia only hosted one event, the 28th race of the 1953 season, and it was the eventual season champ that would go down as the sole NASCAR victor. The race marked Thomas' tenth win on the season. Thomas would record two more victories and secure the season championship, finishing the season 646 points ahead of Lee Petty.

511 The average speed (51.1) in miles per hour by Herb Thomas at Williams Grove Speedway in Mechanicsburg, Pennsylvania in the only NASCAR race held at that site. On June 27, 1954, Thomas held off Dick Rathmann by four car links, averaging just over 51 miles per hour.

512 The number of fans (51.2) in thousands who saw Neil Bonnett beat Richard Petty by two car lengths at the 1977 Los Angeles Times 500 held at Ontario Motor Speedway. Petty and Bonnett, who started one-two, switched positions by the end of the race with Bonnett recording his second career victory.

513 The percentage of races started (.513) by Richard Petty during the 1966 season in which he would place in the top five. Petty recorded 39 starts on the season and finished in the top ten on 20 occasions and almost half of his top five finishes were victories (8 of 20).

514 The speed (51.4) in miles per hour recorded by Rex White on the one-third mile track at the Canadian National Exposition Speedway, good enough for the pole at the only race held at the venue. White would win the pole and lead 71 laps, but faded to seventh place come race's end. Lee Petty, who averaged 43.19 miles per hour, won the July 18, 1958 race, which was also the first race started by son Richard Petty.

The amount of career earnings (5.15) in thousands of dollars by Herb Thomas at the Palm Beach Speedway in West Palm Beach. The track hosted seven races between 1952 and 1956 and Thomas started in six of those events. Thomas dominated the half-mile dirt track, recording four wins and another top five finishes over his six starts. The 1953 race is the only one that caused him troubles. Thomas had a problem with a u-joint, ending his race after 48 of the scheduled 200 laps.

The number of miles driven (5.16) by Marvin Heinis at the Riverside International Raceway on May 21, 1961. Heinis was flagged after the second lap of the 2.58 mile road course, which ended his day and marked the end of his season and NASCAR career.

The total number of laps led (517) by Frank Mundy and Jack Smith while driving for Perry Smith in 1951 and 1952, respectively. Perry fielded cars in 32 races over two years and had six drivers starting for him. Mundy was by far the most successful though. In 1951, Mundy led 331 laps and recorded two victories and eight top five finishes for Perry Smith. The only other driver to record a top five finish that season was Perry himself, who started in one race and finished in fourth place. Jack Smith recorded the remaining 186 laps led at the Central City Speedway in Macon, Georgia, on April 27, 1952, but a wheel problem ended his day and landed Jack in 16th place at the end of the race.

The total number of laps completed (518) by Elmo Langley during the 1955 season. Langley started in four races on the season and completed 59.8% of all possible laps in those starts. Langley also recorded his first career top ten finish during the season, an eighth place finish at Richmond Fairgrounds.

The purse (5.19) in thousands of dollars at the 1967 Islip 300, held at the Islip Speedway in New York. Richard Petty started in the pole position and, after sharing the lead with James Hylton, John Sears, and

Bobby Allison, took the checkered flag by over three laps. He took $1,150 of the total purse for his efforts.

520 The starting position (52.0) of Ned Jarrett during his first race as an owner/driver. On September 7, 1953, the 20-year-old rookie started the Southern 500 52nd in a field of 59 cars. An oil line break would end his race nine laps into the contest and he would finish the race dead last.

521 The number of laps led (52.1) in thousands by Richard Petty over 1,184 starts. Petty led in over 16% of the 307,848 total laps raced over his 35 year career. Petty holds the record in laps led by 20,628 laps over the second ranked driver, Cale Yarborough.

522 The number of laps led (522) over the 34 race career of Parnelli Jones. Jones may not be a household name, but he managed to pull off four victories in just 34 career starts between 1956 and 1970. He never started in more than ten races in any given season, and usually averaged between one to four starts per season raced. He had a pretty good winning percentage in three seasons in particular. In 1958, he led in 148 laps and won one of three races started. The following season he won one of two races and in 1967, he entered one race, led 126 laps of 185 raced, and won it.

523 The percentage of all NASCAR races held (.523) between 1951 and 1954 that were won by a Hudson. The Hudson Motor Car Company may have only built cars between 1951 and 1954, but their cars won over half of all races during that four year span. Hudson cars won 78 of 149 races and collected three manufacturer championships in four years.

524 The percentage of races started (.524) by Marvin Panch during the 1957 season in which he would place in the top five. In what was one of Panch's most successful NASCAR seasons, he would record 22 top five finishes in 42 starts on the season. Panch had a career best in number of starts (42), top five finishes (22), and top ten finishes (27) and would sit second in the final season point standings, also a career best.

525 The percentage of laps raced (.525) led by Kasey Kahne during his 2004 Craftsman Truck Series season. Although Kahne only entered two races of the scheduled 25 race season, he finished the season ranked 47th. Kahne won both races he started while leading 149 of 284 laps raced.

526 The distance (.526) in miles of the shortest track on the NASCAR circuit. The Martinsville Speedway in Martinsville, Virginia is the oldest and shortest track in NASCAR. First used in 1949, the track is just over one-half of a mile . . . that is 80% shorter than the longest track on the circuit, the Talladega Superspeedway (2.66 miles).

527 The margin of victory (5.27) in seconds by Darrell Waltrip over Alan Kulwicki at the 1988 Goody's 500. Even though Kulwicki held and lost the lead and race by under six seconds, it did mark the first race of his NASCAR career in which he would record a top five finish. Waltrip on the other hand, had just come off his third championship season and would finish the season in second place after another strong showing.

528 The average finish position (5.28) of David Pearson during the 1969 season. Pearson started in 51 of 54 races on the season and recorded 44 top ten finishes. Of those top ten finishes, 42 were top fives and, of those, 11 were victories. Pearson went on to win his second consecutive season title and third in four years.

529 The percentage of races entered (.529) by Buck Baker during the 1964 season in which he would finish in the top ten. Baker started in 34 of 62 races held on the season and placed in the top ten in 18 of his starts.

530 The number of points (5.30) in thousands separating 1964 champion Richard Petty from runner-up Ned Jarrett. Jarrett won more races than Petty (15 to nine), but Petty recorded more second and third place finishes (26 to 12) and earned 40,252 points to Jarrett's 34,590 points, earning the championship.

The total number of Sprint Cup points (531) recorded by Frog Fagan during the 1968 season. Fagan only started in 12 races on the season and averaged 44.25 points per start. Had he raced a full schedule, Fagan could have earned a 15th place finish on the year had he kept the same average points earned per start.

The average speed (53.2) in miles per hour recorded by Lee Petty at the only race held at the Louisiana Fairgrounds in Shreveport. Petty would hold off Dick Rathmann for the victory and earn $1,000 for his one hour and 46 minute effort.

The average finish position (5.33) of Rex White during his championship season of 1960. White recorded 35 top ten finishes in 40 starts. Of those 35 top tens, 25 were top five finishes and six were victories. His average finish position was White's personal best in a short and brilliant career.

The margin of victory (5.34) in seconds by Geoff Bodine over Mark Martin at the 1992 Tyson Holly Farms 400. Bodine would lead 312 laps of the 400 laps race after starting in the #3 position and hold off Martin by just over five seconds.

The amount of money earned, in dollars (535), by Cale Yarborough during his first four seasons racing NASCAR. Yarborough only started one race each season and was unable to complete a single race with earnings ranging between $85 and $200 per race/season.

The number of career starts (536) recorded by Elmo Langley in 27 seasons racing NASCAR. Langley started his racing career with limited action between 1954 and 1957, starting in only eight races. He ended his career pretty much the same way, only starting in seven races during his final three seasons. But in between, Langley raced and raced a lot. He started in as many as 52 races in a season and topped the 40 starts mark on five other occasions. Over his career, he recorded 193 top ten finishes and took two trips down victory lane.

The percentage of laps raced (.537) by Fred Lorenzen during the 1964 season in which he would be in the lead. Lorenzen led

2,375 laps of 4,426 laps raced over 16 races and recorded eight victories on the year. Lorenzen finished the season ranked 13th despite the fact that he only started in 16 of the 62 races scheduled.

The average speed (53.8) in miles per hour recorded by Emmanuel Zervakis at the 1961 Yankee 500 held at Norwood Arena in Norwood, Massachusetts. Zervakis earned one of his two season (and career) victories in the only race held at the arena when he beat Rex White by one-fourth of a lap.

The number of miles (539) led by Fonty Flock during the 1953 NASCAR season. Flock would start in 32 of 37 races on the season and complete 1,999 total laps or the equivalent of 1,626 miles.

The difference (54.0) in miles per hour between the race record and slowest race run at the North Wilkesboro Speedway in North Wilkesboro, North Carolina. The first of 93 Sprint Cup Series races held at the track was the slowest with Bob Flock winning the October 16, 1949 race at 53.36 miles per hour. Just under 43 years later, Geoff Bodine would set the track record at 107.36, a full 54 miles per hour faster than Flock's initial race at the track.

The amount of money won (5.41) in thousands of dollars by Walter Ballard at the 1974 Daytona 500. Ballard would record a tenth place finish at Daytona for his highest single race purse in his nine year, 175 start career.

The amount of money earned (542) in thousands of dollars by Darrell Waltrip in 95 career starts on the Busch Series. In 14 seasons spanning a 25 year period, Waltrip would average $5705.52 per start. His most successful season overall was his 1988 campaign in which he would earn $92,873 over 12 starts (four of which were victories). His highest average earnings-per-race was in 2006, when Waltrip earned $23,858 for a 28th place finish at the Goody's 250.

The percentage of races started (.543) by Buck Baker during the 1959 season in which he would finish in the top ten. Baker started in 35 of 44 races on the season and placed in the top ten in 19 of those races.

The average speed (54.4) in miles per hour by Dick Rathmann at the Lincoln City Fairgrounds in North Platte, Nebraska on July 26, 1953. Rathmann earned one of his five victories on the season by holding off Herb Thomas on the half-mile dirt track and finished the season in third place in the point standings, a career best.

The percentage of starts (.545) recorded by Fred Lorenzen during the 1999 season in which he would place in the top five. Lorenzen only started in 11 of 49 races held that season, but still managed to finish the season ranked 23rd, based on the strength of six top five finishes, two of which were wins.

The track race record (54.6) in miles per hour at the Huntsville Speedway in Huntsville, Alabama. The track only hosted one NASCAR event, which occurred on August 8, 1962. Richard Petty lapped Bob Wellborn and company to win the race and set the course speed record.

The number of laps led (547) by Jimmie Johnson during the 2005 season. The laps led by Johnson were a career low since he began racing a full Sprint Cup Series in 2002 as was his finish in the final season point standings. Johnson finished the season with a career low of fifth place in the final season point standings (that's right . . . a career low).

The average speed (54.8) in miles per hour by Junior Johnson at the Columbia Speedway in Columbia, South Carolina on June 5, 1958. Johnson recorded his second of six victories on the season by destroying the competition, beating George Dunn by over eight laps and finding victory lane after 100 miles and 1:49:35 behind the wheel.

The amount of money earned (549) in thousands of dollars by Jimmie Johnson during his 2000 Busch Series rookie season. Johnson started in 31 of 32 races and finished the season ranked tenth. The following year he would earn his sole victory on the Busch Series before transitioning over to the Sprint Cup where he has been very successful, winning 23 races in his first full five seasons.

550 The number of races (550) that Richard Petty and David Pearson drove head-to-head in. Of those 550 races, Petty finished in front of Pearson 289 times. Of the 289 races, Petty went on to not only to beat out Pearson but the rest of the field in 107 races.

551 The percentage of starts (.551) by Bobby Isaac during the 1968 season in which he would finish in the top five. Isaac started in all 49 races on the season and recorded 27 top five finishes. He managed just three wins in those top five finishes and lost the season championship to David Pearson. Isaac would make amends two years later by claiming the championship for himself.

552 The percentage of races entered (.552) by Buddy Shuman in which he finished in the top ten. Shuman started in 29 races between 1951 and 1955 finishing in the top ten in 16 of them. He also recorded his sole victory in 1952, taking the checkered flag at Stamford Park in Niagara Falls, Ontario.

553 The percentage of races (.553) in which Cale Yarborough entered and finished in the top ten. In 559 career starts over 32 years, Yarborough finished in the top ten 309 times. In his career, Yarborough recorded seven seasons with over 20 top ten finishes, with five of those seasons occurring consecutively from 1976 to 1980.

554 The number of laps led (5.54) in thousands by Richard Petty during his amazing 1967 season. Petty not only set the record for victories in a single season, but as it stands to reason, he set the record for laps led by a driver in a single season with 5,537. He ended up leading 43.5% of all laps he completed on the season.

555 The number of career top five finishes (555) recorded by Richard Petty. Of those 555 top five finishes, Petty recorded 200 career wins, a record that may never be broken. Petty's success was incredible with the King finishing in the top five in 46.9% of all races started (555 of 1,184).

556   The approximate space (55.6) in thousands of square feet, of the garages at the Talladega International Speedway. The Sprint Cup holds 32,400 square feet of garage space, while the Busch Series and the Craftsman Truck Series have approximately 23,250 square feet of space.

587   The percentage (.587) of Richard Petty's 1,184 races in which he finished in the top ten. The King finished 694 races in the top ten in his 35 year NASCAR driving career. Petty recorded an incredible nine seasons with 30+ top ten finishes, the first occurring in 1960 and the last in 1971, with a career high of 41 during the 1971 season.

558   The amount of money won (5.58) in thousands of dollars by Lennie Pond at the 1975 American 500 held at the North Carolina Motor Speedway. On October 19, 1975, Pond earned a season-high purse by finishing fourth behind Cale Yarborough, Bobby Allison, and Dave Marcis.

559   The number of career starts (559) recorded by Bobby Hamilton over 18 years racing on all three NASCAR circuits. Hamilton began his racing career on the Busch Series in 1988 and would start in 86 races over 12 years. In 1989 he started driving in the Sprint Cup and, through the 2005 season, would start in 371 races. In 1996, Hamilton began racing on the Craftsman Truck Series and would find his niche. Hamilton started in 102 races, winning ten races (twice as many as his Busch and Sprint Cup totals) and his only NASCAR championship, which he won in 2004 at the age of 47.

560   The number of career starts (560) recorded by Cale Yarborough over 31 years racing NASCAR. Between 1957 and 1988, Yarborough would run at least one race in every season (except in 1958) until his retirement. Entering the 2007 season, Yarborough's 560 career starts ranked him 23rd on NASCAR's all-time list for career starts, while his 83 career victories ranks him fifth in that category.

561   The number of points (561) that separated 1950 Sprint Cup champion Bill Rexford from fifth place finisher, Curtis Turner. Turner dominated a number of categories that season, but couldn't place better than fifth in the final season standings. He completed more laps (1,626) than any other driver, led more laps (1,110), drove more miles (689), led more races (12) than anyone else, and was second to Lee Petty in miles driven (1,390). He started in 16 races, won four of them, and finished in second, third, and fourth one time each. His failure to finish the remaining nine races started killed him in the rankings though and he slid back to fifth place in the standings come season's end.

The percentage of Danny Letner's 1955 earnings (.562) that came from his sole victory at Tucson Rodeo Grounds. On May 15, 1955, NASCAR held its first and only race at the venue and Letner took the checkered flag in the 100 mile race with an average speed of 51.428 mph. Letner took home $1,000 of his season's $1,780 in winnings after the race.

The percentage of laps raced (.563) that Tim Flock led during his 1955 championship season. In Flock's greatest NASCAR season, and one of the greatest seasons by any driver in the history of NASCAR, he won 18 races (three times more than Lee Petty), won 18 poles (three times more than brother Fonty), earned almost twice as much as runner-up Buck Baker ($33,275 to $17,590), beat runner-up Buck Baker by over 1,500 points (9,596 to 8,088) in the final season standings, and led 3,495 laps of 6,208 total laps raced.

The total number of laps led (564) by the three Flock brothers during the 1950 season. Fonty led the brothers with 369 laps led during the season and sat highest in the final season standings at 14th place. Tim led 190 laps over the season and, like Fonty, won one race during the season. His ranking at season's end was 16th. Big brother Bob led five laps over the season and finished in 20th place.

The amount of career earnings (5.65) in millions by Cale Yarborough in 560 career starts. Yarborough, whose career spanned 31 years over four decades, averaged over $10,000 per start, and earned a career-high $623,506 in 1978. That year marked Yarborough's third consecutive championship season, a feat that had not been accomplished before and has not been accomplished since.

The speed record (56.6) in miles per hour set by Tim Flock at the Shangri-La Speedway on July 4, 1952. The track hosted only one NASCAR event which Flock won. He needed each of his eight victories on the season as he won the championship over Herb Thomas by only 106 points.

The percentage of races started (.567) by Darrell Waltrip during the 1982 season in which he would place in the top five. The season marked Waltrip's second consecutive championship year and saw him finish 17 of 30 races in the top five. Of his 17 top five finishes, 12 of them were victories, meaning that Waltrip was victorious in 40% of all races started on the season. For the second straight season Waltrip edged out Bobby Allison for the championship, this time by 72 points.

The average speed of Bobby Allison (56.8) in miles per hour at the first race held at the Oxford Plains Speedway in Oxford, Maine. The track only hosted three races between 1966 and 1968 and Allison claimed the first two races for himself. Allison won the 1966 race by well over a lap and earned $1,100 for his victory over Tiny Lund and the other 25 drivers.

The percentage of top ten finishes (.569) recorded by drivers starting for Junior Johnson at the Atlanta International Raceway in Hampton, Georgia. Between 1965 and 1995, drivers such as Bill Elliot, Cale Yarborough, Geoff Bodine, Terry Labonte, and Darrell Waltrip (just to name a few) started in 72 races at the track and recorded 41 top ten finishes.

The number of careers starts (570) on the Sprint Cup by Geoffrey Bodine. Bodine, who began his career in 1979, became a regular on the circuit in 1982 and pretty much raced a full season schedule for the next 20 years. Entering the 2007 season, Bodine ranks 15th in pole qualifications, 35th on the career victory list with 18 trips down victory lane, and has 100 top five finishes to his name. Lest we not forget, he is also one of NASCAR's 50 all-time greatest drivers.

The percentage of races entered (.571) by A.J. Foyt in the 1971 Sprint Cup Series in which he would finish in the top five. Foyt recorded four top five finishes in just seven starts, including two wins, and had a more successful season than many who raced the entire season.

The amount of money earned (57.2) in thousands by the 1995 Pontiac Excitement 400 runner-up. Seven cars were on the lead lap when Terry Labonte took the checkered flag in the 400 lap race at the Richmond International Raceway, including Dale Earnhardt's. The #3 car finished the race 1.25 seconds behind Labonte with a payday of $57,200.

Entering the 2007 season, the amount of money (57.3) in millions of dollars earned by Tony Stewart in his first eight seasons racing on the Sprint Cup. Stewart started in 184 races between 1999 and 2006, averaging $201,690 per start. His most successful season thus far was his 2005 championship season where his earnings topped $13.5 million.

The number of races run (574) by legendary driver David Pearson. Between 1960 and 1986, Pearson would earn 113 poles, win 105 races along with three Sprint Cup championships, and earn close to $2.5 million over his 27 year Sprint Cup career.

The amount of money earned (57.5) in thousands of dollars by Rex White during the 1960 season. White would start in 40 of 44 races on the season, claiming six victories and 35 top ten finishes en route to his first and only championship while earning an average of $1,438 per start.

The average speed (57.6) in miles per hour by Tommy Thompson at the inaugural Motor City 250 held at the Michigan State Fairgrounds. The track only hosted two races, one in 1951 and the other in 1952, with the latter race won by Tim Flock averaging over two miles per hour faster than the former. Thompson's victory marked the first of his NASCAR career and earned him a payout of $5,000.

The performance points (577) recorded by Fireball Roberts over his 15 year NASCAR career. Under the 10-6-4-3-2-1 point system, Roberts recorded 330 points for victories, 132 points for second place finishes, 36 points for third place finishes, 48 points for fourth place finishes, 26 points for fifth place finishes, and five points for sixth place finishes in just 206 career starts.

578 The amount of money earned (57.8) in thousands of dollars by Davey Allison at the 1988 Miller High Life 400. Allison would start the race from the pole, lead 262 laps of the 400 lap race, and beat Dale Earnhardt by 3.37 seconds to record his second win of the season while earning his fourth highest payday on the season.

579 The career earnings (5.79) in thousands of dollars by Richard Petty at races held at the Savannah Speedway in Savannah, Georgia. Petty started in all ten events held at the track between 1962 and 1970, setting records for poles (three), wins (three), and money earned.

580 The number of points (580) that separated 2007 Sprint Cup champion Jimmie Johnson and Denny Hamlin, the final driver in the chase for the cup.

581 The percentage of races started (.581) by Jody Ridley during the 1980 and 1981 seasons in which he would finish in the top ten. Ridley finished the 1980 season with 18 top ten finishes in 31 starts, a seventh place finish in the final season standings, and the Rookie of the Year Award. The following year, he matched the previous year's numbers, finishing with 18 top ten finishes in 31 starts. The 1981 season saw one minor difference though; Ridley would earn his sole NASCAR victory at Dover Downs International Speedway.

582 The average finish position (5.82) of drivers driving for Petty Enterprises during the 1967 season. While the season was synonymous with Richard Petty, PE had two other drivers that season. Richard had an average finish position of 5.02 over 48 races, while Tiny Lund had an average finish position of 8.5 over four starts and G.C. Spencer had an average finish position of 14 in three starts.

583 Lee Petty's average speed (58.3) in miles per hour at the only race run at the Salisbury Superspeedway in Salisbury, North Carolina. On October 5, 1958, Petty set the track record at just over 58 miles per hour en route to a victory over Buck Baker and a $800 payday.

584 The number of points (584) Curtis Turner fell short on the 1950 NASCAR championship. Turner's numbers on the season were rather impressive. He led the circuit in laps completed (1,626), laps led (1,110 . . . over twice as many as Dick Linder), miles led (689), races led (12), and victories (four). He ranked second on the season for miles driven, just 17 miles short of Lee Petty. Despite leading in so many categories, he only recorded seven top ten finishes and finished the season in fifth place.

585 The amount of money earned (5.85) in thousands of dollars by Curtis Turner in his 17th and final NASCAR season. Turner started in six of 49 races on the season, placing in the top ten four times, and ending his career with a season purse of just under $6,000 and being one of the greatest NASCAR drivers never to win a championship.

586 The amount of career earnings (5.86) in thousands of dollars by Lee Petty at the Lakewood Speedway in Atlanta, Georgia. The track hosted 11 NASCAR races between 1951 and 1959 and Petty started in each event over the years. It wasn't until the last race the track hosted, on June 14, 1959, that Petty would record his first win there.

587 The percentage (.587) of Richard Petty's 1184 races in which he finished in the top ten. The King finished 694 races in the top ten in his 35 year NASCAR driving career. Petty recorded an incredible nine seasons with 30+ top ten finishes, the first occurring in 1960 and the last in 1971, with a career high of 41 during the 1971 season.

588 The percentage of races started (.588) by Fonty Flock during the 1951 season in which he would finish in the top five. In what would be Flock's best season of his nine year NASCAR career, he would record 20 top five finishes in 34 starts, including eight victories, en route to a second place finish in the final season point standings.

589 The percentage of Craftsman Truck Series raced (.589) in which Mike Skinner placed in the top ten. Entering into the 2007 season, Skinner has recorded 76 top ten finishes in 129 races entered. Skinner has been extremely successful on the Craftsman, even more so when comparing his success on the Sprint Cup and Busch Series. Skinner's top ten finish rate is .160 on Sprint Cup and .301 on Busch.

590 The number of miles raced (590) by Johnny Rutherford during the 1963 NASCAR season. Rutherford started in two races that year, the Daytona Qualifier #2 and the Daytona 500. Rutherford took the first 100 mile race, earning his sole NASCAR victory in 35 races started. He also fared pretty well at the 500, finishing in ninth place, with 196 of 200 laps completed (490 miles).

591 The number of top five finishes (591) recorded by Hendrick Motorsports out of 2,242 starts. Between 1984 and 2006, drivers representing Hendrick finished in the top five in over 26% of all races entered. In 1996, drivers Jeff Gordon, Terry Labonte, and Ken Schrader gave Hendrick 45 top five finishes out of 93 races started (an impressive 48.4% rate).

592 Entering the 2007 season, the percentage (.592) of races that Tony Stewart entered in which he placed in the top ten. In 284 races over eight seasons, Stewart has 168 top ten finishes in 284 races started. Of the 168 top ten finishes, 46 can be found in Stewart's two championship seasons of 2002 and 2005.

593 The percentage of races entered (.593) by Frankie Schneider in which he finished in the top ten. Schneider was a NASCAR original who began racing in 1949 and, over the course of nine years, started in 27 races. Of those starts, he finished in the top ten on 16 occasions. Schneider's last season was his best: In 1958, he started in seven races, placing in the top ten in five of those races and earning his sole NASCAR victory.

594 The percentage of races started (.594) by Gwyn Staley in which he would finish in the top ten. In 69 career starts over eight seasons, Staley recorded 41 top ten finishes (including three victories). Twenty-seven of Staley's top ten finishes were recorded during the 1955-56 seasons. Those two seasons coincided with his best season finishes of tenth and 14th place, respectively.

595 The amount of money earned (59.5) in thousands of dollars by Neil Bonnet over six years on the Busch Series. Bonnet started in 13 races, picking up seven top ten finishes, including one win, and earning just shy of $60,000 for his efforts.

596 The length (.596) in miles of the Nashville Speedway in Nashville, Tennessee. The track hosted 42 Sprint Cup races, nine Busch Series races, and five Craftsman Series races before NASCAR moved over to the Nashville Superspeedway. The track hosted its first 15 races as a half-mile paved track before the track was reconfigured to a .596 mile oval.

597 The percentage of races (.597) in which Tim Flock finished in front of older brother Fonty. Tim, the youngest of the three Flock brothers to drive NASCAR, raced against Fonty in 129 total races and finished in front of him 77 times. In addition to beating brother Fonty, Tim beat the rest of the field as well in 28 races.

598 The average speed (59.8) by Junior Johnson at the New Bradford Speedway in Bradford, Pennsylvania on June 12, 1958. The track only hosted one NASCAR race and Johnson held off Lee Petty to earn one of his six victories and $550 to boot. Petty got the last laugh though, winning the season championship while Johnson finished eighth.

599 The number of different races (599) that Richard Petty held the lead. Petty led a total of 52,135 laps over his 1,184 Sprint Cup career and won over one-third of the races in which he held the lead.

600 The percentage of races entered (.600) that "Fireball" Roberts won during his shortened 1958 season. Roberts would only enter ten races on the circuit and win six of those (he placed second and third in two of the remaining four races), finishing 11th in the point standings in a season which ran 51 races long. Also, the distance in miles (600) of the longest race run in NASCAR, at Lowe's Motor Speedway in Concord, North Carolina. The Coca-Cola 600, which runs 400 laps on the 1.5 mile oval, is a good 100 miles longer than most standard NASCAR races.

Jeff Gordon

Busch Series

YEAR	STARTS	WINS	TOP FIVE	TOP TEN	RANK
1990	1	0	0	0	1115
1991	30	0	5	10	11
1992	31	3	10	15	4
1999	6	1	4	4	51
2000	5	1	2	3	57
TOTAL	**73**	**5**	**21**	**32**	-

Sprint Cup Series

YEAR	STARTS	WINS	TOP FIVE	TOP TEN	RANK
1992	1	0	0	0	79
1993	30	0	7	11	14
1994	31	2	7	14	8
1995	31	7	17	23	1
1996	31	10	21	24	2
1997	32	10	22	23	1
1998	33	13	26	28	1
1999	34	7	18	21	6
2000	34	3	11	22	9
2001	36	6	18	24	1
2002	36	3	13	20	4
2003	36	3	15	20	4
2004	36	5	16	25	3
2005	36	4	8	14	11
2006	36	2	14	18	6
TOTAL	**473**	**75**	**213**	**287**	-

Chapter Seven

Gordon

*J*eff Gordon was bound to succeed in NASCAR, he was born for it. As a five-year-old he started his racing career, driving quarter midgets. At six, he had already won over 30 races and set a handful of track records. Jeff moved over to Sprint cars, but couldn't wait to the mandatory 16 years to drive sprints. Persistence and appeal worked, and at 13 he was racing sprint cars. Gordon found success once again . . . off to stock cars.

At the age of 18 Gordon started his NASCAR career. His first start was at the AC-Delco 200. Jeff started in second place and finished in 39th. Welcome to the big leagues, Mr. Gordon. But even at such a young age Gordon knew what he wanted, he knew success and he knew he was meant to be a NASCAR champion. In 1991 he started 30 races and finished the season in 11th place. The following season he started all 31 races on the Busch Series, recorded his first three career wins, and ran one race on the Sprint Cup Series. He apparently liked it. Gordon moved over to the senior circuit full time in 1993 and recorded a 14th place finish in the final point standings, not bad for a 21-year-old. What followed, the level of success, surprised most people, maybe even Jeff himself. Gordon recorded 11 straight top ten finishes, including four Sprint Cup Series championships, earning his first at the ripe old age of 23.

With the exception of an off year in 2005 (Gordon finished the season in 11th place), Jeff Gordon has spent his career in the top ten. Gordon entered the 2007 season with 75 wins at the age of 35. Only Richard Petty reached that mark at an earlier age (he did it at 29 years old). He has been called a wonder-boy (albeit sarcastically by Dale Earnhardt), a racing prodigy, and some other choice words (both good and bad), but no matter what you call him, Jeff Gordon was born to race, born to win, and represents the next generation NASCAR driver and one of the best to get behind the wheel.

Entering the 2007 season, the percentage of races entered (.601) that Jimmie Johnson placed in the top ten at race's end. Johnson, who has started in 183 races in six seasons, has recorded 110 top ten finishes.

The margin of victory (.602) in seconds by Greg Biffle over Jason Keller at the 2001 Pepsi 300. Biffle led 133 laps of the 225 lap race to record his first of five wins on the Busch Series on the season.

The number of career starts (603) recorded by James Hylton between 1964 and 2006. Hylton earned the 1966 Rookie of the Year Award in his first full season of racing, and came close to winning the championship on three different occasions as the Sprint Cup Series runner-up (1966, 67, and 71). His success may have waned later in his career, but his enthusiasm surely didn't. Hylton, who had raced in just a single Busch event (in 1982), jumped back behind the wheel at the Milwaukee Mile on June 24, 2006 and, at the age of 71, ran the AT&T 250. He may have only completed the first four laps before having a brake problem, but he ended his career on a high note and under his terms, 42 years after he first got behind the wheel.

The average speed of Rex White (60.4) in miles per hour at the 1960 Old Dominion 500 held at the Martinsville Speedway in Martinsville, Virginia. White, who started the race in second position, beat Joe Weatherly by a car length and took home $3,110. The race was White's fifth of six on a season that marked his first NASCAR championship.

The percentage of races entered (.605) by legend David Pearson in which he finished in the top ten. Over a career spanning 27 years, Pearson would record 347 top ten finishes out of 574 races started.

The number of laps completed (606) by Sara Christian during the 1949 NASCAR season. Christian, the first female NASCAR driver, was there from the start, placing fourth in the first NASCAR race. Christian would start in six of eight races in 1949 as well as one more race in 1950. She recorded two top ten finishes (including a fifth place finish at the Heidelberg Raceway in Pittsburgh, Pennsylvania) in 1949 and finished the season ranked 13th.

Entering the 2007 season, the percentage of races entered (.607) by Jeff Gordon in which he would finish in the top ten. Gordon has recorded 287 top ten finishes in 473 starts on the Sprint Cup Series between 1992 and 2006.

Entering the 2007 season, the number of career starts (608) by Todd Bodine in the three NASCAR series. On the Sprint Cup, Bodine has started in 228 races; in the Busch Series, he has 315 career starts; and, on the Craftsman Truck Series, Bodine has 65 career starts. It is also where he claimed his first title, the 2006 CTS championship.

The number of laps completed on short tracks (609) by Denny Hamlin while racing on the Craftsman Truck Series. Hamlin started six races between 2004 and 2006, three of them on short tracks (Martinsville Speedway, Indianapolis Raceway Park, and Richmond

International Raceway), placing in the top ten in two of the three events, and earning $24,290.

The race record (61.0) in miles per hour at Soldier Field in Chicago, Illinois. Fireball Roberts won the only race hosted at the half-mile paved track stadium, which occurred on July 21, 1956. The track was torn down in 1970 after protestors objected to the city financing car racing.

The percentage of races started (.611) won by David Pearson during the 1973 season. Pearson, who holds NASCAR's record for highest winning percentage during a single season, won 11 of 18 races started.

The amount of money earned (6.12) in thousands of dollars by David Pearson at the 1971 Southeastern 500. The one-two-three drivers fought most of the race with pole sitter and winner Pearson leading 133 laps. Richard Petty, who started and finished in the #2 position, led a total of 233 laps and Bobby Allison led for 78 laps, but fell from third to fourth by the time the race ended. Pearson's margin of victory was a good four seconds and the Silver Fox averaged 91.704 mph on his trip to victory lane.

The average dollars earned per start ($613) by Dewayne Louis "Tiny" Lund. Lund, who raced between 1955 and 1975, had $185,703 in career winnings in 303 races. Lund's most successful season was his 1963 campaign where he won $49,396 over 22 starts for an average of $2,245 per start.

The percentage of races entered (.614) that Bobby Allison would finish in the top ten. In 717 races entered between 1961 and 1988, Allison would finish in the top ten 440 times. Of Allison's 440 top ten finishes, 84 would be victories and another 86 would be second place finishes.

Ned Jarrett's average speed (61.5) in miles per hour at the Valdosta 75 Speedway in Valdosta, Georgia on August 25, 1962. The course only hosted three races between 1962 and 1965 with Jarrett's speed record and victory coming at the first event held at the venue.

616 The number of points (616) that separated the 2000 Busch Series Champ from the runner-up. Jeff Green, who had the most dominating performance to date on the Busch Series, compiled a line score of four wins, 20 top fives, 25 top tens, and 1,061 laps led en route to a thrashing of the rest of the field, including runner-up Jason Keller.

617 The amount of money won (6.17) in thousands of dollars by Whitey Norman in four years racing NASCAR. Norman recorded 29 career starts between 1956 and 1959 and finished in the top ten in eight races. His best year for earnings was his second. In 1957 Norman recorded 13 starts, finished in the top ten four times, and earned $3,990.

618 The percentage of all races started (.618) by Fonty Flock during the 1951 season in which he would lead at some point in the event. Flock dominated the field, leading in wins (eight), laps completed (2,788), laps led (2,068), miles led (855), miles driven (2,068), and races led (21). Despite his success, he came up short in his quest for the championship, finishing 146.2 points behind champion Herb Thomas.

619 The percentage of races started (.619) by David Pearson during the 1975 season in which he would place in the top five. Pearson started 21 of the 30 scheduled races that year and finished in the top five on 13 occasions.

620 The amount of money ($620) Tiny Lund earned during the final race of his 20 year career. Lund started one race in 1975, the Talladega 500, and crashed on the seventh lap of the race bringing his career and sadly, his life, to an end.

621 The percentage of races started (.621) by Dick Hutcherson in which he would place in the top five. Hutcherson only spent four years racing NASCAR (1964-67) before retiring to concentrate on building chassis for race cars. The four years he spent driving were incredible though: 103 starts, 14 victories, 64 top five finishes, 21 poles won, and close to $170,000 in earnings.

The amount of money earned (62.2) in thousands of dollars by Jimmy Spencer at his last Sprint Cup Series start at the Richmond International Raceway. Spencer, who would be running at finish, recorded a 36th place finish yet still earned his third highest purse in 31 starts at the track.

The number of laps raced (6.23) in thousands by Chuck Bown on the Craftsman Truck Series. Bown, who primarily drove on the Busch Series (187 starts) and the Sprint Cup Series (87 starts), started in 35 races on the CTS during the 1997 and 1998 seasons. When driving a full season on the CTS in 1997, Bown finished the season ranked tenth in the final season point standings. He ended his two seasons with 13 top ten finishes and $363,290 in winnings.

The number of RV spots (624) on the infield of the Chicagoland Speedway in Joliet, Illinois. The infield, which is 1,200 feet by 2,850 feet, also has a 3,500 square foot media center and a 3,900 square foot care center. For the RV fans, there are an additional 85 spots outside the track along the back stretch and 500 in RV Land.

The length (.625) in miles of the Redwood Speedway in Eureka, California. The track, which hosted two races in 1956 and 1957, was a .625 dirt oval that didn't quite live up to the term Speedway. During the 1956 race, Herb Thomas took the checkered flag with an average speed of 38.814 mph. The following year Lloyd Dane picked up one of his four career victories with an average speed that was a bit more respectable, 55.957 mph.

The amount of money earned (62.6) in thousands of dollars by David Pearson over 17 starts on the International Race of Champions. Between 1974 and 1977, the NASCAR legend raced in all four IROC events per season and started one additional race in 1979, recording 15 top ten finishes, ten of which were top fives and one was a victory.

The purse (627) in thousands of dollars of the 2001 CVS Pharmacy 200 Presented by Bayer, held at the New Hampshire International Speedway on May 12 of that year. Jason Keller recorded his only Busch Series win of the season at the track and took home almost $71,000 of the $627,000 purse in the process.

The margin of victory (6.28) in seconds at the 1995 Coca-Cola 600. Bobby Labonte earned one of his three victories on the season by edging out big brother Terry en route to his first top ten finish in the Sprint Cup Series.

The average number of laps led (62.9) per race by Sam Ard during his back-to-back Busch Series championship seasons of 1983-84. Ard, who barely lost the inaugural Busch Series, led 1,862 laps over 35 starts in 1983 and 2,099 laps over 28 starts the following year for an average of almost 63 laps led per race.

Entering the 2007 season, the career earnings (6.30) in millions by Jack Sprague in 11 years on the Craftsman Truck Series. Sprague has started every race on the Truck Series with the exception of the 2002 season (he raced a full Busch Series schedule) and 2003, when he started two of 25 races. In the seasons he raced a full schedule, Sprague has never finished lower than eighth in the final season point standing (which only happened once) and has claimed three championships. Sprague averages just under $25,500 per start on the Craftsman Truck Series.

The average speed (63.1) in miles per hour by Lee Petty on August 29, 1954 at the Corbin Speedway in Corbin, Kentucky. The track only hosted one race and it was Petty who would be victorious, earning one of his eight wins en route to the season championship.

The percentage of races entered (.632) resulting in top ten finishes by Dale Earnhardt during his 17 year Sprint Cup career. In 676 races, the Intimidator would rack up 427 top ten finishes.

The number of laps led (633) by Red Byron during the inaugural NASCAR season of 1949. Byron would win the first championship by competing in six of eight races, recording four top five finishes, to include two victories. Of the 633 laps raced, Red led 103 of them.

634 The percentage of laps completed (.634) by Junior Johnson during the 1960 season. Johnson started in 34 of 44 races on the season, completing 5,096 of a possible 8,041 laps. Johnson also led a total of 320 laps on the season and finished the season ranked seventh, despite starting in six races less than three of the drivers above him.

635 The amount of money earned (63.5) in thousands by Darrell Waltrip in his victory at the 1989 Motorcraft Quality Parts 500. Waltrip collected the victory over Dale Earnhardt by 0.60 seconds to collect his second of six victories on the season that saw Waltrip earn $1.31 million.

636 The number of races started (636) by International Motorsports Hall of Fame inductee Buck Baker between 1949 and 1976. Baker started at the pole in 44 of those races and took the checkered flag 46 times throughout his career, placing him 13th on the all-time list for victories. Baker was the first NASCAR driver to win back-to-back titles when he accomplished the feat during the 1956 and 1957 seasons, beating the season runner-up by over 700 points both times.

637 The percentage of races started (.637) by Bobby Isaac from the pole during the 1970 season that he would win. In Isaac's sole championship season racing NASCAR, he would earn 13 poles in 47 starts and earn seven of his 11 victories on the season when starting from the #1 position.

638 The number of miles driven (63.8) and the percentage of laps completed (.638) by Junior Johnson during his only NASCAR start in 1957. Johnson completed 102 of the scheduled 160 laps at the 1957 Wiles 160 before engine problems ended his day. He finished the race in 20th place, and earned $50 in prize money.

639 Entering the 2007 season, the number of career starts (639) by Dale Jarrett. Jarrett, who has been racing on the Sprint Cup Series since 1984, has collected 32 victories and has finished in the top five in the final season point standings seven times, to include winning the Cup in 1999.

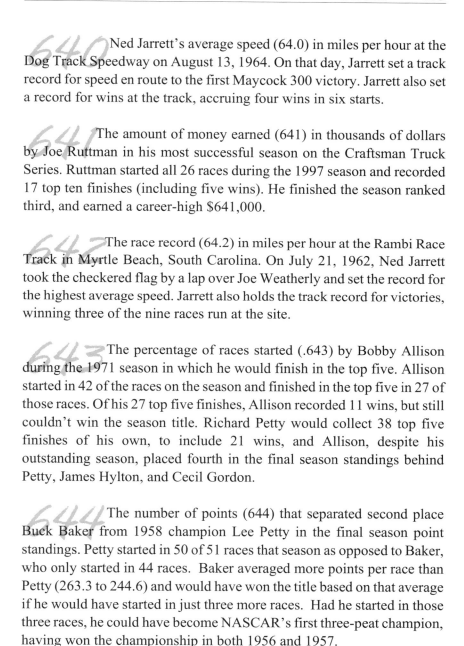

Ned Jarrett's average speed (64.0) in miles per hour at the Dog Track Speedway on August 13, 1964. On that day, Jarrett set a track record for speed en route to the first Maycock 300 victory. Jarrett also set a record for wins at the track, accruing four wins in six starts.

The amount of money earned (641) in thousands of dollars by Joe Ruttman in his most successful season on the Craftsman Truck Series. Ruttman started all 26 races during the 1997 season and recorded 17 top ten finishes (including five wins). He finished the season ranked third, and earned a career-high $641,000.

The race record (64.2) in miles per hour at the Rambi Race Track in Myrtle Beach, South Carolina. On July 21, 1962, Ned Jarrett took the checkered flag by a lap over Joe Weatherly and set the record for the highest average speed. Jarrett also holds the track record for victories, winning three of the nine races run at the site.

The percentage of races started (.643) by Bobby Allison during the 1971 season in which he would finish in the top five. Allison started in 42 of the races on the season and finished in the top five in 27 of those races. Of his 27 top five finishes, Allison recorded 11 wins, but still couldn't win the season title. Richard Petty would collect 38 top five finishes of his own, to include 21 wins, and Allison, despite his outstanding season, placed fourth in the final season standings behind Petty, James Hylton, and Cecil Gordon.

The number of points (644) that separated second place Buck Baker from 1958 champion Lee Petty in the final season point standings. Petty started in 50 of 51 races that season as opposed to Baker, who only started in 44 races. Baker averaged more points per race than Petty (263.3 to 244.6) and would have won the title based on that average if he would have started in just three more races. Had he started in those three races, he could have become NASCAR's first three-peat champion, having won the championship in both 1956 and 1957.

Entering the 2007 season, the number of Sprint Cup starts (645) by Bill Elliot in which he would be running at finish. Elliot has started in 756 races over 31 seasons, making his running at finish percentage .853. Elliot has shared similar success, albeit a bit less, on the Busch Series. On Busch, Elliot started in 43 races over 11 seasons, running at finish in 31 of those races, for a percentage of .721.

646 The margin of victory (646) in points by Herb Thomas over Lee Petty in the 1953 championship. On the strength of 12 wins and eight second place finishes, Thomas earned 8,460 points to Lee Petty's 7,814 points.

647 The percentage of cars running at finish (.647) during the Miller High Life 500 on March 5, 1972 at the Ontario Motor Speedway in Ontario, California. The Speedway, which hosted nine NASCAR races between 1971 and 1980, set three track records that day. A record 51 cars started the race and a record 33 finished it for a running at finish percentage of .647. It was also the slowest race run on that track, with an average speed of 127.082 mph. As a side note, A.J. Foyt pulled off the victory over Bobby Allison.

648 The number of laps led (648) by Marvin Panch during the 1964 season. Panch only started one-half of the races on the season and completed 6,499 laps, of which 648 were with him in the lead. Despite only starting in 31 of 62 races, Panch finished the season ranked tenth on the strength of 21 top ten finishes, four of which were victories.

649 The amount of money won (649) in dollars by Marty Robbins at the 1974 National 500. Robbins was involved in a crash on the second lap of the race and earned a meager $640 for his efforts. The interesting thing about Robbins isn't so much the money earned, but that he started and finished in 42nd place while driving car #42.

650 The distance (650) in feet of the shortest front stretch found on a NASCAR track. The front stretch on the Bristol Motor Speedway in Bristol, Tennessee is only 650 feet, compared to the mammoth 4,300 feet of the longest front stretch in NASCAR found at Talladega.

651 The percentage of laps completed (.651) by drivers starting for Cotton Owens at the Piedmont Interstate Fairgrounds. Between 1960 and 1966, Owens, David Pearson, and Billy Wade recorded 15 starts, completing 1,952 of a possible 3,000 laps, and recording nine top ten finishes.

The total number of fans in attendance (65.2) in thousands at the 1992 Pontiac Excitement 400. The race was run on March 8, 1992 at the Richmond International Raceway and it was a good one; Bill Elliot edged Alan Kulwicki by 18 inches to collect the win. Kulwicki returned the favor at the end of the season, beating Elliot by ten points to win the season championship.

The number of races (653) that J.D. McDuffie raced between 1963 and 1991 without recording a victory. McDuffie, under-funded and usually fielding his own team, never won a race on the NASCAR circuit and tragically died at Watkins Glen International during the early stages of the 1991 Bud at the Glen.

The margin of victory (6.54) in seconds at the 1990 Budweiser at the Glen. The 120,000 fans in attendance saw Ricky Rudd hold off Geoff Bodine to earn his only victory on the season. Bodine, on the other hand, would collect one of his 11 top ten finishes en route to a third place finish on the season.

The average finish position (6.55) of drivers driving for Jack Roush during the 1990 season. Actually, between 1988 and 1991, Roush only had one driver, Mark Martin, driving on the Sprint Cup. In 1990, Martin recorded 23 top ten finishes and three victories on the season. No other driver signed with Jack Roush has been able to duplicate that success. The closest was Mark Martin's 1998 campaign when his average finish was 8.6.

The percentage of races started (.656) by Lee Petty during the 1952 season in which he would finish in the top five. Petty recorded 21 top five finishes in 32 starts on the season and finished his fourth NASCAR season ranked third.

The amount of money earned (657) in thousands of dollars by Tony Raines during the 1999 Busch Series. The Raybestos Rookie of the Year recorded three top ten finishes in 29 starts and finished the season ranked 12th in the final point standings.

658 The number of laps raced (658) by John Rostek during his rookie season of 1960. As an owner/driver, Rostek started in five races in 1960, earning three top ten finishes and his only NASCAR victory, which came at the Copper Cup 100 at the Arizona State Fairgrounds in Phoenix.

659 The percentage of career starts (.659) by Rusty Wallace at the Bristol Motor Speedway in which he would finish in the top ten. Between 1984 and 2005, Wallace recorded 44 starts at the track and placed in the top ten in 29 of those races. His average finish position at the track was 9.6, and Wallace recorded five of his 55 career wins at Bristol.

660 The amount of money earned ($660) by Bill Snowden during NASCAR's inaugural season. In 1949, Snowden started in four of the eight scheduled races, finishing the season with 315 points and an 11th place ranking. Snowden recorded three top ten finishes (including a fifth place showing at Hillsboro) in a pretty successful first season. Two years later, Snowden would finish the season ranked ninth despite only starting in 12 of 51 races on the season. After four years and 24 starts, Snowden called it quits with 15 top ten finishes and $3,640 in winnings to his name.

661 Entering the 2007 season, the career earnings (66.1) in millions by Mark Martin. Martin has done it all and gotten paid for it too. On the Sprint Cup, Martin has earned $59.45 million over 24 years and 674 starts. On the Busch Series Martin has found greater success (statistically speaking), but a lesser payout; $3.5 million over 223 starts and 18 seasons. Martin has only started in 17 Craftsman Truck Series events over three different seasons and has earned approximately $652,000. Finally, Martin has been invited to participate in the International Raced of Champions set 12 times, earning $2.48 million over 47 races.

662 The number of laps led (662) by Carl Edwards on the Busch Series during the 2006 season. Edwards started all 35 races on the

Busch Series, recording four victories and 25 top ten finishes while leading 662 of 6,537 laps raced. He would finish the season second in the final point standings.

663 The number of miles driven (663) by Bill Blair during the 1949 NASCAR season. During the season, Blair would lead the field in miles driven, miles led (199), and laps led (325), and would sit second in laps completed behind Lee Petty. He would also finish five of the six races in the top ten. Despite the success he enjoyed during the season, he finished in fourth place at the end of the season.

664 The average earnings (664) in dollars per start by Curtis Turner during his 20 year NASCAR career. Turner, one of NASCAR's originals, competed in 184 races between 1949 and 1968, and tallied $122,155 in career winnings.

665 The percentage of laps completed (.665) by Banjo Matthews in seven starts at the Lowe's Motor Speedway. Of the 2,201 laps run in the seven events, Banjo completed just under one-third of them. In races Matthews was running at finish, which consisted of his first three events at the track, he completed 95.6% of all laps run (702 of 734). The final four races gave Matthews problems though; two engine failures, a crash, and a differential problem cut his races short and he was only able to complete 761 laps of the 1,467 scheduled in the final four races (51.2%).

666 The final lap of the 2001 Daytona 500.

667 The average finish position (6.67) of drivers driving for Richard Howard during the 1972 season. Bobby Allison started all 31 races on the season and had an average finish position of 5.3. The only other drivers to race that season were Lem Blankenship, who started one race and finished in 39th place, and Jim Paschal, who also started in one race and finished in 16th place.

668 The amount of money earned (6.68) in thousands of dollars by LeeRoy Yarbrough during the 1963 season. Yarbrough would record 14 starts on the season, five of which ended in top ten finishes. In these top ten finishes, Yarbrough would earn $2,605 dollars of his season's winnings.

The number of laps completed (669) by Davey Allison in his first Busch Series season. Allison started four races on Busch in 1983, completing 669 of 731 possible laps and recording three top ten finishes. He would earn $15,310 on the season and continue to race periodically on the Series until his death in 1993.

The amount of winnings (670) in dollars earned by Buck Baker during the 1973 season. Baker would crash in Rockingham during his first race of the season and he would not race again until 1976. His earnings were the lowest since his rookie year in 1949 when he earned $50 over two races.

The amount of money earned (67.1) in thousands of dollars by Harry Gant at the 1991 Peak AntiFreeze 500 held at Dover Downs International Speedway. Gant would beat runner-up Geoff Bodine by over a lap to record his third of four consecutive wins on the season.

The amount of money won (672) in thousands by Dale Earnhardt in 1980. In what would be Earnhardt's first championship season, the Intimidator took the checkered flag five times and finished in the top ten in 24 of 31 races started. Earnhardt's winnings would be the highest of his career and he would not surpass that amount until he won his second championship six seasons later.

The number of laps raced (6.73) in thousands by Cotton Owens during the 1959 season. The season ended with a number of career highs recorded by Owens; he started in 37 races, completed 6,733 laps, earned $14,639, and finished the season ranked second despite having five fewer starts than the champion, Lee Petty.

Entering the 2007 season, the number of career starts (674) recorded by Mark Martin. Martin, who began his Sprint Cup career in 1981, has averaged approximately 28 starts per active season racing on the circuit (he did not compete in 1984 and 1985).

675 The percentage of laps raced (.675) that Chuck Stevenson led during the 1956 season. Stevenson only started one race during the season and led 54 of 80 laps raced en route to his sole NASCAR victory. In fact, Stevenson only raced two NASCAR events, the first race of both the 1956 and 1957 seasons, ending his career with a wining percentage of .500.

676 The percentage of races (.676) in which Kevin Harvick would place in the top five during his two Busch Series championship seasons. In 2001, Harvick recorded 20 top five finishes in 33 races started and five years later he recorded 23 top five finishes in 35 races.

677 The average speed (67.7), in miles per hour, by Jimmy Pardue at the Southside Speedway in Richmond, Virginia on May 4, 1962 . . . good enough for the track record. The quarter-mile paved track only hosted four events between 1961 and 1963 with four different victors but they were dominated by Pontiacs. Three of the four winners, including Pardue, drove a Pontiac to victory lane.

678 The amount of money earned (678) in thousands of dollars by rookie Steve Park during the 1997 Busch Series season. Park started in all 30 events and recorded 20 top ten finishes (to include three wins) en route to a third place finish in the final season point standings and the Raybestos Rookie of the Year Award.

679 The number of laps raced (679) by Leon Sales over three seasons. Sales, who started in just eight races between 1950 and 1952, achieved more than many drivers who have since followed. He has the distinction of winning a NASCAR race and, to make that win even more impressive, he got it on the first race he started. On September 24, 1950, Sales, starting in the 11th position, ran 200 of his career laps en route to a victory at the Grand National race held at the North Wilkesboro Speedway in North Wilkesboro, North Carolina.

680 The pole speed (68.0) in miles per hour by Bob Flock in the first NASCAR race in 1949. Flock suffered from engine problems though and Jim Roper, driving a '49 Lincoln, overcame a 13th place start and held off Fonty Flock for his first and only NASCAR victory. Roper would race one more event, placing 15th at Hillsboro a few weeks later.

681 The average finish position (6.81) of Bobby Isaac during the 1970 season. Isaac started in 47 of 48 races on the season and placed in the top ten in 38 of those races. After placing second and sixth in the previous two seasons, Isaac, on the strength of his consistency, finally won his NASCAR championship.

682 The number of laps raced (682) on the Craftsman Truck Series by Jeff Burton. Burton, who started in four races during the 1996 season (three top ten finishes, average finish 8.5), also raced one race on the Busch Series (31 laps) as well as 30 races on the Sprint Cup (8,592) that season; his total laps raced on the three circuits was 9,305 laps. Entering the 2007 season, Burton has raced a total of 168,953 laps since he began his NASCAR career in 1988 on the Busch Series,

683 The percentage of laps raced (.683) by Curtis Turner during the 1950 season in which he would be in the lead. Turner started in 16 races on the season consisting of 1,626 laps. Of those laps, he would hold the lead in 1,110 of them. Over half of the laps led (599) were recorded in the four wins Turner recorded over the course of the season.

684 The average speed (68.4) in miles per hour by Jack Smith in the first Volunteer 500 race held at Bristol International Raceway. On July 29, 1961, Smith would take the checkered flag and beat Fireball Roberts by over two laps.

685 The number of career starts (685) recorded by Geoff Bodine between the Sprint Cup, Busch, and Craftsman Truck Series. Bodine started 570 races on Sprint, 94 on Busch, and 21 on the CTS. Bodine's busiest season was in 1999, when he started all 34 races on the Sprint Cup Series as well as 11 races on the Busch Series.

686 The average speed (68.6) in miles per hour by Richard Petty at the 1970 Albany-Saratoga 250 at the Speedway in Malta, New York. The track held two races, both won by Petty. The second race at the track, held on July 14, 1971, saw Petty win with an average speed of 66.7

miles per hour. As there were only two races run at the track and they were both won by Petty, he holds the record for slowest race winner and race record.

687 The margin of victory (.687) in seconds at the 1999 Sam's Town 300. The race, held at the Las Vegas Motor Speedway on March 6, saw Mark Martin edge Joe Nemechek by a slim margin. Martin would record one of six victories in just 14 starts on the Busch Series while Nemechek recorded one of six top five finishes in 12 starts.

688 The percentage of races started (.688) by Dick Rathmann between 1952 and 1954 in which he would place in the top ten. Rathmann only raced NASCAR for five seasons and had 128 career starts, but for a three year period, he was in the hunt for the championship despite starting in only 93 of the 108 scheduled races during that time. Rathmann recorded 14 top ten finishes in 27 starts during the 1952 season, 24 top ten finishes in 34 starts in 1953, and 26 top ten finishes in 32 races started in 1954. Rathmann finished those seasons fifth, third, and fourth, respectively.

689 The average speed (68.9) in miles per hour at the 1966 Maryland 200 at the Beltsville Speedway. The August 24 race was won by Bobby Allison, but it was the slowest NASCAR race of the eight run at the site. Bobby Allison would set the record for the slowest race that day, but won his third season (and career) NASCAR race which helped him to a tenth place finish in the final season standings.

690 The race record (69.0) in miles per hour at Jacksonville Speedway Park in Jacksonville, Florida. The track hosted six races between 1951 and 1963 with the record being set on February 13, 1955 when Lee Petty took the checkered flag over Dick Rathmann.

691 The margin of victory (6.91) in seconds at the 1995 Detroit Gasket 200. The Busch Series race was held at the Michigan International Speedway and saw Mark Martin beat Terry Labonte by just under seven seconds for the win. Both drivers were full-time on the Sprint Cup Series, but still raced 15 and 19 races on the Busch Series, respectively. Martin earned one of his three wins on the season, while Labonte recorded one of his nine top fives on the season.

The percentage of races started (.692) that Lloyd Dane would place in the top ten. Dane, who raced in 11 seasons over a 14 year period, started in a total of 52 races, recording 36 top ten finishes. He never started in more than ten races in any given season and, on average, started in less than five races per season, but he was consistent in placing in the top ten and recorded four victories between 1951 and 1964.

The percentage of laps completed (.693) by Fireball Roberts at races held at the Richmond International Raceway. Between 1956 and 1963, Roberts recorded five starts at the track, completing 783 of 1,130 possible laps at the venue. Roberts was unable to post a win at the track, but did record two of his career 93 top five finishes there.

The average speed (69.4) in miles per hour by Dick Rathmann at the Morristown Speedway in Morristown, New Jersey. The half-mile dirt track hosted five races, one each year between 1951 and 1955. Rathmann set the course speed record the third year it was held and earned $1,000 for his efforts.

The number of Sprint Cup points (695) owned by Davey Allison after the fourth race of the 1992 season. After a fourth place finish at the Motorcraft Quality Parts 500, Allison held a lead of 58 points over Bill Elliot and Harry Gant. Allison would hold the point lead from week one through week 16, when Bill Elliot took over the lead. Allison would take the lead back the following week, then relinquish until the 28th race of the season, when he recaptured the lead. Allison finished the final race of the season in 27th place, allowing both Bill Elliot and Alan Kulwicki to pass Allison in the final point standings and ending what could have been Allison's first championship season.

The percentage of races started (.696) by Ned Jarrett in which he would be running at finish. In 352 career starts, Jarrett would be running at finish in 245 of those, including 50 races in which he would be the victor. His most successful season in this category was his last championship season. Jarrett would be running at finish in 45 of 54 races started (.833).

The amount of money won (6.97) in thousands of dollars by Neil Bonnet during the 1987 Busch Series. Bonnet would start three races on the season and would complete 351 laps and a top five finish. The season also marked the only of his six in which he would lead a lap.

The percentage of races started (.698) in which Dale Earnhardt Jr. would place in the top ten during his back-to-back Busch Series championships. Earnhardt Jr. had impressive and similar seasons during his 1998-99 reign as Busch champion. He had 44 total top ten finishes in 63 starts. In 1998 he had 22 top ten finishes, including 16 top five finishes and seven victories. The following season, Earnhardt Jr. had 22 top ten finishes again, of which 18 were top five finishes and six were victories.

The number of races run (699) by Buddy Baker during his 34 year NASCAR career. During his career, Baker won 19 races, earned $3.6 million in race winnings, and finished a career best fifth in the Sprint Cup Series standings in 1977. In 1997, Buddy joined his father Buck in the International Motorsports Association Hall of Fame.

The percentage of races entered (.700) by Rex White in which he placed in the top ten. In his nine year career, White would place in the top ten in 163 of 233 races entered. His two best seasons were in 1960 and 1961, when he placed in the top ten in 35 out of 40 races (.875) and 38 out of 47 races (.801), respectively.

DAYTONA 500 FACTS

Most Victories	7	Richard Petty (1964, 66, 71, 73, 74, 79, 81)
Most Consecutive Victories	2	Richard Petty (1973-74); Cale Yarborough (1983-84); Sterling Marlin (1994-95)
Most Career Starts	33	Dave Marcis
Most Consecutive Starts	32	Dave Marcis (1968-99)
Most Pole Positions	4	Cale Yarborough (1968, 70, 78, 84); Buddy Baker (1967, 73, 79-80)
Most Wins from the Pole Position	2	Cale Yarborough (1968, 84); Bill Elliott (1985, 87)
Most Consecutive Pole Positions	3	Fireball Roberts (1961-63); Bill Elliott (1985-87); Ken Schrader (1988-90)
Longest Span Between First and Last Victory	17	Richard Petty (1964-81)
Most Starts Before Winning	20	Dale Earnhardt
Most Races Led	20	Richard Petty
Most Laps Led, Career	780	Richard Petty
Most Times Led, Race	21	Bobby Allison (1981)
Most Laps Led, Race	184	Richard Petty (1964)
Driver Leading the Most Laps and Winning	184	Richard Petty (1964)
Driver Leading the Most Laps and Not Winning	170	Fireball Roberts (1961)
Driver Leading the Fewest Laps and Winning	4	Benny Parsons (1975) & Kevin Harvick (2007)
Lowest Winning Starting Position	34th	Kevin Harvick (2007)
Widest Winning Margin	2 laps	Richard Petty (1973)
Closest Winning Margin	2 feet	Lee Petty (1959)
Fastest Winning Speed	177.602 mph	Buddy Baker (1980)
Slowest Winning Speed	124.740 mph	Junior Johnson (1960)
Youngest Winner	25 yrs, 6 mos	Jeff Gordon (1997)
Oldest Winner	50 yrs, 2 mos	Bobby Allison (1988)

Chapter Eight

Daytona and the 500

*T*here is probably no track (or maybe professional sports stadium) more awe inspiring than the Daytona International Speedway. Each year the track hosts a number of racing events, but NASCAR is still king in Daytona. The 500 has been run at Daytona for 50 years and it remains the biggest fish in the NASCAR Sea. Every driver strives to win just one and doing so solidifies you as a NASCAR great, even if just for one day, one season, or perhaps forever. The 500 started off with a bit of controversy. On February 22, 1959, Johnny Beauchamp and Lee Petty crossed the finish line in a race too close to call. Joe Weatherly, down a lap, crossed with Petty and Beauchamp, making the race almost impossible to call on the ground. Beauchamp was initially awarded the win but lost it after a couple days and news footage showed Petty take the race by a couple of feet. So began the legacy of the Daytona 500 . . . exciting from day one.

The excitement of Daytona was brought to the world when, in 1979, it was broadcast on live television. As Cale Yarborough and Donnie Allison battled for the win on the final lap, the two drivers touched, lost control, and spun into the infield off turn three. Richard Petty would come from half a lap back, battling Darrell Waltrip, to win the race. Cale and Donnie proceeded to discuss who was at fault and, when Bobby Allison pulled up, all hell broke loose. A fistfight erupted on the infield, live on national television.

Daytona and the 500 are more than just a track and a race. They mark the beginning of another NASCAR season and an opportunity for eternal glory. It is a place where forty-some drivers, their teams, and almost 200,000 people get together with dreams and aspirations of a successful season, a chance to hoist the Harley J. Earl trophy, and an opportunity to take the first step to that coveted season championship. There is no better atmosphere for racing, no greater history in the sport, and nowhere a driver or fan would rather be come the start of the season.

701 The total purse (70.1) in thousands of dollars at the 1979 Sun-Drop Music City USA 420 at the Nashville Speedway in Tennessee. Approximately 16,000 fans saw Cale Yarborough edge Richard Petty by 2.8 seconds to win the race and a $12,275 cut of the purse.

702 The number of laps raced (702) by Kevin Harvick on the Busch Series following his 2001 season championship. Harvick was a two-series driver in 2001, winning the Busch Series and placing ninth in the Sprint Cup Series, in a truly remarkably season. In 2002 though, Harvick only started in four Busch series events, completing 702 of a possible 816 laps in the races started, and recording one top ten finish.

703 The race record (70.3) in miles per hour at the Old Dominion Speedway located in Manassas, Virginia. The .375-mile paved track hosted seven NASCAR races between 1958 and 1966 with Ned Jarrett and Richard Petty each recording two victories at the track.

The King set the speed record in the second race at the track while Jarrett had the second quickest run at 68.8 mph.

704 Entering the 2007 season, the number of career starts (704) recorded by Ken Schrader. In 23 years, Schrader has started an average of just under 31 races per season and has racked up over $32 million in earnings.

705 The number of laps led (705) during the 2005 Busch Series by champ Martin Truex Jr. Truex, in his second consecutive championship season, held the lead in 19 of the 35 races on the season and averaged over 20 laps per race in the lead position.

706 The number of races started (706) over 26 years of competition by Rusty Wallace. Wallace would leave active racing with 55 victories (eighth on the all-time list), and approximately $49.7 million in winnings (fourth on the all-time list), but he would not go far. He owns Rusty Wallace Inc. and fields the #66 car in the Busch Series. His current driver is his son, Steve.

707 The margin of victory (7.07) in seconds at the 1987 Winston Classic. The race, held on November 1 of that year, saw Jimmy Hensley start from the pole and finish with a victory over Mike Alexander. The victory would be the only one recorded by Hensley on the Busch Series that year and it would help him secure a second place finish in the final season point standings.

708 The number of people in attendance (70.8) in thousands to watch Tiny Lund beat Fred Lorenzen at the 1963 Daytona 500. It was an amazing race for Lund, not just because he won the race by 24 seconds, but because it was his first career victory and he was driving the car of Marvin Panch, whose live he saved after a crash during practice runs.

709 The number of races started (709) by Kenny Wallace between the Sprint and Busch Series. Wallace has started 327 races on Sprint Cup Series and 382 on Busch. Despite a superior performance on the Busch Series (nine wins, 63 top five finishes, 156 top ten finishes vs. zero wins, six top five finishes, and 27 top ten finishes on the Sprint Cup

Series), Wallace has earned well over twice as much on the Sprint Cup. Entering the 2007 season, Wallace has $14.1 million in earnings on Sprint versus $5.4 million on Busch.

710 The number of fans in attendance (71.0) in thousands to watch the Atlanta 500 held on March 27, 1966. The fans saw Jim Hurtubise record his only NASCAR victory in his 13 year career by beating Fred Lorenzen and the rest of the pack by over a lap.

711 Entering the 2007 season, the number of career starts (711) recorded by Sterling Marlin. Marlin, who has been racing on the Sprint Cup Series since 1976, has collected ten victories, 83 top five finishes, and 216 top ten finishes over the past 30 years.

712 The number of top ten finishes (712) recorded by Richard Petty between 1958 and 1992. The King ended his career finishing in the top ten in approximately 60% of all races started (712 of 1,184).

713 The percent of laps completed (.713) by Marvin Porter during his rookie season racing NASCAR in 1957. Porter started in six races on the season completing 771 of 1,082 total laps. He also recorded one of his two career victories during the season. On the final race of the season and the only NASCAR race held at the Santa Clara Fairgrounds in San Jose, California, Porter took the checkered flag as one of only five cars running at finish from the original field of 22.

714 "Golden Boy" Fred Lorenzen's winning percentage (.714) at Martinsville Speedway between 1963 and 1966. Lorenzen would win five of seven races run at the track during that time frame, taking the 1963, 1964, and 1966 Old Dominion 500 as well as the 1964 and 1965 Virginia 500. Martinsville would be the site of almost 20% of all of Lorenzen's NASCAR victories.

715 The amount of money earned (7.15) in thousands of dollars by Benny Parsons at the 1972 Daytona 500. Parsons finished the race in fourth place and earned his second highest payday on the season. The only race that was more lucrative to Parsons was his fourth place finish at the World 600, which netted him $7,350.

The pole speed recorded (71.6) in miles per hour by Wendell Scott at the Savannah Speedway in Georgia on June 20, 1962. Scott earned his first and only pole of his career at the venue, but faded and finished in eighth place. Scott recorded 19 top ten finishes in 41 starts on the season and would earn his first NASCAR win two years later.

The number of races (717) that Bobby Allison started in 18 years of racing. Allison would earn 58 poles and take the checkered flag 84 times over his career. Allison's career was cut short when, at the age of 50, he suffered career ending injuries at Pocono during the 1988 season. Allison earned his first and only Sprint Cup Series title in 1983, edging Darrell Waltrip by 47 points. Allison would finish his career with over $7.6 million in winnings, earning $10,688 per start.

The percentage of laps completed (.718) by Richard Petty during his 1959 season. Petty would start in 21 of 44 races held that year and completed 3,648 of a possible 5,084 laps in races he started. The season would also be the last one in which the King would be held winless for 19 years.

The record speed in miles per hour (71.9) recorded at a NASCAR race run at the Arizona State Fairgrounds. The one mile dirt track hosted four races between 1951 and 1960, with the speed record occurring on April 3, 1960 when John Rostek took his 1958 Ford to victory lane and set the course speed record in the process. Rostek would collect $800 in earnings for his sole NASCAR victory.

The margin of victory (7.20) in seconds by Dick Brooks over Buddy Baker at the 1973 Talladega 500. Brooks started from the #24 position and held off Baker, who started three spots higher, and recorded his only NASCAR career victory in 358 starts over 17 seasons.

The number of laps raced (721) by Roscoe Thompson during the 1961 season. Thompson started at least one race in nine seasons and recorded 29 career starts between 1950 and 1963. Thompson's best overall season was in 1961 where he set career marks in top ten finishes (recording both of his career top ten finishes), laps run, winnings ($2,535), and final season ranking (40).

722 The number of points (722) separating 1975 champ Richard Petty from runner-up Dave Marcis. Petty won 13 of 30 races and dominated the season, earning 4,783 points in the final season point standings versus Marcis' 4,061 points.

723 The margin of victory (.723) in seconds by Jimmie Johnson over Kyle Busch at the 2007 Jim Stewart 400. Johnson began the race in the #4 position and led a total of 105 laps while Busch started in the #34 position and was able to lead 27 laps himself. Throughout the 400 lap race, 11 different drivers held at least a lap-long lead, but in the end it was Johnson who would win the race at the Richmond International Raceway.

724 The percentage of starts (.724) by Fred Lorenzen during the 1963 season in which he would finish in the top five. Lorenzen started in 29 of the 55 races scheduled on the season and recorded 21 top five finishes. Despite starting in just over half of the races on the season, Lorenzen's success landed him third in the final season point standings.

725 The average speed (72.5) in miles per hour by the winner of the first Southeastern 500 race held at the Bristol International. On October 22, 1961, Joe Weatherly took the checkered flag after starting in the #2 position by edging out Rex White. It was one of Weatherly's nine victories on the season, but White would get the better of Weatherly on the season, placing second in the final season point standing to Weatherly's fourth place finish.

726 The amount of money earned (726) in thousands of dollars by Ted Musgrave in his first full season racing trucks. Musgrave had raced in three Craftsman events in 1995 and 1996, and didn't return until 2001, when he left the Sprint Cup Series to focus on the truck series. It paid off. Musgrave recorded 18 top ten finishes, including seven wins, to finish the season with almost three-quarters of a million dollars and a second place finish in the final season point standings. After three consecutive third place season finishes between 2002 and 2004, Musgrave would hit pay-dirt with his first NASCAR championship in 2006.

The number of points (727) Tony Stewart had after the sixth race of the 2002 season. After a 15th place finish at the Ford City 500 at Bristol Motor Speedway on March 24, Stewart found himself ranked 12th in the point standings, a full 204 points off the lead after six of 36 races on the season. On the strength of 18 top ten finishes in the next 30 races, to include two victories, he was able to pull off his first championship season, edging out Mark Martin by 38 points.

The amount of career earnings (7.28) in thousands of dollars by Fireball Roberts in five starts at the Raleigh Speedway in Raleigh, North Carolina. Roberts won two of the final three races held at the track, earning 93.5% ($6,800) of his earnings at Raleigh in those two races.

The amount of money earned (7.29) in thousands of dollars by Jeff Gordon at the 1992 Budweiser 500. Gordon, who started in the #2 position, finished the race in fifth place (one of ten top five finishes on the season), and earned his tenth highest payday on the season.

The number of fans (73.0) in thousands that saw Bobby Allison edge out Buddy Baker by two car lengths at the 1972 National 500. On October 8th at the Charlotte Motor Speedway, Allison and Baker dominated the race, together leading a total of 307 of the 334 lap race, but in the end it was Allison who led the most important lap of all, the one that led to victory lane.

The percentage of laps completed (.731) by Fred Lorenzen in his last NASCAR season. In his final eight career starts, Lorenzen completed 1,801 of a possible 2,464 laps and recorded four top ten finishes of which three were top fives.

The record speed (73.2) in miles per hour at the Montgomery Motor Speedway in Montgomery, Alabama. The half-mile track hosted six Grand National Races between 1955 and 1969. Bobby Allison, who took the checkered flag on the last race the track hosted, the second race of the 1969 season, set the speed record.

The percentage of races started (73.3) by Eddie Pagan during the 1957 season in which he would finish in the top five. Pagan started 15 races on the season and placed in the top five in 11 of those races. He also recorded three victories on the season, which accounted for three-fourths of his NASCAR career total.

The percentage of laps completed (.734) by Parnelli Jones during his rookie season of 1956. Jones entered the NASCAR circuit in 1956 and, over the next 13 years, started in a total of 34 races. In 1956, the 22-year-old Parnelli started in three races and completed 592 of a possible 805 laps. He recorded his first of six career top five finishes by placing third in his first race at Merced while completing 181 laps of the 200 lap race. In San Mateo, Parnelli would complete all 241 laps and record another top ten finish, this time placing seventh.

Bobby Allison's speed (73.5) in miles per hour at the Meyer Speedway in Houston, Texas. On June 23, 1971, Allison won the Space City 300 by more than two laps over James Hylton in the only race run at the site.

Richard Petty's average speed (73.6) in the inaugural race at the Kingsport Speedway in Kingsport, Tennessee. On June 19, 1969, Petty would set the race speed record on the 0.400 mile paved track en route to a victory at the Kingsport 250.

The average earnings per start (737), in dollars, by Bob Welborn during the 1958 season. Welborn, who had his career best numbers in victories (five), top five finishes (ten), and top ten finishes (15) that season, earned $13,270 in 18 races started, yet, due to entering just over one-third of the season's races, finished the season ranked well out of the top ten.

The number of points earned (738) by Ted Chamberlain and Neil Roberts during the 1953 NASCAR season. The season spanned 37 races and the only driver to start in all events is the one who took the title. Chamberlain and Roberts raced in all of 11 races between them; Chamberlain in nine and Roberts in two. Roberts recorded one top ten finish and had an average finish position of 11.5 in his two starts.

Chamberlain recorded three top ten finishes, but had an average finish position of 19.2 on the season. Both drivers finished the season behind champ Herb Thomas by 7,722 points.

739 The margin of victory (.739) in seconds by Jeff Gordon over Dale Jarrett at the 1998 NAPA 500 at the Atlanta Motor Speedway in Hampton, Georgia. Gordon would start the race in 21st position (compared to Jarrett's third place start) and edge out Jarrett to win the race. Gordon became only the fifth driver on the Sprint Cup to win both the final race of the season and the season championship.

740 The number of dollars earned (7.40) per every mile raced by Paul Goldsmith between 1956 and 1969. Goldsmith started in 127 races over 11 different seasons completing 26,897.3 miles en route to nine career victories and $198,977.

741 The average speed of Lloyd Dane (74.1) in miles per hour at the inaugural race at the California State Fairgrounds on July 8, 1956. Dane set the record on the one mile dirt track and beat Chuck Meekins to earn his first career NASCAR victory.

742 The percentage of all laps raced (.742) by Fonty Flock during the 1951 season in which he was in the lead. Fonty led almost three-quarters of the laps he raced. Flock completed a total of 2,788 laps on the season and led 2,068 of them. Flock would finish his third NASCAR season ranked second despite starting in only 34 of 41 races.

743 The amount of money won (7.43) in thousands of dollars by Owner Fred Lovette during the 1961 and 1962 seasons. Brian Naylor made his NASCAR debut for Lovette at the 1961 Daytona Qualifier #2 and finished in 32nd place. Earnings from the qualifier: $200. The following season, Johnny Allen started 12 races, recorded five top ten finishes, and earned Lovette his sole owner victory . . . and $7,230.

744 The number of laps led (744) on the Sprint Cup by Kasey Kahne during the 2006 season. Kahne, in only his third season on the series, recorded six victories on the strength of 744 laps led of 10,044 laps raced and six poles. Kahne finished the season ranked eighth in the final point standings.

745 The amount of money earned (745) in thousands of dollars by Jack Sprague during the 1998 Craftsman Truck Series season. Sprague recorded 23 top ten finishes, to include 16 top five finishes and a career high five victories, but was beat out by Ron Hornaday by a mere three points for the season title and what could have been his second consecutive championship.

746 The total number of laps led (746) by Kurt Busch during his 2004 Sprint Cup championship season. Over half of all of Busch's laps led came in the victories he claimed on the season (119 laps led at the Ford City 500, 110 laps led at the Siemens 300, and 155 laps led at the Sylvania 300). The rest of his laps led were spread out over 15 other races throughout the season and Busch never held the lead in a total of 15 starts. It did not matter too much as Busch put together a strong season with 21 top ten finishes (including ten top five finishes and his three victories) in order to claim his first Sprint Cup championship.

747 The amount of money won (7.47) in thousands of dollars by Dave Marcis at the 1980 Southern 500. Marcis recorded an eighth place finish, one of 14 top ten finishes on the season, and picked up his second highest payday on the season.

748 The amount of money won (7.48) in thousands of dollars by Herb Thomas at the 1955 Southern 500. Thomas lapped Jim Reed at the Darlington Raceway to record the victory and take almost three times as much in winnings as the nearest driver.

749 The amount of money earned (74.9) in thousands of dollars by Dale Jarrett at the 1991 Daytona 500. Jarrett collected his biggest payday of the season with his sixth place finish. Only his win at Michigan came close in the earnings category ($74,150). The remaining races Jarrett started had paydays ranging from $5,475 to $27,400.

750 The percentage of races started (.750) by Greg Biffle during the 2000 Craftsman Truck Series in which he would place in the top five.

During the 24 race season, Biffle recorded 18 top five finishes, including five victories. He would win the championship that year and earn more than $1 million in the process.

The amount of money earned (7.51) in thousands of dollars by Rusty Wallace for a fifth place finish at the 1984 Holly Farms 400. Wallace would record his second best finish on the season (fifth) and his seventh highest payday in 30 races started.

The percentage of laps completed (.752) by Cale Yarborough in 27 starts during the 1975 season. Yarborough completed 7,353 laps of a possible 9,784 laps on the season and ended up finishing the season ranked ninth with three wins and 13 top five finishes. The next three seasons, Yarborough would complete 92.6%, 98.8%, and 94.8% of all laps in races started and, showing the importance of consistency, won the championship three years in a row.

The average speed (75.3) of Johnny Mantz, in miles per hour, at the first running of the Southern 500 at Darlington Raceway. On September 4, 1950, Mantz took the checkered flag in Hubert Westmoreland's '50 Plymouth. Mantz's margin of victory was an amazing 9+ laps over Fireball Roberts.

The margin of victory (7.54) in seconds at the 1995 Carolina Pride/Red Dog 250. Two-time Busch Series champion Larry Pearson held off Jason Keller to record one of his two season wins en route to a sixth place finish in the final season standings.

The performance points (755) recorded by Jim Paschal over his 23 year NASCAR career. Under the 10-6-4-3-2-1 point system, Paschal recorded 250 points for victories, 204 points for second place finishes, 124 points for third place finishes, 102 points for fourth place finishes, 50 points for fifth place finishes, and 25 points for sixth place finishes in 421 career starts.

Entering the 2007 season, the number of career starts (756) recorded by Morgan Shepherd. Shepherd began his NASCAR career in 1970 and raced sparingly until he became a regular on the NASCAR scene in 1981. All told, Shepherd has 513 career starts on the Sprint Cup, 192 on the Busch Series, and 51 on the Craftsman Truck Series. Going into the 2007 season, Shepherd is still racing on the Busch and Craftsman Truck Series at the age of 65.

757 The number of laps led (757) by Ted Musgrave on the Craftsman Truck Series during the 2002 and 2004 seasons. In both years, Musgrave would record 16 top ten finishes and finish in third place in the final season standings.

758 The amount of money earned (75.8) in thousands of dollars by Mike Bliss at the 2002 Kroger 225. On July 13, 2002, Bliss pulled off his third victory of the season, beating out Dennis Setzer by over 18 seconds. Bliss would pick up an additional two wins over the last 11 races en route to his first Craftsman Truck Series championship. The season was by far his most lucrative driving on the truck series. In 22 starts Bliss would earn just shy of $900,000.

759 The percentage of races (.759) that Shorty Rollins started during his rookie season that he would finish in the top ten. In 1958, the 29-year-old rookie started in 29 of the 51 races of the season, most often driving his own car. He managed 22 top ten finishes and recorded his sole NASCAR victory at the Stateline Speedway in Busti, New York on July 16th. Rollins only started in 14 more races over the following two seasons, and recorded an additional five top tens to finish his career with 27 top ten finishes in 43 races started.

760 The average finish position (7.60) of Lee Petty over 427 career starts. Petty may have won only 54 races (12.6% winning percentage) over his career, but he consistently placed in the top ten and his average finish position is the best in the history of NASCAR.

761 The percentage of races started (.761) by Bobby Allison during the 1970 season in which he would place in the top ten. Allison started in 46 races on the season, recording 35 top ten finishes en route to his best season finish to date, a second place position in the final season point standings.

The length (76.2) in miles of the IROC race held at the Riverside International Race Way in Riverside, California. Between 1974 and 1988 the track hosted 15 events on the 2.54 mile track with each race running 30 laps on the road course.

The number of laps completed (763) by Bill Blair during the 1949 NASCAR season. Blair completed more laps than every other driver other than Lee Petty, who completed 890 laps on the season. Neither Blair nor Petty would win the championship though. Red Byron won the first NASCAR championship with Petty finishing second and Blair in fourth, behind Bob Flock.

The number of laps raced (764) by Michael Waltrip over eight career starts on the Craftsman Truck Series. Waltrip hasn't spent too much time behind the wheel of the trucks, well, at least in comparison to his Sprint and Busch history. Waltrip has 44,157 laps under his belt on the Busch Series and an additional 189,449 laps on the Sprint Cup for a total of 234,370 laps raced on the three circuits entering the 2007 season.

The amount of money earned (7.65) in millions of dollars by Jimmie Johnson during his second Sprint Cup championship season. Johnson earned approximately $500,000 more than series runner-up, teammate, and friend Jeff Gordon.

The number of laps led (766) by Glen Wood during the 1960 season. Wood only started in nine races over the 44 race season, but won three of his starts. Wood led from pole to finish in two of those victories, which accounted for over half of his laps led (400 of 766 laps).

The amount of money earned (7.67) in millions by Bobby Allison over 25 years racing on the Sprint Cup. Allison made his debut in 1961 as a 23-year-old rookie and started in four of the 52 races scheduled and claimed $650 in earnings. After four years away from the sport, he returned and went on to become a regular on the circuit. Eighteen years later, Allison would claim his first (and only) championship and his highest season payout, $883,009.

768 The number of laps led (768) by Buck Baker during the 1954 season. Baker started in 34 of 37 races on the season and raced a total of 5,730 laps on the season, leading 13.4% of all laps completed. Baker would have his best season to date, recording 28 top ten finishes, including four wins.

769 The race speed record (76.9) in miles per hour at the South Boston Speedway in South Boston, Virginia. The quarter-mile paved track hosted ten NASCAR events between 1960 and 1971 and was dominated by Richard Petty, who won half of all the races run at the track. Even though Petty was the king of this track, it was Bobby Isaac who holds the speed record. Isaac set the record on August 21, 1969 and, in the process, ended Petty's string of four consecutive victories there.

770 The amount of money earned (770) in dollars by Ned Jarrett in his victory in NASCAR's only race at the Dixie Speedway. Located in Birmingham, Alabama, the speedway hosted race number 28 in the 1960 Grand National series and saw Jarrett take his own 1960 Ford to victory, leading pole to finish, and beating out Richard and Lee Petty, who placed second and third, respectively.

771 The number of laps completed (771) by Marvin Porter during the 1957 NASCAR season. Porter started in six races on the season and was running at finish in four of those events. He finished on the lead lap in his final two starts and in those two races earned $1,350 of his season's $1,770 purse. Porter recorded a second place finish at the Sacramento State Fairgrounds on September 8th to earn his first career top five finish. One week later, on September 15th, Porter was in the lead at the Santa Clara Fairgrounds when the race was called due to a crash and he was declared the winner.

772 The purse (7.72) in thousands of dollars for the May 30, 1956 race held at the New York State Fairgrounds. The one mile dirt track hosted three NASCAR events between 1955 and 1957. The '55 and '57 races had a purse of $4,335 and $4,635, respectively, and were only 100 laps in length. The '56 race was 150 laps with a much higher purse. Buck Baker took that race by three laps over Jim Paschal and earned $1,900 for the victory.

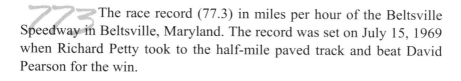

773 The race record (77.3) in miles per hour of the Beltsville Speedway in Beltsville, Maryland. The record was set on July 15, 1969 when Richard Petty took to the half-mile paved track and beat David Pearson for the win.

774 The percentage of races started (.774) by Jeff Gordon during the 1996 season in which he would finish in the top ten. Gordon started a full 31 race schedule and recorded 24 top ten finishes. Most of those top tens (21) were top five finishes, with ten of those being victories. Despite a dominating season, teammate Terry Labonte edged Gordon out for the championship by 37 points.

775 The amount of money earned (77.5) in thousands of dollars by Rusty Wallace at the 1993 Slick 50 300. Wallace started the race in the #33 spot, ended up leading for 106 laps of the 300 lap race, and beat Mark Martin by 1.31 seconds to claim the victory and one of his ten victories on the season.

776 Al Keller's speed (77.6) in miles per hour at the Linden Airport at the only race held at the two mile road course. On June 13, 1954, Al Keller took his Jaguar to victory lane to earn his second and final NASCAR victory by beating out Joe Eubanks and delaying his first win by four years.

777 The car number (777) driven by Tom Suligoy in his sole NASCAR start. On August 12, 1951, Suligoy raced his 1951 Packard at the Motor City 250 at the Michigan State Fairgrounds in Detroit, Michigan. Just over halfway through the 250 lap race, Suligoy was involved in a crash, ending his race and NASCAR career. He finished his only race in 39th place in a field of 59 cars.

778 The percentage of races started (.778) in which Lee Petty would place in the top ten. Petty, who holds the best average finish in the history of NASCAR at 7.60, recorded 332 top ten finishes out of 427 career starts.

779 The amount of money earned (7.79) in thousands of dollars by Richard Petty in 11 starts at the Augusta International Speedway. The track hosted 12 NASCAR races between 1962 and 1969 with Petty earning two wins, seven additional top five finishes, and over $2,800 more than the next closest competitor.

780   The number of laps led (780) by Richard Petty at the Daytona 500 over his career. Petty's number of laps led is a Daytona 500 record, but not the only one that belongs to the King. Petty also holds the record in victories (seven), consecutive victories (two), longest span between first and last victory (17 years), races led (20), miles completed (12,150), laps led in a race (184), widest winning margin (two laps), and driver leading the most laps and winning a race (184).

781   The number of miles driven (78.1) by Herb Thomas at the first of two NASCAR events held at the Eureka Speedway in California. On May 30, 1956, Thomas won the race, which was scheduled to be a 100 mile event on a .625 mile dirt track. Due to track conditions (rain and darkness), the race was shortened to 125 laps with Thomas the only driver on the lead lap, completing 78.1 miles when the race was called.

782   The amount of money earned (78.2) in thousands of dollars by David Pearson during his first championship season. In 1966, Pearson started in 42 of 49 races on the season, recording 33 top ten finishes, of which 15 were victories. Pearson's average earnings per start was about $1,860.

783   The number of laps raced (783) in the NASCAR circuit by Trans-Am and USRRC champ Mark Donohue. Donohue started in six NASCAR races during the 1972 and 1973 seasons. In four races in 1972, Donohue only managed to complete 390 laps. A crash and mechanical difficulties limited him to 13, 18, and 45 laps completed in the first three races he entered. In his final race of the season at Atlanta, he completed 314 laps and recorded a 15th place finish. The following season was much better for Donohue. He captured the checkered flag at the 1973 Winston Western 500 and led 138 of the 191 laps. He finished in 30th place at the Atlanta 500 in his last NASCAR event, falling victim to engine problems after completing 202 of 328 laps.

784 The number of square feet (7.84) in millions of the infield of the Daytona International Speedway. That converts to 180 acres in the infield, 29 acres of which is Lloyd Lake. Race fans can also find specialty vehicle parking, Paddock Club Suites, and the D500 Club.

785 Entering the 2007 season, the number of career starts (785) recorded by Kyle Petty. Of these starts, 448 have come while driving for Petty Enterprises. Interestingly enough, Petty, who has only recorded eight victories since entering the Sprint Cup Series in 1979, has not been able to muster a victory while driving for the family business.

786 The percentage of races started (.786) during the 1953 season in which Dick Passwater would finish in the top ten. Passwater only raced NASCAR for two years and only started a total of 20 races over that span, but during his second and final season, he recorded 11 top ten finishes in 14 races started. One of those top ten finishes would be his sole NASCAR victory, which he recorded at the Charlotte Speedway on April 5.

787 Marvin Burke's average speed (78.7) in miles per hour on October 14, 1951 at Oakland Stadium in Oakland, California. Burke would be victorious in the first race hosted by the stadium. The final two races at the track had average speeds in the low 50s after alterations to the track banks and straightaways.

788 The number of consecutive races (788) that Ricky Rudd qualified for prior to taking a year off in 2006. Rudd's amazing streak began in 1981 and ended in 2005. Along the way he qualified 29 times at the pole position and captured the checkered flag 23 times.

789 The number of laps completed (7.89) in thousands by Herb Thomas during the 1956 season. Thomas started in 48 of 56 races on the season and was almost a lock to win his third championship until a wreck that put him in a coma in the fourth to last race of the season and opened the door for Buck Baker to win the season championship.

790 The amount of money (790) in dollars that Bobby Allison won during the 1969 season when driving the car he owned. In two races, he had a top ten finish and failed to complete the other race. By comparison, Allison won over $64,000 driving Mario Rossi's car in 23 races and earned an additional $1,275 driving a Bill Ellis car in two events.

The amount of money earned (7.91) in thousands of dollars by Darrell Waltrip for his second place finish at the 1976 Southeastern 400 at Bristol. Cale Yarborough lapped Waltrip, who himself lapped third place driver Benny Parsons, to win the race and deny Waltrip his first win of the season (he would get it six races later though).

The track length (7.92) in thousands of feet of Lowe's Motor Speedway in Concord, North Carolina. The front stretch measures 1,980 feet, the back stretch 1,500 feet, banks one and two measure 2,400 feet, and banks three and four measure 2,040 feet. The track hosted its first race in 1960 with Joe Lee Johnson taking the checkered flag in the World 600.

The amount of money won (7.93) in thousands of dollars by Earl Ross at the 1974 Motor State 360. Ross recorded his best finish and payday to date when he finished the race under caution, sandwiched between winner Richard Petty and David Pearson.

The performance points (794) recorded by Bobby Isaac over his 15 year NASCAR career. Under the 10-6-4-3-2-1 point system, Isaac recorded 370 points for victories, 222 points for second place finishes, 108 points for third place finishes, 54 points for fourth place finishes, 30 points for fifth place finishes, and ten points for sixth place finishes in 308 career starts.

The amount of money earned (7.95) in thousands of dollars by David Pearson over six career Busch Series starts. Pearson started in five races in 1982 and one race in 1983, earning one win and four top ten finishes. Pearson also won the pole in half of his Busch starts, having an average start position of 1.2 on the series.

The number of laps completed (796) by Jeff Gordon at the Martinsville Speedway while racing on the Busch Series. Gordon started in four races during the 1991-92 seasons and completed 99.5% of all possible laps (800). He recorded two top ten finishes at Martinsville and earned $11,260 at the track.

797 The performance points (797) recorded by Herb Thomas over his ten year NASCAR career. Under the 10-6-4-3-2-1 point system, Thomas recorded 480 points for victories, 150 points for second place finishes, 76 points for third place finishes, 60 points for fourth place finishes, 20 points for fifth place finishes, and 11 points for sixth place finishes in just 228 career starts.

798 The NASCAR race record (79.8) in miles per hour at the Raleigh Speedway in Raleigh, North Carolina, set on July 4, 1956. Fireball Roberts set the track record at the Raleigh 250 by beating out Speedy Thompson by two laps and earned $3,000 on the day.

799 The amount of money earned (7.99) in thousands by Ned Jarrett at races started at the Piedmont Interstate Fairgrounds in Spartanburg, South Carolina. Jarrett started in 12 races, winning six of them, and earning a full $2,340 more than any other competitor over the 22 race history at the track.

800 The average amount of money earned per race (800) in dollars by Tim Flock in the only two NASCAR races run on the Lakeview Speedway in Mobile, Alabama. The third and 41st race of the 1951 season were held at the track in Mobile. Flock won the first race on the track driving a '51 Olds and earned $1,000. In the second race that season, Flock finished in the runner-up position in his '51 Hudson, earning $600.

Fabulous						
YEAR	CAR	STARTS	WINS	TOP 5	TOP 10	RANK
1951	Hudson	13	5	5	5	1
1951	Others	21	2	11	13	1
1952	Hudson	32	8	19	22	2
1953	Hudson	37	12	27	31	1
1954	Hudson	34	12	19	27	2
1955	Hudson	6	1	4	4	5
1955	Others	17	2	10	11	5
TOTALS	Hudson	122	38	74	89	-
	Others	38	4	21	24	-

Chapter Nine

THE Fabulous Hudson Hornet

*H*erb Thomas really was fabulous. Thomas was with NASCAR from day one. As a 26-year-old rookie in 1949, he started in four of the inaugural season's eight races driving a Ford. He managed a fifth place finish in the final race, earned $225, and finished the season ranked 25th. Not fabulous just yet. Season two saw Thomas start in 13 of 19 races. After running a Ford for the first three races, Thomas switched over to a Plymouth. After a shaky start, Thomas found his groove, recording four top five finishes in the final eight races of the season, including his first career victory. Not fabulous, but respectable.

Thomas started 34 of 41 races during the 1951 season. Twenty of his starts came behind the wheel of a Plymouth, one behind Hubert Westmoreland's Oldsmobile, and the remaining 13 in a Hudson. Enter Fabulous. Thomas recorded five of his seven season victories in the Hudson and he was sold. Thomas continued driving a Hudson and earned an additional 33 wins behind the wheel of the Hudson Hornet. Of

Thomas' 48 career wins, 38 trips down victory lane came at the wheels of a Hudson.

Regrettably for Thomas, Hudson Motor Car Company and Nash-Kelvinator Corporation merged on January 14, 1954 and the Hudson as Herb knew it was no longer produced. The Fabulous Hudson Hornet only lasted from August 12, 1951 through August 7, 1955, but what an era it was. While Thomas holds the NASCAR record for winning percentage at 21%, his success driving Hudson is even more impressive. Over 122 starts behind the wheel of a Hudson, Thomas won 38 races for a winning percentage of 31.1%. Thomas would record 79.2% of his career wins, 60.7% of his top five finishes, and 73% of his top ten finishes driving a Hudson and he recorded both of his season championships on the strength of the Hornet. Fabulous indeed.

The percentage of laps completed (.801) by Wendell Scott during the 1962 NASCAR season. In his second year on the circuit, Scott completed 8,542 of 10,662 laps and recorded his first top five finish (he had four on the season). Two years later, Scott would record his first NASCAR victory.

The amount of money won (8.02) in thousands of dollars by Cale Yarborough at the 1969 Rebel 400. Yarborough finished the race in second place after starting from the pole. He lost the race by over a lap to LeeRoy Yarbrough, who earned $14,700 for the victory.

The percentage of laps completed (.803) by Harry Gant in starts at the Daytona International Speedway. Between 1978 and 1994, Gant started in 32 races and completed 4,660 of a possible 5,800 laps. He led a total of 86 laps at Daytona, but was never able to pull off a victory, although he did manage seven top ten finishes.

The amount of money earned (804) in thousands of dollars by Harry Gant during the 1985 Sprint Cup season. Gant started in all 28 races on the season and recorded, what was to date, career high wins (three), poles won (three), laps led (1,270), and earnings.

805 The amount of money earned ($805) by Bob Welborn during his final NASCAR season. In 1964, Welborn started in three races and, despite having an average finish position of seventh, only mustered up $805 in winnings.

806 The percentage of all races started (.806) in 1981 by Darrell Waltrip in which he would finish in the top ten. The season marked the first of two consecutive championship seasons for Waltrip and three in five years. Waltrip would finish in the top ten in 25 of 31 races started and record 12 victories en route to a 53-point victory in the final season standings over Bobby Allison.

807 The total number of laps led (807) by Joe Ruttman in 20 years racing on the Sprint Cup Series. Ruttman started in 225 races in his career and recorded a career high in starts and laps led during the 1983 season. He started in 30 races and led 397 total laps, but was unable to post a victory (although he did record ten top ten finishes). In fact, Ruttman was never able to lead the lap that mattered . . . the one that led to victory lane.

808 The number of laps led (808) by Buck Baker during the 1955 season. Baker started in 42 of the 45 races on the season, leading 808 of 6,705 total laps completed. Baker would finish the season with 34 top ten finishes, but would come up short in his quest for the championship. Tim Flock won 18 races on the season and beat Baker in the final point standings, 9,596 to 8,088.

809 The number of career starts (809) by Darrell Waltrip in 29 years on the Sprint Cup Series. Waltrip averaged just under 28 starts per season on the series. He started another 95 races on the Busch Series and an additional 17 on the Craftsman Truck Series, bringing his career total starts to 921.

810 The amount of money earned ($810) by Sara Christian in seven NASCAR starts during the 1949 and 1950 seasons. Christian, the first female driver in a NASCAR race, earned $760 over seven races in 1949 and earned another $50 in one start during the 1950 season.

The average speed (81.1) in miles per hour by Tim Fedewa at the 1995 Meridian Advantage 200 held at Nazareth Speedway in Nazareth, Pennsylvania. The race marked Fedewa's first NASCAR victory and, along with three other top ten finishes, marked his best Busch Series finish . . . seventh place.

The number of miles raced (812) by Bubba Adams in 13 races over a three year span. Adams, who raced between 1984 and 1986, entered 13 races, finishing in the top ten five times. He completed 1,910 laps, although he never held a lead, and earned just under $8,000.

Percentage of races started (.813) that Buck Baker would finish in the top ten during his 1956 championship season. Baker started 48 races, finishing 39 of those in the top ten. Of those top ten finishes, 14 were victories.

The percentage of laps completed (.814) by Dale Earnhardt racing Busch Series races at Bristol. Between 1982 and 1991, Earnhardt started in 14 races and completed 2,360 of a possible 2,900 laps at the track. He also earned one of his 21 Busch Series wins there.

The number of thousands of fans in attendance (81.5) to see Buddy Baker take the 1972 World 600. Baker led 39 of the 400 lap race at the Charlotte Motor Speedway to Allison's 239 laps led, but Baker held the lead in the most important lap of all, crossing the finish line 23.7 seconds in front of Allison.

The amount of money won (81.6) in thousands of dollars by Tony Stewart in his last start at the North Carolina Speedway in Rockingham. Stewart would start the race in the pole position, but faded to finish in 18th place at the AC Delco 200 on October 31, 1998.

The pole speed (81.7) in miles per hour recorded by Tim Flock at the Orange Speedway on October 30, 1955. Flock started in the pole position and led start to finish for one of his 16 victories from the pole. He also became the first driver in NASCAR to win the final race of the season and the championship.

The number of laps led (818) by Brett Bodine on the Busch Series. Bodine raced a total of 12,868 laps on the Busch Series over 77 races in a seven year span. He fared better on the Busch Series than the Sprint Cup, taking five checkered flags and placing in the top ten in over 67% of the races he started.

The number of races entered (.819) in which Mike Bliss would place in the top ten during his 2002 championship season on the Craftsman Truck Series. Bliss entered all 22 races, finishing 18 of them in the top ten, en route to his most successful season in NASCAR and his first and only championship thus far.

The amount of money earned ($820) by both Wendell Scott and Donnie Allison at the 1971 American 500. Allison started the race from the #3 position and overheated after completing 63 laps. He finished the race in 39th place. Scott, on the other hand, started in 36th place and finished in 21st. He was running at finish, but 71 laps off the 492 laps that made up the race.

The average amount of money earned per start ($821) over Ned Jarrett's 352 career races. Jarrett's career winnings totaled $289,146 over 14 years of racing. His best season for earnings per start was in 1965 where Jarrett earned approximately $1,734 per start.

The speed record (82.2) in miles per hour at the Martinsville Speedway in Martinsville, Virginia. The .526 mile track is the shortest on the Sprint Cup and has only seen the winner's average speed top 80 miles per hour twice. On April 24, 1996, Rusty Wallace broke the elusive 80 mph mark by averaging 81.4 mph. The record didn't last long though . . . just five months and a day later, Jeff Gordon topped the mark by averaging 82.2 mph.

The number of laps raced (8.23) in thousands by Possum Jones in ten years racing on the NASCAR circuit. In 47 starts, Jones averaged 175 laps per start. He never won a NASCAR race, but did place in the top ten 13 times over the course of his career.

Heading into the 2007 season, the amount of dollars (82.4) in millions that Jeff Gordon has won en route to becoming NASCAR's all-time leading money winner. Gordon, in just 473 starts, has earned almost $23 million more than #2 on the list, Mark Martin (who needed 674 starts to reach just under $60 million in winnings). 824 is also the number of points that separated Busch Series champ Kevin Harvick from runner-up Carl Edwards during the 2006 season.

The number of spectators (8.25) in thousands to see the 1967 Beltsville 200 at the Beltsville Speedway in Maryland. On May 19, 1967, Jim Paschal recorded his first victory of the season by beating Richard Petty by five seconds. In what would be Paschal's most active season on the circuit, he would record career bests in victories (four) and earnings ($60,122) and he would finish the season ranked sixth in the final point standings. Paschal would only race in nine more events between 1967 and 1972.

The average speed recorded (82.6) in miles per hour by Dick Hutcherson at the 1965 Pennsylvania 200 Classic held at the Lincoln Speedway in Abbottstown, Pennsylvania. The race marked the last time a NASCAR event was held at the site and Hutcherson won and won big. Not only did he cut 0.39 seconds off the previous track record, he beat G.C. Spencer by a full eight laps.

The number of laps led (827) by Curtis Turner during the 1958 season. Turner only started in 17 of 51 races on the season, completing 3,068 total laps of which he would lead 27% of them. Despite racing in only one-third of the races on the season, Turner finished the season ranked 20th.

The amount of money earned (82.8) in thousands of dollars by Lake Speed during the 1986 season. That season marked Speed's fewest starts in a season in his 19 year career and the money earned, which to most people in 1986 would have been awesome, was the fifth lowest earnings in his career.

829 Herb Thomas' average speed (82.9) in miles per hour on June 19, 1954 at the Hickory Speedway in Hickory, North Carolina. Thomas set the NASCAR speed record on the track in the third of 35 races held in Hickory by beating Lee Petty in front of 4,000 spectators.

830 The number of points (830) that separated the 1961 season champion from the runner-up driver. Ned Jarrett only won one race on the season, but displayed consistency by placing in the top ten in 34 of 46 races. Jarrett scored 27,272 points on the season compared to Rex White, who finished the season ranked second with 26,442 points.

831 The average speed (83.1) in miles per hour at the first NASCAR race held at Watkins Glen International. On August 4, 1957, driver/owner Buck Baker took his '57 Chevy to victory lane. It was his seventh win on the season and helped catapult Baker into NASCAR fame as he became the first back-to-back champion.

832 The percentage of total laps raced (.832) that Herschel McGriff completed during his most successful season racing NASCAR. Between 1950 and 1993, McGriff started in a race in 27 different seasons, typically racing in about two events a season. In 1954 though, he started in 24 races and completed 3,891 laps of the 4,675 laps scheduled. He also recorded all four of his NASCAR victories in 17 top ten finishes and a sixth place finish come season's end.

833 The percentage (.833) of his first six seasons that Jimmie Johnson raced in which he finished in the top five in the final point standings. Johnson failed to finish in the top five only once. In his rookie season in 2001, Johnson placed 52nd in the championship series points, but since has placed fifth twice, second twice, and won his first championship in 2007, his sixth season on the senior circuit.

834 The amount of money earned (834) in thousands by Jack

834 The amount of money earned (834) in thousands by Jack Sprague

during his second Craftsman Truck Series championship season of 1999. Sprague who claimed his first CTS title two years earlier, actually earned over $45,000 less the second time around (due in part to one less race run in 1999), but still averaged $33,360 per start.

835 The number of miles driven (835) by Red Byron during the 1950 season. In the year after his championship season, Byron started in just four of 19 races on the season, but found a fair amount of success in his limited action. Red finished the first three races he started in second, fourth, and third place, earning $3,300 in those races and actually improving his average finish position from the year before.

836 The percentage of laps completed (.836) by THE Fabulous Hudson Hornet during the 1952 season. Herb Thomas started in 32 of 34 races the season after his first championship and completed 5,134 of 6,141 laps on the season. Thomas was fabulous on the season again, recording eight wins and 19 top five finishes, but lost the season championship to Tim Flock, who started one more race than Thomas, yet only beat him by 106 points (6,859 to 6,753).

837 The number of laps raced (8.37) in thousands by Tom Cox during the 1962 season. Cox started in 42 of 53 races on the season, completing 8,370 of a possible 10,672 laps. Cox recorded three top five finishes and 20 top ten finishes, earned $10,181, and finished the season ranked 18th. The following year Cox started in just two races, completed just eight laps, and never won the series again.

838 The race record (83.8) in miles per hour at the West Virginia International Speedway. The 0.4375-mile paved track located in Huntington, West Virginia hosted four Sprint Cup events from 1963 through 1971. The last race saw Richard Petty take the checkered flag, beating the previous record by over five seconds. In fact, Petty set the record in three consecutive starts, bettering Fred Lorenzen's original record set in 1963 by over 24 mph.

839 The percentage of laps completed (.839) by Dale Earnhardt Jr. in his first season racing on the Sprint Cup. Junior started in five races in 1999, completing 1,363 of 1,625 laps on the season, and earned his first top ten finish. That year was also the second consecutive Busch Series championship for Junior, who transitioned over to the Sprint Cup Series as his primary tour the following season.

The number of points earned (840) by Bill Blair over the course of the 1951 NASCAR season. Blair started in 18 of 41 races on the season, recorded seven top ten finishes, and finished the season ranked 16th, a full 3,368 points off Herb Thomas' total.

Entering the 2007 season, the number of races started (841) by Kyle Petty. Petty has spent most of his time on the Sprint Cup (785 starts over 28 seasons), but also raced a fair amount on the Busch Series (55 starts over nine seasons) and even gave the Craftsman Truck Series a try in 1994 (one start).

The amount of money won (84.2) in thousands of dollars by Dale Earnhardt Jr. at the 2006 Winn-Dixie 250. Junior started five races on the Busch season and, despite his limited action, was ranked fourth in wins on the season with two. Earnhardt picked up over $220,000 for his five starts, making it a rather lucrative part-time ride.

The percentage of laps completed (.843) by Terry Labonte during the 1985 Sprint Cup Series season. Labonte started all 28 races on the season, but could not quite duplicate the success he enjoyed in his championship season the year prior. Labonte's lap completion percentage dropped from 96.0% the year prior, as did his top ten finishes, top five finishes, and wins. That is not to say that Labonte's season was a failure though . . . he still finished the season ranked seventh and earned roughly $695,000.

The percentage of races started (.844) by Lee Petty during the 1952 season in which he would finish in the top ten. Petty started in 32 of 34 races on the season and recorded 27 top ten finishes. Of those 27 top ten finishes, 21 were top five finishes and of the top five finishes, three were victories.

The amount of money earned (845) by Jerry Wimbish on the NASCAR circuit. Between 1950 and 1954 Wimbish would start in nine races. He placed in the top ten in four of those events and earned $500 of his career earnings in two of those races, both fifth place finishes. His average earnings-per-race was just shy of $100.

Entering the 2007 Sprint Cup season, the percentage of races started (.846) that Jeff Gordon would be running at finish. In 473 career starts over 15 years, Gordon would be running at finish 400 times. Statistically, 1998 was his best season in this category. That season, Gordon was running at finish in 31 of 33 starts (.939).

The percentage of laps completed (.847) by Rex White in 14 starts at the Asheville-Weaverville Speedway in Weaverville, North Carolina. White completed 3,410 laps of a possible 4,025 over seven seasons and the track was nice to him when his car cooperated. Three of White's 14 races ended in mechanical failure or a crash, but the remaining 11 resulted in a top ten finish. Of those 11 finishes, ten were top five finishes; of those top five finishes, five were wins.

The number of races (848) that Terry Labonte competed in between 1978 and 2006. Labonte would earn 22 victories, start in 655 consecutive races, and bank over $40 million in winnings during his impressive career.

The percentage of laps completed (.849) by David Pearson at the Riverside International Raceway. Between 1963 and 1979, Pearson started in 20 races, completing 2,715 of 3,199 possible laps, and recording three of his 105 career wins.

The allowable horsepower (850) at 9000 rpm for vehicles competing in Sprint Cup Series races. That compares to 750 hp at 8400 rpm for vehicles in the Busch and Craftsman Series.

The number of laps led (851) by Neil Bonnet during his first season racing on the Busch Series. Bonnet, who had already spent nine seasons on the Sprint Cup, raced a full season on that circuit and an additional five races on the Busch Series in 1983. In five races started, he led 851 laps, averaging over 170 laps per race in the lead.

852 The margin of victory (.852) in seconds by Jamie McMurray over Dennis Setzer in the 2004 Kroger 200 held at Martinsville Speedway. McMurray started a total of 50 races on the season, 36 on the Sprint Cup Series, 14 on Busch, and three on the Craftsman Truck Series. The third race started by McMurray on the CTS saw him start his last race on the circuit, but record his first win. McMurray started mid-field (18 of 36) and won the race with an average speed of 60.819 mph.

853 The amount of money won (8.53) in thousands of dollars by Rick Newsom during the 1973 season. Newsom recorded career highs in starts (12), laps raced (3,209), and ranking (34), and his earnings were the sixth highest in Newsom's 14 year NASCAR career.

854 The amount of career earnings (8.54) in millions of dollars by Harry Gant in 22 years of racing NASCAR. Gant started in 474 races during his career, earning an average of just over $18,000 per start. His most lucrative season came in 1991, when he earned just under $1.2 million while finishing fourth in the final season standings. The season in which Gant earned the least was his third. In 1975 Gant started in one race, the World 600, and was forced to retire after 306 laps due to engine problems. His race (and season) earnings were a paltry $1,130.

855 The margin of victory (8.55) in seconds by Darrell Waltrip over Terry Labonte at the 1986 Busch 500 at Bristol International Speedway. Waltrip started the race in tenth place, three spots behind Labonte, and ended up taking the lead and holding it for 179 of 500 laps. Waltrip recorded one of his three season victories by denying Labonte his second on the season. Waltrip would finish the season in the runner-up position behind Dale Earnhardt while Labonte finished the season ranked 12th.

856 The number of laps raced (856) on the NASCAR circuit by Grand Prix legend Jim Clark. Clark, who won 25 of 72 Grand Prix starts in championship races, started in seven NASCAR races in 1952 and 1954. In 1952, he drove 125 of 200 scheduled laps at the Playland Park Speedway in South Bend, Indiana before mechanical problems ended the race for him. Two years later Clark entered six races and ran 721 laps. His

last race was his most successful; Clark recorded a sixth place finish at Charlotte and landed his biggest payday, $250.

The number of Sprint Cup points (8.57) recorded in thousands by Herb Thomas during the 1956 NASCAR season. Thomas started in 48 of 56 races held on the season, recording five wins and 36 top ten finishes en route to a second place finish on the season behind Buck Baker, who benefited from Thomas' misfortune. Thomas was critically injured in the fourth to last race of the season, allowing for Baker to win the championship.

The number of laps led (858) by Buck Baker during his second consecutive championship season. Baker started in 40 of 53 total races in 1957, completed 8,068 laps and led approximately 10.6% of all laps raced. He recorded ten wins on the season and 30 top five finishes to beat out Marvin Panch for the championship.

The percentage of races started (.859) by Dale Earnhardt on the Sprint Cup Series in which he would be running at finish. Earnhardt started in 676 races on the Sprint Cup, was running at finish in 581 of those races, and finished on the lead lap in 352 races.

The number of laps led (860) by LeeRoy Yarbrough in the seven races he won during the 1969 season. Yarbrough earned half of his career victories during the '69 season and dominated those races, leading a total of 860 laps of the 2,107 laps raced. During the remaining 23 races and 6,083 laps, he only managed to lead an additional 295 laps.

The percentage of laps completed (.861) by Tammy Jo Kirk over 19 starts on the Craftsman Truck Series in 1997. In her first year on the CTS, Kirk completed 3,102 of a possible 3,601 laps and finished the season ranked 20th in the final season point standings.

The average speed (86.2) in miles per hour by Buck Baker at the New York State Fairgrounds. The track only hosted three races between 1955 and 1957 with Baker winning the second event on May 30, 1956 and setting the race record for speed.

863 The approximate speed (86.3) in miles per hour that Fireball Roberts averaged at the Augusta International Raceway on November 17, 1963. In his 33rd and final victory on the NASCAR circuit, Roberts won the first and only race run on the three mile paved road course, beating out Dave MacDonald by over a full lap.

864 The purse (86.4) in thousands of dollars for the 1971 Southern 500. On September 6, Bobby Allison won the race by over one lap and claimed $22,450 of the total prize money.

865 The number of performance points (865) recorded by Benny Parsons over his 21 year Sprint Cup career. Under the 10-6-4-3-2-1 point system, Parsons earned 210 points for victories, 186 points on runner-up finishes, 204 points for third place finishes, 126 points for his fourth place finishes, 108 points on his fifth place finishes, and 31 points on his sixth place finishes.

866 The career earnings (8.66) in thousands of dollars by Buck Baker at the Occoneechee Speedway in Hillsboro, North Carolina, a track record. The track hosted 32 races between 1949 and 1968. Baker holds the track record for starts (22), wins (three), and money earned ($8,660).

867 The average finish position (8.67) by Dick Hutcherson over 103 races. Between 1964 and 1967, Hutcherson would record 73 top ten finishes in 103 starts and, in the only two seasons he raced more than half the season races, he would finish second and third in the final season standings. His average finish is second best in NASCAR history, behind Lee Petty.

868 The amount of money earned (86.8) in thousands of dollars by Dale Earnhardt for his second place finish at the 1995 UAW-GM Quality 500. The race held on October 8 at the Charlotte Motor Speedway saw Mark Martin hold off Earnhardt by 0.97 seconds. Martin earned about $20k more for the victory than Earnhardt did for a second place finish.

869 The percentage of laps completed (.869) by Harry Gant in 14 starts on the 1992 Busch season. Gant, on top of driving a full 29 race season on the Sprint Cup (which he would finish in fourth place), completed 2,265 of a possible 2,605 laps on the Busch Series. He would also win two races on the season and finish the season ranked 19th despite starting in less than half of the scheduled races.

870 The points (870) separating the 1996 Craftsman Truck Series champion from its Rookie of the Year come season's end. Ron Hornaday Jr. would finish the series' second year as champ with 3,831 points while rookie Bryan Reffner would take home the series first Raybestos Rookie of the Year Award with 2,961 points and a ninth place finish on the season.

871 The amount of money earned (8.71) in thousands of dollars by Jeff Gordon at the 1993 Hooters 500. Gordon would crash after completing 193 laps and finish the race in 31st place. His earnings were well below his season average of almost $21,000 per race, but the race marked the end of the Sprint Cup season and opened the door to the 1994 season, which would mark Gordon's breakout year.

872 The amount of money earned (872) in thousands of dollars by Travis Kvapil during his 2003 Craftsman Truck Series season. Kvapil, the 2001 Rookie of the Year, placed in the top ten in 22 of 25 races and, based on that consistency, won the championship despite only earning one victory on the season. The earnings recorded by Kvapil remain a career high on the truck circuit.

873 The amount of money won (8.73) in thousands of dollars by Gordon Johncock in six career starts at Daytona. Johncock's career lasted six seasons and he recorded 21 starts between 1966 and 1976. Daytona was pretty good to Johncock; he recorded one of his three career top five finishes at Daytona, two of his four top ten finishes, and one-third of his career winnings.

874 The amount of money earned (8.74) in thousands of dollars by Richard Petty in ten starts at the South Boston Speedway in South

Boston, Virginia. Petty won five of the races he started and earned $6,750 of his track winnings in his victories.

875 Entering the 2007 season, the number of career starts (875) by Ricky Rudd on the Sprint Cup Series. Of the 875 races entered, 192 races started were with Rudd as both driver and car owner. Rudd has been a relatively successful NASCAR driver, finding victory lane on 23 occasions, most recently in 2002.

876 The number of miles driven (87.6) by Fats Caruso in two career starts at the Oxford Plains Speedway in Maine. Caruso's NASCAR career consisted of these two starts and Fats was plagued by mechanical problems which held him to completing just 263 of a possible 600 laps on the .333 mile track.

877 The number of laps (877) raced by Danny Graves in two seasons racing NASCAR. Graves started in nine races during the 1957 and 1958 seasons, finishing four of those races in the top ten and earning his sole victory at the California State Fairgrounds in Sacramento.

878 The number of laps led (878) over 53 starts by Joe Weatherly during the 1963 season. Weatherly started 53 of 55 races on the season and completed 11,343 of 13,671 laps. He won his second consecutive championship with 35 top ten finishes, 20 top five finishes, and three victories.

879 The margin of victory (.879) in seconds at the 1999 Hotwheels.com 300 held at the Homestead-Miami Speedway. Joe Nemechek edged out Dale Earnhardt Jr. by under nine-tenths of a second to earn his only victory in 12 starts on the Busch Series. Junior on the other hand recorded another of his 18 top five finishes on the season en route to his second consecutive Busch title.

880 The number of fans (88.0) in thousands that saw Rusty Wallace edge out Mark Martin at the 1998 Budweiser at the Glen. Wallace earned one of his six victories on the season by holding Martin to one of his five second place finishes by a margin of 1.06 seconds. It was a season of bests for both drivers on the Sprint Cup though. Martin finished the season ranked third in the final season point standings while Wallace earned his first championship.

881 The average amount of money earned (881) per start, in dollars, by Junior Johnson during his 14 year career driving on the NASCAR circuit. Johnson, whose driving career lasted between 1953 and 1966, earned $275,910 over 313 starts.

882 The margin of victory (.882) in seconds by Matt Kenseth over Michael Waltrip at the 2003 1-800-Pitshop.com 300. Kenseth catapulted from a #19 start position to beat both Waltrip (who started #2) and third place finisher Kevin Harvick, who had started the race in the pole position. Kenseth only started in 14 races on the Busch Series in 2003 and won two consecutive starts. Kenseth won the Carquest Auto Parts 300 a month later, this time under caution, over Kyle Busch.

883 The number of career starts (883) on the Sprint Cup by Dave Marcis. While Marcis may not have had the numbers that many associate with success (only five victories, eight top ten final season rankings over 35 seasons), he was an independent owner/driver who managed a runner-up season in 1975 and recorded 222 top ten finishes while racing over 35 years in his famed wingtip shoes.

884 The amount of money earned (88.4) in thousands of dollars by Kenny Wallace during his 1989 Busch Series Rookie of the Year campaign. In his first full season racing Busch, Wallace recorded 16 top ten finishes and placed sixth in the final season point standings.

885 The percentage of races started (.885) by Richard Petty at Bowman-Gray Stadium in which he would finish in the top ten. Petty started in 26 of the 29 races held at the track, completing 5,089 of a possible 5,408 laps in races started and finished 23 races in the top ten. Twenty of those top ten finishes were top five finishes and four were victories. The track was kind to the King, who averaged a start position of 3.5 and a finish position of 5.2.

886 Rex White's average speed (88.6) in miles per hour at the 1960 Empire State 200 held at Montgomery Air Base in Montgomery,

New York. White won the race by a lap over Richard Petty in the only race run at that venue.

887 Entering the 2007 season, the number of career starts (887) recorded by Ken Schrader. Schrader first began racing NASCAR on the Sprint Cup during the 1984 season. Three years later, he began racing on the Busch Series as well and, in 1995, he began driving the trucks on the Craftsman Truck Series. Still going strong at the age of 52, Schrader has recorded 704 career starts on the Sprint Cup, 115 starts on the Busch Series, and an additional 68 starts on the Craftsman Truck Series.

888 The car number (888) driven by Chuck Hansen on four occasions in both the 1957 and 1958 seasons. Hansen raced between 1954 and 1958 and recorded 26 career starts. He never won a race nor placed in the top five, but there was something interesting about Hansen: In each of his 26 starts, the number eight was to be found on his car. Hansen raced the #888 car eight times, the #88 car three times, the #148 car three times, the #48 car three times, the #348 car three times, the #80 car twice, the #48 car once, the #8 car once, the #83 car once, and the #89 car once. (Hansen seemed to like the #8).

889 The percentage of races started (.889) during the 2005 Busch Series in which Ryan Newman would finish in the top ten. Driving mainly on the Sprint Cup (36 starts), Newman only started in nine races on the Busch Series, but he was incredible. He placed in the top ten in eight of the nine races (only failing to do so at the O'Reilly challenge) and had a string of five consecutive victories finishing the season with six wins and ranked 34th, despite only entering a quarter of the races run on the season.

890 The average number of laps led (8.90) per race recorded by Buck Baker over 26 years racing on the Sprint Cup Series. Baker led a total of 5,662 laps over his 636 career starts. During his back-to-back championship seasons of 1956-57, Baker led 2,259 laps, averaging 25.67 laps in the lead during each of the 48 races started.

891 Entering the 2007 season, the percentage of races started (.891) on the Sprint Cup that Jimmie Johnson was running at finish.

Johnson, in his first six seasons on the series, started in 183 races and was running at finish in 163 of them. He wasn't just running at finish, he was winning. Johnson recorded 23 victories in the 183 starts and finished in the top ten 110 times.

892 The track speed record in a NASCAR event (89.2) in miles per hour at the Birmingham International Raceway. Between 1958 and 1968, the track hosted eight races. The final race at the track was held on June 8, 1968 and Richard Petty collected his second victory and set the track record at 89.2 mph.

893 The number of laps Dave Marcis led (893) during the 1976 season. In the season following his best season finish (second in the final standings), Marcis set career high marks in laps led, victories (three), average start position (4.4), and poles won (seven).

894 The percentage of laps completed (.894) by Bob Welborn during the 1964 season. Welborn started in just three races in what would be his final NASCAR season and completed 506 of a possible 560 laps in those races. He went out strong, compiling two fifth place finishes and one 11th place finish.

895 The track record (89.5) in miles per hour at the Thompson International Speedway in Thompson, Connecticut. The track hosted three events in a 20 year span, one in 1951, one in 1969, and one in 1971. David Pearson set the track record on July 10, 1969 when he took the race in the Thompson 200 averaging just shy of 90 mph.

896 The length of the 1957 Indian River Gold Cup 100 (89.6) in miles held at the Titusville-Cocoa Speedway in Titusville, Florida. On December 30, 1956, Fireball Roberts took the checkered flag at the only race held at the track. Curtis Turner, Marvin Panch, and Ralph Moody were the only other drivers on the lead lap of the 1.60 mile road course when Roberts crossed the finish line.

897 The amount of money earned (89.7) in thousands of dollars by Jimmie Johnson at the 2004 Siemens 300 held at the New Hampshire International Speedway in Loudon. Johnson's payday was not too shabby, but the race must have been a disappointment to Johnson. He started from the #2 position but finished in 11th place while Kurt Busch, starting from the #32 spot, won the race. While this race occurred mid-way through the season, it was one of many with potential end of season implications; Busch beat Johnson by a mere eight points for the season championship.

898 The average finish position (8.98) of Rex White over nine seasons racing NASCAR. In just 233 career starts, White recorded 163 top ten finishes of which 110 were top fives and 28 were victories. His average finish position ranks him third on NASCAR's all time list for best average finish position.

899 The Memphis-Arkansas Speedway record (89.9) in miles per hour, held by Fonty Flock. The record was set by Fonty Flock on August 14, 1955 in the second of five races hosted by the speedway. Flock held off Speedy Thompson to win his second race of the season and win $2,950.

900 The length of the track (.900) in miles at the Bremerton Raceway in Bremerton, Washington. The track hosted one Sprint Cup Series race on August 4, 1957. Parnelli Jones recorded his first career NASCAR victory at the track, and in the process denied Lloyd Dane his second victory of the season.

THE FLOCK BROTHERS

TIM

300 91

FONTY

14

BOB

23

Chapter Ten

The Flocks

hen NASCAR started its first season back in 1949, three brothers were there and ready to make their mark on the world of stock car racing. Bob Flock would be the first to make his mark on NASCAR. It made sense; he was the eldest of the three brothers. Born in 1918, he was 31 when he made his NASCAR debut. In his third start, he earned his first victory. Brothers Fonty and Tim actually both recorded top five finishes in the first ever NASCAR race (finishing second and fifth, respectively), while Bob started from pole but finished 32nd.

The youngest of the Flock brothers, Tim, would be the next to record a win. He got his first one in the second race of the 1950 season by beating big brother Bob by half a lap. Fonty would also earn his first victory in 1950 on his fourth start of the season. Fonty beat Bill Blair by a good half-mile at the Langhorne Speedway on September 17. The three brothers would end up racing together from 1949 until 1956 when Bob bowed out. The following season Fonty retired, and for the last four years

Brothers Flock

Bob

YEAR	STARTS	WINS	TOP 5	TOP 10	RANK
1949	6	2	3	3	3
1950	4	0	1	3	20
1951	17	1	4	9	14
1952	2	1	1	1	73
1954	2	0	0	0	-
1955	1	0	1	1	62
1956	4	0	1	1	77
TOTAL	**36**	**4**	**11**	**18**	-

Fonty

YEAR	STARTS	WINS	TOP 5	TOP 10	RANK
1949	6	0	3	3	5
1950	7	1	2	3	14
1951	34	8	20	22	2
1952	29	2	14	17	4
1953	32	4	17	17	5
1954	5	0	2	2	-
1955	31	3	12	14	11
1956	7	1	1	4	50
1957	2	0	1	1	63
TOTAL	**153**	**19**	**72**	**83**	-

Brothers Flock, Continued					
Tim					
YEAR	STARTS	WINS	TOP 5	TOP 10	RANK
1949	5	0	2	3	8
1950	12	1	4	7	16
1951	30	7	19	21	3
1952	33	8	22	25	1
1953	26	1	11	18	6
1954	5	0	1	3	35
1955	39	18	32	33	1
1956	22	4	11	14	9
1957	1	0	0	0	93
1958	3	0	0	0	-
1959	2	0	0	1	31
1960	2	0	0	1	63
1961	7	0	0	3	-
TOTAL	187	39	102	129	-

of his career, Tim had no sibling to drive against, which was unfortunate for Tim because he excelled against his big brothers.

The career stats show Tim as the most successful of the three Flocks in NASCAR, followed by Fonty, with Bob pulling up the rear. The same held true in the more important sibling rivalry. Head-to-head, Tim was the most successful of the three. Against Fonty, Tim finished in front of him in 77 of 129 races. Against Bob, Tim finished ahead of his eldest brother in 22 of 32 events. When it came down to head-to-head competition between Fonty and Bob, Fonty finished in front of Bob in 20 of 32 races. Combined though, the Flocks had a huge impact on the young days of NASCAR; they recorded 62 wins, 185 top five finishes, 230 top ten finishes, and a championship.

901 The average finish position (9.01) of Herb Thomas over his ten-year NASCAR career. In 228 career starts, Thomas recorded 156 top ten finishes of which 122 were top five finishes and 48 were victories. His average finish position ranks Thomas fourth on NASCAR's all-time list. Thomas' most successful season came during his second championship. In 1953, Thomas started in 37 races, averaging a 5.2 finish position. He would have an average finish position of better than tenth an additional four times.

902 The percentage of laps completed (.902) by Johnny Yountz at the 1951 Southern 500, his only NASCAR start. On September 3 at Darlington Raceway, Yountz started mid-field, 41st in the 82 car field, and finished the race seven spots higher. Yountz completed 361 laps of the 400 lap race before being taken out in a wreck. His purse for the day was $50.

903 The amount of money earned (90.3) in thousands of dollars by Joe Nemechek at the 2000 Daytona 500. In an example of just how big an event this is, Nemechek's purse was for a 42nd place finish in a field of 43. He completed 131 laps of the race before he retired due to an oil pressure problem. By way of comparison, Nemechek started in five races during his rookie season in 1993, finished each race higher, yet only earned $56,000 over those starts.

904 The percentage of laps completed (.904) by Davey Allison during the 1991 Sprint Cup Series. Allison started in all 29 races and completed 8,770 of a possible 9,699 laps on the season. He also recorded 16 top ten finishes and five victories while finishing the season in what would be the first of two consecutive third place finishes in the final point standings.

905 The percentage of IROC races started (.905) by two-time Sprint champ Tony Stewart in which he would finish in the top ten. Over six seasons racing in the International Race of Champions, Stewart has started in 21 events, placing in the top ten in 19 of those races and recording four victories. He has also earned over $1.3 million for his efforts, averaging out to over $62,000 per race . . . not a bad supplement to your $7 million a year NASCAR job.

906 The margin of victory (.906) in seconds by Ted Musgrave over Jack Sprague at the 2001 Orleans 350 held at the Las Vegas Motor Speedway. Sprague started in the pole and led 104 of the 146 lap race, but it was Musgrave who came from a tenth place start to secure the win. In the end though, it didn't matter too much. Sprague beat Musgrave by 73 points to win the season championship.

907 The average speed (90.7) in miles per hour by Ned Jarrett on March 17, 1965 at the Occoneechee Speedway. Jarrett recorded his third victory on the season of what would be a 13-win season. In what would be his next-to-last season, Jarrett won his second and final NASCAR championship.

908 The number of miles driven (90.8) at the Charlotte Speedway by Ned Jarrett in his only race at the track. On November 20, 1955, Jarrett started and finished in the #13 spot, earning $60 after completing 121 of the 134 laps on the .750 mile dirt track.

909 The percentage of races started (.909) by Lee Petty at the Wilson Speedway in Wilson, North Carolina that he would finish in the top ten. The track hosted 12 races with Petty starting in all but the first one held in 1951. Petty recorded a top ten finish in each of his 11 starts except for the eighth race of the 1956 season. On March 18, 1956, Petty had to pull out due to a bearing problem and finished the race in 13th place.

910 The amount of money won ($910) by Herb Thomas in his first and last race at the Merced Fairgrounds Speedway in Merced, California. In fact, the speedway only held one NASCAR event and that was race number 24 on the 1956 Grand National schedule. Thomas, driving car #300B, took the checkered flag beating out Harold Hardesty while averaging 47.325 mph on the .20 mile dirt track.

Entering the 2007 season, the number of career starts (911) by Mark Martin. Martin began his NASCAR career in 1981 on the Sprint Cup Series and became a regular on the circuit during his sixth season. Martin has started 674 Sprint Cup races and has picked up 35 victories, good enough for 17th all-time on the series. Martin has been even more successful on the Busch Series, where he has recorded 220 starts since making his first appearance in 1982 and has recorded 47 victories. Finally, Martin has started in 17 races on the Craftsman Series and has recorded an additional seven victories racing trucks. Martin's combined career line is rather impressive: 911 starts with 89 of those being victories.

The amount of money earned (9.12) in thousands of dollars by David Sisco at the 1975 Southern 500. Sisco recorded a career best third-place finish at Darlington on September 1 and earned a career-high purse in the race. Sisco ended up racing for seven years and started in 133 races, earning $251,359 and placing in the top ten on 31 occasions.

The total number of laps led (913) by drivers of the #90 car since the inception of Sprint Cup Series. In the first 916 races, only Jody Ridley was able to take #90 down victory lane, but he only accounted for 20 of the laps led. Dick Brooks accounted for most of the laps led by the #90 car, accounting for 401 laps led. Charlie Glotzbach also led a number of laps in the #90 car, 105 to be exact.

The performance points earned (914) by Buddy Baker over his 33 year NASCAR career. Under the 10-6-4-3-2-1 rating system, Baker earned 190 points on victories, 252 points on runner-up finishes, 236 points on third place finishes, 126 points on fourth place finishes, 80 points of fifth place finishes, and 30 points on sixth place finishes.

The amount of money earned (915) in thousands of dollars by Ron Hornaday Jr. during the 1998 Craftsman Truck Series season. Hornaday would capture his second championship title in four years with six wins and 22 top ten finishes in 27 starts. His average purse per race was just under $34,000.

916 The amount of money earned (9.16) in millions of dollars by Tony Stewart during the 2002 Sprint Cup Series season. In his fourth full season, Stewart recorded 21 top ten finishes, including three wins, and earned his first championship. The money earned was a career high for Stewart (although he would surpass it three years later during his second championship season), and equated to about $255,000 per start.

917 The amount of money earned (9.17) in thousands of dollars by Buddy Baker in his final race at the North Carolina Motor Speedway. On March 6, 1988 at the Goodwrench 500, Baker placed 11th, finishing two laps off race winner Neil Bonnett and earning his final payday at the track, which was his fifth largest earned over 44 starts.

918 The average finish position (9.18) by Ned Jarrett in his 13 year NASCAR career. In 352 career starts, Jarrett recorded 239 top ten finishes. Of those top tens, 185 were top five finishes and 50 were victories. Jarrett's average finish position ranks him fifth on NASCAR's all-time list.

919 The percentage of laps completed (.919) by Harry Gant during his first NASCAR race. Gant's first race was the 1973 National 500 held at the Charlotte Motor Speedway in Concord, North Carolina on October 7, 1973. Gant started 17th in the 41 car field and completed 307 of the 334 laps. Gant was running at finish and won $2,620 for an 11th place finish.

920 The number of fans (9.20) in thousands who watched Bobby Isaac take the checkered flag at Hickory Speedway in Hickory, North Carolina on June 20, 1970. The crowd saw Isaac lead the Hickory 276 from start to finish and win the race with Dick Brooks being the closest competitor over two laps back.

921 The number of starts (921) recorded by Darrell Waltrip over his Sprint Cup, Busch Series, and Craftsman Truck Series career. Waltrip spent most of his career on the Sprint Cup Series, recording 809 career starts between 1972 and 2000. From 1982 through 1995, Waltrip started 94 races on the Busch Series. He would come back to the Busch Series 11 years after his last race in 1995 to record one more start at the age of 59.

Waltrip also started a total of 17 races on the Craftsman Truck Series, averaging between one and five starts over six different seasons.

The number of laps completed (922) by Curtis Turner at the Daytona International Speedway. Turner started 11 races at the track, completing 67.9% of the 1,358 laps possible in those events. Turner was also only able to break the top ten on two of the 11 races, making it one of the less friendly tracks to Turner over the years.

The amount of money earned (9.23) in thousands of dollars by Bobby Allison at the 1972 Yankee 400 held at the Michigan International Speedway in Brooklyn, Michigan. The race was really a three-man race between David Pearson, Bobby Isaac, and Allison. Even though Richard Petty started at pole, he only led six laps with Isaac leading 34, Allison leading 26, and eventual winner Pearson leading 124 laps. Allison finished the race in second place and earned just over $9,000.

The number of laps raced (924) during Swede Savage's final NASCAR season. Savage started in nine races between 1967 and 1969, with his final four starts occurring in 1969. Savage recorded a fifth place finish at Daytona Qualifier #2 and a seventh place finish at Martinsville, which were the only two races he finished. On the season, Savage completed 924 of 1,084 laps.

The amount of money earned (925) in dollars by Mario Andretti during his last race on the NASCAR circuit. Andretti entered one race in 1969, the Motor Trend 500, and completed 132 of 186 laps before engine problems ended the race for him. He finished the race in 18th place and earned $925 for his efforts. In 14 starts over four seasons, Andretti recorded one victory and earned a total of $58,075.

The percentage of IROC races entered (.926) by Cale Yarborough in which he would finish in the top ten. Yarborough, on top of being one of NASCAR's greatest drivers, was just as impressive driving on the International Race of Champions circuit. In eight seasons, Yarborough entered 27 races on IROC, finishing in the top ten 25 times, including 17 top five finishes, and five victories while completing each race entered.

927 The number of miles driven (92.7) by Banjo Matthews during the 1958 season. Matthews was never a full-time driver, recording only 51 career starts over a ten year period, but 1958 was an especially disappointing season for him. He made three starts on the season but was unable to complete as much as half a race. Rear-end and axle problems along with a crash left Matthews unable to complete even one-quarter of the possible laps in the three events started.

928 The margin of victory (9.28) in seconds by Darrell Waltrip over Dale Earnhardt at the 1992 Bud 500. On August 19 at the Bristol International Speedway, Waltrip, who started the race in the ninth position, led a total of 247 laps and held off Dale Earnhardt, who charged from a 23rd place start to finish in second. Waltrip earned his second of three victories on the season en route to a ninth place finish on the season. Earnhardt, on the other hand, had an off-season that year, placing 12th in the final point standings and breaking what could have been a string of five consecutive championships (he won the championship in 1990, 1991, 1993, and 1994).

929 The amount of money earned (92.9) in thousands of dollars by Robby Gordon at the 2007 Toyota/Save-Mart 350 at the Infineon Raceway in Sonoma, California. Gordon would fall 14 spots over the course of the race to finish in 16th place in what was surely a disappointing race for Gordon as he started the road course in second, especially after leading a total of 48 of the 110 lap race.

930 The number of miles driven (93.0) by Tex Brooks in his two career NASCAR starts. Brooks made his NASCAR debut on June 13, 1954 at the Linden Airport in Linden, New Jersey and finished in 20th place after completing 86 miles, 14 miles back of winner Al Keller. Six weeks later Brooks would only finish seven miles or 14 laps at the Morristown Speedway due to a hub problem. Brooks would end his NASCAR career with just $35 in winnings, but able to claim that he was a NASCAR professional.

The amount of money earned (9.31) in millions of dollars by Jeff Gordon during the 1998 Sprint Cup season. Gordon, who won the championship with a dominating 13 wins on the season, had a career high in earnings and it still remains his second highest season earnings in his 15 year career.

The amount of money earned (932) in thousands of dollars by the 2006 Busch Series Rookie of the Year. Danny O'Quinn Jr. won the Raybestos award with five top ten finishes in 33 starts and a final season ranking of 19. O'Quinn could not repeat his success during the 2007 season though; he only started ten races during the season and was unable to record a single top ten finish. His earnings on the season were just under $185,000.

The amount of money earned (9.33) in thousands of dollars by David Pearson at the 1961 Dixie 400. On September 17, Pearson would take the checkered flag after starting in the #5 position and beating Junior Johnson by five seconds. His purse was $9,330, his second most lucrative payday on the season behind a victory nine races earlier at Charlotte.

The percentage of laps completed (.934) by drivers of Petty Enterprises at the Nashville Speedway in Tennessee. Between 1958 and 1984, Jimmy Thompson, Lee Petty, Richard Petty, Jim Paschal, and Kyle Petty recorded 54 starts at the track, completing 19,672 of 21,063 possible laps. Together they led 4,286 laps at the track and recorded 31 top five finishes, which included 11 victories.

The amount of money earned (935) in thousands of dollars by Mike Bliss during his second most lucrative year on the Busch Series. During the 2003 season Bliss, in his first full season, recorded 14 top ten finishes in 34 starts to secure a tenth place finish on the season, earning just shy of the $1 million mark. The following year, Bliss bettered his numbers, to include winning three poles and earning his sole Busch Series victory, while finishing the season ranked fifth and earning $1.3 million.

The number of laps completed (936) by Joe Kelly during the 1984 Busch Series. The season marked two of Kelley's six top ten finishes and his sole top five finish, which occurred at Darlington. Kelly's lap total on the season was also approximately one-quarter of his total laps completed during 30 starts on the Sprint Cup and Busch Series over a 25-year span dating back to 1961.

The number of laps completed (937) by Bobby Hamilton over six career starts at the Texas Motor Speedway. Hamilton completed 99.7% of all laps possible in his six starts, and recorded five top ten finishes at the Ft. Worth track. In his six starts, Hamilton won $102,950, making it the fifth most lucrative venue in his Craftsman Truck Series career.

The amount of money earned (93.8) in thousands of dollars by Greg Biffle for a 14th place finish at the 2005 Dodge/Save Mart 350 held at the Infineon Raceway in Sonoma, California. Biffle started in the #41 spot, but worked his way up to finish 14th. His money earned was the ninth lowest purse in 36 starts and accounted for just over 1% of his annual winnings.

The margin of victory (9.39) in seconds by Chad Little over Mark Martin at the 1995 Goodwrench 200 at the North Carolina Motor Speedway in Rockingham. Little and Martin both started in the top five (second and fifth, respectively), but Martin couldn't take hold of a lead. Little led 177 of the 197 laps and earned his second consecutive victory to start the season.

The margin of victory (.940) in seconds by Mark Martin over Dave Blaney at the 1999 Dura Lube 200 at Darlington Raceway in Darlington, South Carolina. Martin started from the #2 position, led the race for 104 of 147 laps, and held off Dave Blaney who had started in the #12 position, by under a second. The victory was worth $41,550 and marked one of Martin's six victories on the Busch Series.

The number of laps completed (9.41) in thousands by Benny Parsons during the 1977 NASCAR season. Parsons, in the midst of nine consecutive top five finishes in the final season point standings, completed a career-high in laps as of the end of his tenth season (he would break his personal best record the following year, but never top it again). Parsons led 1,398 of the laps raced, just shy of 15% of all laps he completed.

942 The amount of money earned (9.42) in millions of dollars by Matt Kenseth during the 2003 Sprint Cup season. Kenseth started in all 36 events (and 14 of 34 on the Busch Series just for good measure) and recorded a single victory and 25 top ten finishes. Kenseth became one of only four drivers to take the championship with a single victory on the year and earned over $9.4 million for his efforts.

943 The number of laps completed (943) by Gober Sosebee during the 1953 NASCAR season. Sosebee would start in 17 races of the 37 scheduled and record nine top ten finishes. His number of starts and laps completed would be career best up to that point (although surpassed the following season), and Sosebee would finish the season ranked a career high 14th.

944 The percentage of total laps completed (.944) by Darrell Waltrip during his third and final Sprint Cup championship season. In 1985 Waltrip completed 8,933 of 9,458 total possible laps over 28 starts. In what would be a rather strange season compared to his other two championships, Waltrip would take the Cup with just three wins (compared to 12 wins in both the 1981 and 1982 seasons), and he led just 10.8% of all laps raced compared to 26.3% and 32.0% in 1981 and 1982, respectively.

945 The total earnings (945) in dollars by Dick Passwater in his first season racing NASCAR. Passwater started in six races during the 1952 season, recording three top ten finishes, and finished the season averaging $158 per start. The following season, which would be his last, Passwater recorded 16 starts, earned his sole career victory, and earned $4,555 dollars to finish his career with $5,550 in earnings.

946 The career earnings (94.6) in thousands of dollars by Richard Petty in eight starts at the Texas World Speedway in College Station, Texas. Petty started in every race run at the venue, recording

three victories, and finishing, on average, in just better than fifth place over his eight starts.

The percentage of laps completed (.947) by Carl Edwards during his first season driving on the Sprint Cup Series. In 2004, Edwards started in 13 races and completed 4,056 laps of a possible 4,238 laps in the races he started. The following season he would race in all 36 events on the Sprint Cup Series and 34 of 35 races on the Busch Series. The total number of laps completed was 16,658 and Edwards finished both series ranked third in the final season point standings.

The number of laps led (948) by Bobby Allison during the 1980 season. Allison completed 8,244 total laps, leading 11.5% of them, en route to a sixth place finish on the season and a fifth consecutive top ten placing in the final point standings.

The margin of victory (.949) in seconds by Johnny Benson Jr. over Ron Hornaday Jr. at the 2007 Toyota Tundra Milwaukee 200. On June 22 at the Milwaukee Mile in West Allis, Wisconsin, Benson, who started from the fourth position, held off Hornaday who started at #14, to earn his first victory of the 2007 season.

The percentage of races entered (.950) by Buck Baker in 1957 in which he finished in the top ten. Baker, in his second consecutive championship season, placed in the top ten in 38 of 40 races entered. 950 is also the amount of money won in dollars by Baker the year prior in the only NASCAR race held at Chisholm Speedway in Montgomery, Alabama; a race that he also won.

The number of laps completed (951) by Fonty Flock during the 1950 season. Flock would finish the season ranked 14th, starting in only seven of the 19 races, but he proved to be pretty successful in the few starts he made. Flock recorded one win, three top ten finishes, and led a total of 369 of the 951 laps he ran.

Entering the 2007 season, the number of career starts (952) recorded by Michael Waltrip. Waltrip began his NASCAR career on the

Sprint Cup in 1985 and, over 22 seasons, started 675 races. In 1988, Waltrip started racing the Busch Series as well and started in an additional 269 races over 19 seasons. Waltrip made the move over to the Craftsman Truck Series in 1996 and started an additional eight races over five seasons.

The number of laps completed (9.53) in thousands by Dale Earnhardt during the 1996 Sprint Cup season. Earnhardt started all 31 races on the season and was running at finish in 29 of those races. His laps completed total that season marked the fourth of seven consecutive seasons in which Earnhardt completed around 9,500 laps on the year.

The number of laps led (954) by Darrel Waltrip on the Busch Series. Waltrip, who was a Sprint Cup regular, started 95 races on the Busch Series and won 13 of them, making him more successful on the Busch Series (.137 winning percentage) than on the Sprint Series (.104 winning percentage).

The percentage of laps raced (.955) at the Las Vegas Park Speedway on October 16, 1955 that were led by Norm Nelson. In the only NASCAR race held at this venue in Nevada, Nelson started at pole, led 106 of the 111 laps raced, and finished in style, winning his first and only NASCAR race. Nelson only had five career starts over 14 years, but recorded his victory from the pole, making him one of only 80 drivers to accomplish that feat in the storied history of the Sprint Cup.

The amount of career earnings (956) in thousands of dollars by Geoffrey Bodine over 94 starts on the Busch Series. Predominately a Sprint Cup driver, Bodine started 94 races over 13 different seasons spanning a 24 year period. He averaged just over seven starts per season he raced and, on two occasions, actually started more races on the Busch Series than the Sprint Cup. In 2001 he started 17 Busch races versus two Sprint races and in 2005 he only raced on Busch, starting in eight races.

The percentage of laps completed (.957) by Jeff Gordon in his first 30 starts on the Sprint Cup Series at Daytona. Between the first race of the 1993 season and the 18th race of the 2007 season, Gordon completed 5,049 of 5,274 laps. He led approximately 10% of all laps completed, finished in the top ten in 56.7% of his starts, and recorded six wins at the track. He has also earned over seven million dollars at Daytona, averaging $235,631 per start.

The percentage of races entered (.958) by Ron Hornaday Jr. during the 1996 Craftsman Truck Series in which he would finish in the top ten. After placing third during the inaugural season in 1995, Holladay took advantage of 23 top ten finishes in 24 starts. He needed every one of them as he edged out Jack Sprague by 53 points to take the championship.

The amount of money earned (959) in thousands of dollars by Ron Hornaday Jr. during his rookie season on the Busch Series in 2000. Hornaday started in 32 races on the season, recorded two victories and 13 top ten finishes, and finished the season ranked fifth. Despite his success, he was not able to take home the Rookie of the Year Award. That went to Ken Harvick, who finished the season with three wins, 16 top ten finishes and a third-place ranking in the final season point standings.

The amount of money earned (960) in dollars by Buck Baker at the Langhorne Speedway in Langhorne, Pennsylvania on September 15, 1957. Baker started the 45th race of the season in the #12 spot and worked his way up to fifth by race's end. He finished the race five laps off the leader, Gwyn Staley, and earned $960 as the owner/driver.

The margin of victory (.961) in seconds by Ron Hornaday Jr. over Jack Sprague in the 2006 City of Mansfield 250. The two-time Craftsman Truck Series champ edged the three-time Craftsman Truck Series champ after coming from a 17th place start to take the lead and hold it for over half of the race.

The percentage of laps completed (.962) by Skip Hudson in his only NASCAR top ten finish. Hudson started one race in each season between 1963 and 1966, but only placed in the top ten in one of those four races. At the 1964 Motor Trend 500 at the Riverside International Raceway in California, Hudson completed 178 of the 185 lap race and was running as Dan Gurney took the checkered flag. Hudson finished the race one spot better than his ninth place start.

963 The total number of laps completed (963) by John Ruttman during the 1987 Sprint Cup Series. Ruttman only started in four of 29 races on the season and completed just 963 laps, numbers that were lower than any put up in his previous seven seasons. Ruttman started off poorly at Talladega when a transmission problem ended his race just 27 laps into the 178 lap race. The following three races, Ruttman finished all but three laps (936 of 939 laps completed), and recorded a seventh, tenth, and 11th place finish. Despite the troubles at Talladega, Ruttman completed 86.2% of all possible laps in races he started.

964 The percentage of laps completed (.964) by Kenny Irwin Jr. during his only full Craftsman Truck Series season. Irwin started in all 26 races during the 1997 season, completing 4,668 of 4,840 laps. He also recorded ten top ten finishes, to include two wins, and finished the season ranked tenth in the final point standings.

965 The number of laps completed (965) by James Hylton during the 1975 season. Hylton started in all 30 races of the season and was running at finish in all but three of the races he started. Hylton didn't win a race on the season and only recorded two top five finishes, but he did finish in the top ten 16 times and finished the season in third place (and in the top five for the eighth time in ten years).

966 The number of miles completed (96.6) by Dick Hutcherson in his sole race at Watkins Glen International in New York. Hutcherson started the 151.8 mile race in the pole position, but was only able to complete 42 laps of the 66 lap, 2.30 mile road course.

967 Entering the 2007 season, the number of career starts (967) recorded by Dale Jarrett on the Sprint Cup and Busch Series. Jarrett began his career on the Busch Series in 1982 and moved over to the Sprint Cup Series as his primary ride in 1987. In 22 seasons on the Sprint Cup, Jarrett has recorded 639 starts and 32 victories. On the Busch Series he has an additional 328 starts and 11 victories, giving him a total of 967 career starts and 43 victories between the two.

968 The percentage of races started (.968) by both Richard Petty and Bobby Allison during the 1972 season in which they would lead a race. In his first 30 starts, Allison would hold a lead in each race, but failed to do so at the Texas 500, the last race of the year (he still finished fourth in the race). The only race Petty failed to hold a lead in was the World 600, where engine problems shut him down 328 laps into the 400 lap race.

969 The number of laps led (969) by Darrell Waltrip during the 1985 Sprint Cup Series. Waltrip held leads in 21 of 28 starts on the season, but led only half as many laps as Bill Elliot (1,920) did on the season. Despite that fact, and the fact that Elliot recorded 11 wins to Waltrip's three, it was Waltrip who beat Elliot for the season title, winning on the strength of consistency by 101 points.

970 The number of miles driven (97.0) for Robert Dixon as a NASCAR owner. At the 1949 Wilkes 200 at the North Wilkesboro Speedway in North Carolina, Raymond Lewis made his only NASCAR career start taking Dixon's 1949 Caddy to an eighth place finish and earning the pair $75.

971 The percentage of laps completed (.971) by Richard Petty during the 1972 NASCAR season. Petty would complete 10,282 laps of a possible 10,592 laps in the 31 starts on the season, be running at finish in 27 races, and earn his fourth championship despite a win total (eight) that was the lowest for Petty in six years.

972 The average number of laps led (972) by Greg Biffle during his championship seasons on the Busch Series and Craftsman Truck Series. In 2000, Biffle would lead 833 of 4,038 laps raced on the Craftsman Truck Series en route to his first championship in NASCAR. Two years later, Biffle would lead 1,061 of 6,077 laps raced on the Busch Series to capture that series championship.

973 The total number of laps led (973) by Terry Labonte during his second championship season on the Sprint Cup Series. In 1996, Labonte led 973 of 9,443 laps raced and recorded 21 top five finishes (including two wins) to win the championship. Labonte needed it all, edging out Jeff Gordon by a mere 37 points to capture the championship despite Gordon's ten victories on the season and 21 top five finishes.

974 The percentage of laps completed (.974) by Ernie Young at the Santa Clara Fairgrounds in San Jose, California on September 15, 1957. In what would be Young's sole top five finish in 14 starts over five years, he would complete 113 of 116 laps before crashing his 1957 Pontiac.

975 The number of laps led (975) by Buddy Baker during his most successful season racing. Baker, one of NASCAR's 50 greatest drivers, raced between 1959 and 1992 but could never win the championship. In 699 races over 33 years, Baker's best finish was fifth during the 1977 season. Baker didn't win a race that year, but had 20 top ten finishes in 30 races, and led 975 laps out of 8,369 laps raced.

976 The number of miles driven (97.6) by Tammy Jo Kirk in her sole start at the Louisville Motor Speedway. On July 12, 1997, Kirk started and finished in 14th place at the Link-Belt Construction Equipment 225, completing 223 laps of the 225 lap race, which equated to 97.6 miles completed of the 98.4 mile race.

977 The percentage of laps completed (.977) by Mark Martin in both his 1997 and 1999 Sprint Cup Series. In 1997 Martin completed 9,567 of a possible 9,822 laps over 32 starts. Two years later, Martin would complete 9,903 of a possible 10,132 laps over 34 starts. His lap completion was not the only similarity for Martin that season . . . he would finish each season ranked third in the final season point standings.

978 The total number of laps led (978) by Jeff Burton during the 1998 Sprint Cup Series. Burton started in all 33 races on the season, completing 9,488 laps and leading 10.3% of those laps. Burton recorded two wins on the season and in those races he led a total of 394 laps. The race he led the most laps on the season wasn't one he won though. Burton led 273 of 367 laps at the Pepsi Southern on September 6, but lost the lead and race to Jeff Gordon.

979 The percentage of laps completed (.979) by Bobby Allison in races started at the Beltsville Speedway in Beltsville, Maryland. Allison had six career starts at the track and finished in the top three in five of those starts. His only problem at the track was the 1966 Beltsville 200 where a differential problem ended his race after 174 laps. The next five races, which included one victory, two second place finishes, and two third place finishes, saw Allison only fail to finish six of 1,300 laps.

980 The amount of money earned (980) by Billy Myers at the 1957 Virginia 500 held at Martinsville Speedway in Martinsville, Virginia. Myers and Tom Pistone were involved in a crash on lap 441, resulting in the race being called 59 laps short of the scheduled 500 lap event. Myers would officially finish in fourth, and earn just shy of $1,000.

981 The number of laps led (981) by Fred Lorenzen during the 1965 NASCAR season. Lorenzen started in 17 races on the season, completing 3,677 total laps, leading approximately 27% of all laps he raced. Lorenzen recorded 655 of the total laps led in his four victories on the season, with a bulk of them coming at the Virginia 500 at Martinsville Speedway.

982 The number of laps completed (9.82) in thousands by Jeff Gordon during his 1998 championship season. In what would be his third championship and second consecutive Sprint Cup championship, Gordon held off Mark Martin despite trailing him in laps completed (by 12 laps) and laps led (1,731 to 1,706). Gordon won 13 races on the season to Martin's seven and was consistent with 15 additional top ten finishes to win the title by almost 400 points.

983 The percentage of possible laps (.983) that were completed by Johnny Rutherford during his first year racing NASCAR. Rutherford recorded two starts in 1963 and completed 236 of 240 possible laps. Rutherford also has the distinction of winning his first race (1963 Daytona 500 Qualifier #2), but not being able to repeat the feat in the 34 race career that followed over 12 seasons spanning 26 years.

984 The number of thousands of laps (9.84) raced by drivers driving under Bob Adams between 1963 and 1967. Elmo Langley, Larry Manning, Don Tarr, Melvin Bradley, and Bill Dennis raced in 43 events for Bob Adams. Manning was the most successful driver, recording 33 starts and finishing in fourth place twice and finishing in the top ten an additional eight times.

985 The number of laps led (985) by Cotton Owens in 15 years racing NASCAR. Owens led 23 of 511 laps raced his first season and did not find himself in the lead again until his eighth season. From season eight until 11, Owens found himself up front quite often. Between 1957 and 1960, Owens led 179, 241, 209, and 185 laps, respectively, accounting for 814 of his career total of laps led.

986 The number of top ten finishes (986) recorded by Hendrick Motorsports entering the 2007 season. Between 1984 and 2006, drivers representing Hendrick started in 2,243 races, finishing in the top ten almost 44% of all races started.

987 The margin of victory (9.87) in seconds by Chuck Bown over Steve Grissom at the 1991 Pontiac 200 at Nazareth Speedway in Nazareth, Pennsylvania. Starting the Busch Series event in the number two position, Bown recorded one of his three wins on the season by beating out Grissom, who had started in tenth place.

988 The percentage of laps completed (.988) of all laps scheduled during the 1998 Sprint Cup Series season. Gordon started all 33 races on the season and completed 9,818 of 9,933 possible laps on the season. Of those laps completed, Gordon led a total of 1,717 laps.

989 The price per ticket ($989) that the SBTN guys would pay to go to the 50th running of the Daytona 500 on Sunday, February 18, 2008. Those seats, located in Row F36 of the tower, sit directly across from the Start/Finish line with a perfect view of Pit Row and the entire 2.5 mile track.

990 The number of laps completed (9.90) in thousands by Harry Gant during the 1984 Sprint Cup season. Gant would start in all 30 races on the season and complete more laps on the season than any other of his 21 years on the circuit. His lap total was the highest on the season and his laps led (1,186) was his best to date. Gant would also finish the season ranked second, a career best.

991 The number of laps completed (9.91) in thousands by Tony Stewart during his first year on the Sprint Cup. Stewart would complete the second most laps on the season behind Bobby Labonte and would lead the second most number of laps behind Jeff Gordon . . . not bad for a rookie. Stewart would finish the season ranked fourth in the final point standings, take home the Rookie of the Year Award, and solidify himself as one of the strongest up-and-coming drivers on the Sprint Cup.

992 The amount of money earned (992) in thousands of dollars by Matt Kenseth during his first full season racing on the Busch Series. In 1998 Kenseth started in all 31 races on Busch, earning three wins and 23 top ten finishes en route to a second place finish in the final season point standings. He followed up his success the next season by topping $1 million in earnings and getting a third place finish before jumping ship to the Sprint Cup as his primary series.

993 The number of laps raced (993) by Clifton "Coo Coo" Marlin during the 1969 NASCAR season. Marlin started in seven races during the season and placed in the top ten in two of those races. Marlin ran into mechanical problems in five of seven races, and was unable to effectively compete that season. Marlin never won a Sprint Cup race over his 165 starts, but he was a fan favorite and respected driver. Upon Marlin's passing in 2005, Richard Petty said, "I don't remember him ever causing any trouble, running over anybody or beating on anybody's head as far as Cup racing. I guess they'll remember him as a happy-go-lucky guy. That was my perspective of him."

994 The percentage of total laps possible (.994) that Kurt Busch completed at the Richmond International Raceway through 2007. Busch has started in 13 events at the track and completed 5,162 of 5,193 total laps. He finished all 13 races, four of them on the lead lap, and most of the remaining races one or two laps off the leader. He also earned one of his three victories in 2005 on the track.

995 The amount of money earned ($995) by Mike James in his fifth and final race on the Sprint Cup. On June 9, 1974, James started 28th in the Tuborg 400 at Riverside Raceway in Riverside, California. He would complete 103 of the scheduled 138 laps and finish a career best 18th, a full ten positions better than his career average.

996 The number of miles driven (99.6) by Bobby Isaac at the 1965 Tidewater 300 at Dog Track Speedway in Moyock, North Carolina. The race marked the first time that a driver other than Johnson had driven his car. Johnson had recorded 37 starts as a driver/owner up through the 55th race of the 1965 season and had recorded 13 wins in 19 top ten finishes. Isaac drove Johnson's car in the final race of the '65 season, started at pole, and finished in second place. Not a bad showing for Johnson's first race as "just" an owner.

997 The number of laps raced (997) by Ron Barfield Jr. on the Craftsman Truck Series in races held at the Phoenix International Raceway. Between 1996 and 1999, Barfield started in six races, completing an impressive 95.5% of all possible laps. Despite his consistency in lap completion, he was never able to finish higher than fifth in any of the races, and had an average finish position of 19.8 at the venue.

998 The length (99.8) in miles of four of the final five races held at the Charlotte Speedway in Charlotte, North Carolina. The track hosted 12 NASCAR events between 1949 and 1956. Buck Baker favored the shorter races, claiming his only three victories at the track in the 99.8 mile race configuration. Speedy Thompson took the other short race. The track also hosted races between 100.5 miles and 150 miles.

999 The number of miles raced (99.9) by Ned Jarrett during the 1965 Tidewater 300. Jarrett, the only car on the lead lap come the end of the 300 lap race at the Dog Track Speedway in Moyock, North Carolina, won the season's last race and the championship, only the third driver to accomplish the feat of winning both the final race and NASCAR championship during the same season.

1000 Dale Earnhardt Jr.'s winning percentage (.1000) on the Busch Series during the 2003 season. Junior won the only three races he entered on Busch that season, two races at Daytona and one at Talladega. His average start position was second, his average finish position first. Junior had similar luck the year prior, winning two of the three races entered (he crashed at Charlotte during his second race of the three race set).

Bibliography

Putting this book together has been extremely educational as well as incredibly enjoyable. It is not until you have undertaken a task like this that you truly appreciate the history and significance of NASCAR.

Much of the information held within these covers was found by sorting through countless pages of facts, figures, and records from a number of sources including books, articles, newspapers, and websites. We decided to list and discuss a few of the major sources, those most readily available to NASCAR fans.

Of course, NASCAR's website is an ideal place to start doing research about the history of the sport. But that was just the first of many resources we came across in our journey to bring SBTN to the NASCAR and NASCAR to SBTN. One of our friends along the way was Racing-Reference (www.racing-reference.com). It is an amazing website that provides an in-depth history of racers, drivers, and tracks and is one of the most complete resources that we came across. Another benefit of RR is that it is not specific to one series; it covers the Sprint Cup, Busch Series, and Craftsman Truck Series in a great amount of depth.

There were so many resources that helped us to create this book, each of which contributed to our effort to bring you what we hope is an amazing NASCAR experience. Websites dedicated to the greats of NASCAR, both official and unofficial, gave us a feel for the person behind the wheel. The websites of each of the tracks that host NASCAR events provided interesting information, not only about the configuration of the track, its seating capacity, and its winners and losers, but about some interesting bits of trivia, like how many hotdogs are sold during race weekends.

Two books were especially useful in our fact-finding mission. They were well-written and researched and assisted us in finding and checking facts to put into the SBTN NASCAR book:

Golenbock, Peter and Fielden, Greg (2002), *NASCAR Encyclopedia*, USA: MBI Publishing Company.

The Sporting News (2007), *NASCAR Record & Fact Book,* USA: Sporting News Books.

It is important to note that the history of NASCAR proper is closing in on 60 years. Record keeping was not always as good as it is today, therefore we must stress that there are bound to be statistical discrepancies between sources. Typically the discrepancies we found were small, almost insignificant, but nevertheless, we want to ensure NASCAR fans that we put forth our best efforts to sort through the information in order to get it right.

Index

NOTES

NOTES

NOTES

NOTES

NOTES